PILGRIM TO
THE HOLY LAND

H. J. RICHARDS

PILGRIM TO THE HOLY LAND

A Practical Guide

(Third edition)

Drawings and maps by
CLARE RICHARDS

McCrimmons

Great Wakering, Essex

First published in Great Britain in 1982 by
MAYHEW McCRIMMON LTD
Great Wakering Essex England

Second edition 1985
Reprinted 1987,1988
Third edition 1992
© H.J. Richards

ISBN 0 85597 321 8

Illustrations by Clare Richards
Cover design by Nick Snode
Cover illustration taken from a painting by
Marie Iatchenko which appeared in
Children of the World Paint Jerusalem
published by Keter Publishing House Jerusalem Ltd

Typesetting and lithographic artwork by Barry Sarling, Rayleigh
Printed by WBC Print Ltd, Bridgend, Mid Glamorgan

Dedicated to our twins
Pedro Benjamin and Blanca Rebecca
who made their first pilgrimage
to the holy places
without the aid of this book

ACKNOWLEDGEMENTS

Biblical quotations, except where noted, have been taken from the *Revised Standard Version of the Bible,* copyrighted ©1946,1952, 1971, 1973.

We also thank the following copyright holders for permission to use their material:

Brummer, Nadine: the poem *Pilgrim* on p.256.
The Collect for Purity is from The Order for Holy Communion Rite A in *The Alternative Service Book 1980* and is © the Central Board of Finance of the Church of England. Reproduced with permission.
De Rosa, Peter: *A Bible Prayer Book for Today* (referred to as BPB), Fontana, 1976.
Doubleday, London: *The Scriptures of the Dead Sea Sect.*
The Grail: *The Psalms: A New Translation.*
Macaulay, Rose: for the extract from *Towers of Trebizond,* 1956.
Oosterhuis, Huub: for material from *Ten Table Prayers.*
Prayers on pp. 103, 105, 109, 159 (referred to as DH), appeared in *Prayers for the Church Community* compiled by Roy Chapman and Donald Hilton, used by permission of the National Christian Education Council.
Reform Synagogue of Great Britain: *Forms of Prayer.*
Robson, Jeremy: an extract from *Adam International Review.*
SCM Press Ltd: for the prayer on p. 187 which appeared in *URC Book of Services.*
United Reformed Church: worship material from *A Book of Services.*

Hymn Section
Most of the hymns are taken from *Celebration Hymnal Volumes 1 and 2* published by McCrimmon Publishing Co Ltd.
Hymns 36, 63 and 71 are taken from *Songs of the Spirit,* published by Kevin Mayhew Ltd.
We acknowledge with thanks the following copyright holders:
Franciscan Communications Centre of Los Angeles for *Make me a channel;* Kevin Mayhew Ltd for *Laudate sii* and *Ask and it shall be given;* Stainer and Bell Ltd for *Lord of the Dance* and *Were you there?;* Thankyou Music for *Colours of Day;* Vanguard Music for *God's Spirit;* World Library Publications for *Keep in Mind.*
Every effort has been made to trace the owners of copyright material, and we hope that no copyright has been infringed. Pardon is sought and apology made if the contrary be the case, and a correction will be made in any reprint of this book.

CONTENTS

PREFACE TO THE SECOND EDITION

The first edition of this guide book appeared in 1982. It is encouraging that it has proved useful to so many pilgrims that a second edition is already required.

In preparing this new edition, I have taken the opportunity to make a number of revisions:

☐ In the Introduction, where many readers have asked for help in planning an itinerary. A number of long-length and short-length suggestions have been added.

☐ In some of the details of the sites listed, where the information given in the first edition was either unclear or outdated or plain wrong! It goes without saying that all guide books need continual revision on this score.

☐ In the material for worship, which in the first edition had in view only a Roman Catholic readership. Non-Roman readers have rightly pointed out that their needs would be met if this section could provide not the full text of any one service, but resource material taken from several traditions, which all Christians could use as they saw fit. I have gladly fallen in with this ecumenical suggestion in the hope that those who are not familiar with prayer patterns or traditions other than their own will find themselves enriched.

☐ In the hymn section, where again the first edition offered too narrow a choice. The newly enlarged section will hopefully allow Anglican and Free Church pilgrims, as well as Roman Catholics, to break into song, and to learn from each other how much they hold in common.

The preparation of the last two sections (worship and hymns) would have been quite beyond me if I had not been constantly advised and helped by the Revd Donald Hilton, of the United Reformed Church. He has not only gently drawn my attention to my Roman Catholic bias, but also gracefully accepted it. He has not only made the most valuable suggestions (and painfully typed them out for me), but provided some two dozen new prayers, most of them composed especially for this edition. He knows how grateful I am; but, publishers being what they are, he knows too that he will only get the reward due to him in heaven.

H.J.R.
1985

PREFACE TO THE THIRD EDITION

I am happy that continued demand has justified yet another edition of this guidebook. A recent visit to the Holy Land has given me the opportunity to update the information offered in earlier editions, and to realise that there is scarcely a page which did not need some emendation, however minor.

Recent events have understandably curtailed the number of visitors to the Holy Land. Yet it remains important that western Christians continue to show support for their fellow Christians in the East, lest they emigrate in even greater numbers than they have been since 1948, and leave the holy places as mere museum pieces. There is no better way of 'Praying for the peace of Jerusalem' (Psalm 122) than by showing solidarity with our elder Christian brothers and sisters there.

H.J.R.
1992

PRAYER FOR TRAVELLERS

May the God who called our father Abraham
to journey into the unknown,
and guarded him and blessed him,
protect me too and bless my journey.
May his confidence support me as I set out,
may his Spirit be with me on the way,
and may he lead me back to my home in peace.
Those I love, I commend to his care.
He is with them, I shall not fear.
As for myself,
may his presence be my companion,
so that blessing may come to me
and to everyone I meet.
Blessed are you, Lord,
whose presence travels with his people.

Jewish Prayer Book

FOREWORD

Why another Guide Book?

This journey cannot be made quickly, nor can all the holy places in Jerusalem and other localities be hurried through.... Nor is it possible to visit and explore all the sacred places without a good guide and interpreter.

Russian pilgrim, 1106 AD

The average pilgrim is not well served by guide books. Some offer him so much information irrelevant to his needs that he feels disheartened. Some are so laced with a saccharine piety that he feels sick. And if he turns to more popular publications, he may well feel angry that they hardly ever answer the questions he is actually asking.

The average pilgrim is not interested whether the capitals of the pillars he is looking at are proto-Aeolic or protoplastic. Nor does he want every detail of every site turned into a pious thought. His actual needs are far simpler.

He wants to be told where the holy places are, and if necessary the unholy ones too. He wants to be told clearly and simply what there is to see there. He wants some of the actual biblical texts they refer to placed in his hands, instead of being told to look them up in his bible. He wants examples of the kind of prayers and hymns he could use, should he feel so inclined. And most important, he wants to be regularly informed where he may find food, drink, toilets and, above all, slides.

These are the needs I have tried to answer in the present book. It is based on the observations of a considerable number of groups that have come with me to the Holy Land. I am grateful to them for making it clear to me over twenty years what the actual needs and interests of the average pilgrim are. I hope that their experience and mine will prove useful to other pilgrims and to those who, even at a distance, wish to recall, or prepare for, or simply dream of, their visit to the holy places.

Those who have already visited them will warm to the maps, plans and drawings with which my wife Clare has enlivened the text, and recognize that she is as infatuated with the Holy Land as I am myself.

This is all absurdly inadequate to convey to you my overwhelming love for Jerusalem and for Palestine — you can't believe how lovely they are.

Eric Gill, 1934 AD

INTRODUCTION

The city of Bethlem is as far from Jerusalem as Wansworth from London. Joppa is from Jerusalem as Ailsbury from London.... Mount Sion adjoins to J. as Southwark to L.

Henry Timberlake + 1626

A little geography (see map)

The Holy Land is a small country, only 350km. in length, and less than 100km. across at its widest point. If its coastline were superimposed on the south of England, it would look as in fig. 1, with Tel Aviv at Worthing, Jerusalem at Croydon, and Damascus no further away than Cardiff.

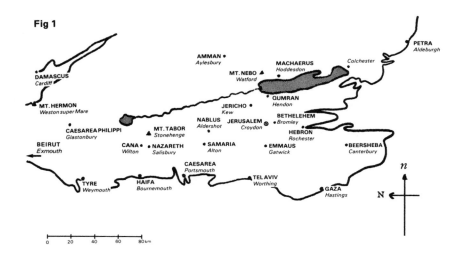

Fig 1

It is a mountainous country, the range rising at times to heights over 1000m., higher than any of our English mountains. Agriculture of an extensive kind is possible only on the coastal strip, in the vast plain that cleaves the mountain range to separate Galilee from the rest of the country, and in the Jordan valley.

The Jordan separates the country from the continuation of the mountain range to the east. It is part of the great geological Rift stretching from Syria to Africa, which imprisons the Jordan in a ditch below sea level. By the time it reaches the Dead Sea the ditch has sunk 400m. below.

17

The land enjoys a warmer and drier climate than other Mediterranean countries, though it yields similar produce. The plains are subtropical and the Jordan valley tropical. The hill-country remains pleasantly cool in the summer, and has some sunshine throughout winter.

A little history

The history of the Holy Land is long and complex, and those who wish to understand the Judaism and Christianity to which it gave rise will need to study it carefully. To summarize it shortly for the purpose of this book would criminally oversimplify it. What the pilgrim would probably appreciate much more would be a list of the key dates to which he can refer:

BC	3000	*Canaanite Rule*
	1800	Hebrew Patriarchs
	1250	Exodus from Egypt
	1200	Joshua's Conquests
		Judges
	1050	Samuel
		Israelite Rule
	1000	David
	960	First Temple
	930	Schism between North and South
	721	Exile of North
		Assyrian Rule
	586	Exile of South
		Babylonian Rule
	538	*Persian Rule*
		Return of Jewish Exiles
		Second Temple
	332	Alexander the Great's Conquests
		Greek Rule
	167	Maccabee rebellion
	63	*Roman Rule*
	37	Herod the Great
AD	27—30	Ministry of Jesus
	66	First Jewish revolt
	70	Destruction of Jerusalem
	132	Second Jewish revolt
		Bar Kokhba
	330—640	*Byzantine Rule*
	570	Muhammad born
	640—1100	*Arab Rule*
	1054	Schism between eastern and western Christianity

1100—1200	*Crusader Rule*
1200—1500	*Mameluke Rule*
1500—1918	*Turkish Rule* (Ottoman)
1914	First World War
1920	*British Rule*
1939	Second World War
	Immigration of Jewish refugees
1948	British hand over to United Nations
	Partition
	State of Israel
1967	Six Day War
	Israeli occupation of West Bank and Golan.
1973	Yom Kippur War

Those for whom even that table of dates is daunting could perhaps be helped, as I was in the early stages of my studies, by the magic word AMDEX, whose initials stand for the great turning points in BC history (Abraham, Moses, David, Exile, Xt). They fall roughly (but only very roughly) into periods of 500 years. So do the turning points of the AD period, for which I have hopefully added another memory-aid, eXBeCTeM:

Abraham	2000	BC
Moses	1500	
David	1000	
Exile	500	
Xt	0	
Byzantines	500	AD
Crusaders	1000	
Turks	1500	
Modern	2000	

Documents

Travellers to the Holy Land need a full and updated passport - a visitor's pass will not do. Visas are not required by British citizens. English-speaking nationals from a number of other countries (Australia, Canada, Ireland, New Zealand, South Africa, U.S.A.) are given a visa at the frontier free of charge. Vaccination is no longer required except for those who have recently visited an infected country. Travel agents will be able to advise about insurance: a package deal (comprising accident, delay, money, medical, curtailment, liability, cancellation and baggage) would seem to be best.

Health

Anyone already on a prescribed regime will presumably take his own drugs with him: chemists in the Holy Land are helpful and efficient, but expensive. The change of weather and diet gives some people 'tummy'; this can generally be overcome with Enterosan or something similar, either as a preventative or as a cure. Pilgrims may not be aware that a small dose of the local *arak* can settle stomachs as well as refresh spirits. Water in hotels is normally safe enough, but care should be taken about unpeeled fruit and the excessive use of iced drinks in warm weather. Those liable to sunburn should take their own lotion. Those exhausted by the heat may find relief with half a teaspoon of salt in water.

Aspirins, kwells and footpowder hardly need mentioning, but people may need to be told of the benefits of wax earplugs if their room is shared by others or overlooks the bus station.

Clothes

The Holy Land varies from the tropical in the Jordan valley, to the subtropical on the coast, to the almost alpine in the hill country. Visitors to the holy places will go to all three regions, sometimes in the same day, and should be prepared for considerable variations in weather.

For the heat, sunhats and sunglasses would seem essential, and presumably costumes for those who want to swim. Flip-flops will be useful for the beach. For the cold, it is useful to have sweaters which can be donned or shed as needed. Rain is almost unknown from April to October, but for winter on the hills some kind of windproofing and waterproofing is important. Shorts and bare shoulders are frowned on at some holy places.

The following rough temperature guide may be useful.

	Jerusalem	**Sea of Galilee**
Christmas	40°—55° F(5°—14° C)	48°—68° F(9°—20° C)
Easter	50°—70° F(10°—20° C)	52°—80° F(12°—26° C)
Mid Summer	65°—85° F(18°—30° C)	73°—100° F(24°—37° C)

Those who commendably intend to get the feel of the land by doing an amount of walking should bring sensible shoes. Those who wish to be elegant of an evening (and this too is commendable) should bring the appropriate clothes. A shoulder bag is obviously useful for expeditions and shopping.

Shopping

Handbags, like shoulder bags, should have a strap and be kept zipped. The crowded markets are a happy hunting ground for bag snatchers and pickpockets — some of them fellow pilgrims. Shoppers may wish to know that most of the goods they are familiar with, like Marmite, sellotape, baby nappies and Nescafé, are available in east and west Jerusalem (though not necessarily in Nazareth). Film is expensive, and photographers should bring their own supply.

Hotels

It would be pointless to give advice about hotels in a book of this kind. Travel agents and the local Israeli Government Tourist Office will provide a far fairer and more up-to-date selection, and moreover will be able to advise about rising prices. It is worth mentioning however, that youth and school groups who don't mind dormitory accommodation will find Youth Hostels throughout the country.

Single rooms in hotels are of course limited, and not always available, and it would be good to come to terms early with the likelihood of having to share a room. English electrical appliances will work normally on the hotel sockets (220 volts, AC), with the appropriate continental two-pin plug. Others may need an adaptor.

Most pilgrim hotels turn a benevolently blind eye to the sharing of preprandial drinks, and many groups have found that this use of their Duty Free is a most effective way of fostering a sense of community. It should of course be done discreetly. A tip of at least 10 per cent of the hotel costs is advisable. Some tour leaders include this (as well as tips for drivers and official guides) in their quotation.

Tickets

Admission to many of the sites in the Holy Land is by ticket only. Thoughtful leaders will take this into account and include the cost in their quotation. A useful 14-day season ticket is issued by the National Parks Authority, covering many of the sites listed in this book (Ashkelon, Bet Alfa, Belvoir, Bet Shean, Bet Shearim, Caesarea, Hammat Tiberias, Hazor, Herodium, Jericho, Jerusalem Walls, Korazin, Kursi, Masada, Megiddo, Qumran, Samaria, Ummayad Palace). These season tickets are available at many of the listed sites, but are only worthwhile if a good number of the sites are visited.

Opening hours have been quoted below wherever possible, though circumstances may alter them. Tickets for some sites, though they are open on the Jewish sabbath, must be obtained beforehand.

Those who wish to hold a service at the Roman Catholic shrines must also book beforehand, the earlier the better. For sites controlled from Jerusalem, permission is given at the Christian Information Centre, in the square inside the Jaffa Gate. This Office will also supply information on times of services, including non-Catholic ones, and (for a small cost) a colourful signed certificate verifying that one has visited the holy places (closed 12.30 - 15.00, Saturday p.m. and Sunday).

Non-Catholic groups are sometimes welcome to hold services at Roman Catholic shrines, but may feel more at home in their own churches. The Garden Tomb in particular (p. 71) willingly provides facilities for all comers, though booking is important.

Money

Hotels will gladly exchange bank notes and travellers cheques. So will numerous money changers, who ply their trade quite legally. It does no harm to compare rates; they will usually be slightly better than those given by banks at home.

Darmstadt

A community of German Lutheran nuns has taken pains to go round the Christian shrines in the Holy Land, and put up a distinctive black plaque in most of them, offering an apposite thought in different languages. They are well worth the attention of the pilgrim, even if his own reflections cause him to differ.

War and peace

Many prospective pilgrims ask worried question about the continuing tension between Israel and its neighbours, especially if some conflict has made headlines in news bulletins at home. It is not cynical to say that this tension has existed for the last forty years and may be expected to continue. Obviously the occasional visitor has been involved, but thousands have gone and returned less aware even of local incidents than newspaper readers at home.

Most pilgrims will want to include in their prayers some hope for reconciliation and peace. They should take care not to make these prayers unrealistic. It is easy to pray for reconciliation. The question to ask is how one would begin to help towards its realization.

Further reading

In spite of what I said above about other guide books, it would be ungracious, not to say dishonest, to hide the fact that I could not have written this book without them. Three of them above all I am happy to recommend to anyone who wishes to delve further into the historical and archaeological aspects of the holy places which, for practical reasons, this book has kept to a minimum:

Itinéraires Bibliques (Guide de Terre Sainte), Cerf and Mame 1966, second ed. 1974. This excellent guide has been put together by a team of experienced French pilgrimage leaders. It covers Lebanon, Syria and Jordan, as well as Israel, and is visually a joy to use.

J. Wilkinson, *Jerusalem as Jesus Knew It (Archaeology as Evidence)*, Thames and Hudson 1978. A learned but most readable discussion of the sites in and around Jerusalem which the gospels associate with the life of Jesus. Numerous informative plans and photographs. The author is Director of the British School of Archaeology in Jerusalem.

J. Murphy O'Connor, *The Holy Land (An Archaeological Guide from Earliest Times to 1700)*, Oxford University Press 1980. The New Testament professor at Jerusalem's Ecole Biblique has led numerous field trips in the Holy Land, and here wittily shares his experience. Valuable historical summaries and detailed site plans.

Suggested Itineraries

Most pilgrims to the Holy Land plan to spend at least two weeks there. The most important sites cannot be adequately visited — nor will they cohere into a clear pattern — in less time than that. Still, one is aware that many visitors, for a variety of reasons, will have far less time at their disposal. What must they at all costs *not* miss if they have only ten days to play with? Or only six? Or only three? Or if their Mediterranean cruise allows them only one day ashore from Haifa? Here are a few suggestions:

14 days

Day 1: Mount of Olives for a panorama of the city (p. 53). Walk back via Dominus Flevit (p. 53), Gethsemane (p. 37), Western Wall (p. 80) and the Suk (p. 75). Afternoon free.

Day 2: Jordan Valley via Good Samaritan Inn (p. 124). Jericho (p. 132), Umayyad Palace (p. 133) and Qumran (p. 162). Swimming at Ein Fashkha (p. 164).

Day 3: Via Garden Tomb (p. 71) to Russian excavations (p. 45) and Holy Sepulchre (p. 41). Afternoon walk down Kidron Valley (p. 48) to Gihon, Hezekiah's Tunnel and Siloam (p. 50). Thence to Peter in Gallicantu (p. 60), Cenacle (p. 59) and Dormition (p. 58).

Day 4: Lithostropos (p. 35) and Temple area (p. 76). Afternoon coach to Bethlehem (p. 98) and environs.

Day 5: Desert tour to Solomon's Pools (p. 173), Hebron (p. 127), Beersheba (p. 92) and Masada (p. 138). Swimming at En Gedi (p. 123).

Day 6: Free day.

Day 7: Walk via Bethesda (p. 27) and Tomb of Virgin (p. 39) to Mount of Olives to visit Ascension, Paternoster and the Darmstadt Sisters (p. 55). Thence via Bethphage (p. 104) to Bethany (p. 93). Local bus back. Afternoon free.

Day 8: Short walking tour of New City (north) (p. 69ff). Visit one of Jerusalem's museums (p. 63 and 71). Afternoon free.

Day 9: Coach tour of New City (west) (p. 62ff), not omitting Shrine of the Book (p. 63), Yad Vashem (p. 64) and Model of Jerusalem (p. 64). Possibly on to Emmaus (p. 119).

Day 10: Transfer via Jacob's Well (p. 149), Nablus (p. 149), Mount Gerizim (p. 151) and Sebastiya (p. 165) to Nazareth or Tiberias.

Day 11: Tour of Nazareth (p. 154ff), especially of the Basilica, Synagogue church, Greek Orthodox church and Little Sisters. The tour should begin or end with the Salesian School for the panorama. Afternoon free.

Day 12: Via Cana (p.111) to the Sea of Galilee (p. 168), especially Mount of Beatitudes (p. 144), Tabgha (p. 174) and Capernaum (p. 112). (Those who wish to visit Capernaum by boat must arrange for their coaches to meet them there.) Swimming at Tiberias (p. 168) and paddling at Jordan Bridge (p. 171). For Tabor (p. 146) and Nein (p. 160) taxis are needed.

Day 13: Free day.
Optional visits to Acre (p. 88), En Gev (by boat) (p. 170) or Banyas-Dan (p. 90).

Day 14: Megiddo (p. 141), Mount Carmel (p. 143) and Caesarea (p. 107). Swimming. So on to the airport.

10 days
As above, omitting days 6, 8 and 13, and combining days 11 and 12 into one.

6 days
Day 1: As day 1 above.

Day 2: Lithostrotos (p. 35) and Temple area (p. 76). Holy Sepulchre (p. 41). Coach to Bethlehem(p. 98).

Day 3: As day 9 above.

Day 4: Jericho (p. 132), Qumran (p. 162), Masada (p. 138).

Day 5: As day 10 above.

Day 6: Combine days 11 and 12 above.

3 days
Day 1: By coach to Mount of Olives for a panorama of the city (p. 53). Return to visit Gethsemane (p. 37) and Holy Sepulchre (p. 41).

Day 2: Walk to Lithostrotos (p. 35) and Temple area (p. 76). Coach to Bethlehem (p. 98).

Day 3: Coach to Nazareth (p. 154). Basilica and Greek Orthodox church. Tour of Sea of Galilee (p. 168), especially Mount of Beatitudes (p. 144), Tabgha (p. 174) and Capernaum (p. 112).

1 day
From Haifa one can visit *either* Galilee *or* Jerusalem, not both. In Galilee, one would go to the Nazareth Basilica (p. 154), and down to the Sea of Galilee to see the Mount of Beatitudes (p. 144), Tabgha (p. 174) and Capernaum (p. 112). In Jerusalem, one would go to the Mount of Olives for a panorama of the city (p. 53), and then spend the rest of the time available in the Holy Sepulchre (p.41) and the Temple area (p. 76).

JERUSALEM

(see plan enclosed)

> If I forget you, Jerusalem,
> let my right hand wither,
> let my tongue cleave to my mouth,
> if I remember you not.
>
> *Psalm 137*

IT is impossible to capture in words the magnetism of Jerusalem. It draws Jews, Christians and Muslims by the hundred thousands, all bent on seeing this place where Solomon built the Temple, where Jesus preached and died, and where Muhammad dreamed of the Dome of the Rock. For all three faiths, the city has become a symbol of the New Jerusalem that men yearn for.

Yet one does not need to be a believer to be drawn to Jerusalem. Its delightful position on the Judean heights, the gentleness of its climate even in winter, its walled compactness happily holding the tension between the changing and the changeless, and above all the courtesy and warmth of its Arab population — these exercise an appeal that few can resist. No one visits Jerusalem without hoping one day to return.

The walls which the visitor sees today enclose what is known as East Jerusalem. The name West Jerusalem is given to the (largely Jewish) town outside it. The walls are less than 450 years old, the work of the Turk, Suleiman the Magnificent. Yet they rest generally on foundations going back another 450 years, the work of the Crusaders. The Jerusalem of New Testament times covered about the same area as the present walled city, but 500m. further south, so that it included a large area now outside the southern wall, and excluded the quarter which Christians later built around the Holy Sepulchre, then outside the northern wall.

PRESENT JERUSALEM (BLACK LINES)

NT JERUSALEM (DOTTED LINES)

For most of the Old Testament period Jerusalem was considerably smaller. David's city occupied only a tiny hillock south of the Temple area, now totally outside the walls.

Inside the walls the city is divided into four roughly equal quarters by its two main thoroughfares, one running north-south from the Damascus Gate to the Zion Gate, and the other east-west from the Temple to the Jaffa Gate. Clockwise, the northwest area around the Holy Sepulchre is known as the Christian Quarter. The Muslim Quarter to its right is attached to the Dome of the Rock which now occupies the old Temple area. To the southeast, also keeping in touch with the Temple which is no more, lies the Jewish Quarter. To its left is the Armenian Quarter.

'Thoroughfares' may be thought too grandiose a name for the arcaded roads of the Old City. They are generally too narrow for vehicles, and often stepped — G.K. Chesterton called the town 'a city of staircases'. Cars are allowed to enter for only short stretches inside three of its gates, and apart from these stretches the town is a pedestrian area, where everything needed for survival, from building materials to baby powder, is humped on handcarts, donkeys or human backs. This gives the place a homely air, and visitors quickly respond to the gentle pace it induces. The main markets or *suks* tend to be crowded, but there are countless side alleys and lanes where the silence is broken only by children at play or a muezzin calling to prayer.

In the market, goods can still be purchased by discussion and agreement rather than by fixed price, and everyone finds favourite shops to which they wish to return. Snack foods, hot and cold, familiar and strange, are available in abundance, as are coffee, tea and other drinks. A rush stool outside the cafes at the Damascus or Jaffa Gate provides an ideal setting for observing the world go by, quite literally, as fellow Europeans on pilgrimage jostle with hooded Armenians, bearded Greeks with stately Ethiopians, and Jews of all cultures, in prayer shawls or trilbys or both, weave their way through to the Temple Wall.

Some Key Dates		
BC	1000	David's City
	950	Solomon's Temple
	586	Destruction by Babylon
	520	Second Temple
	160	Maccabees
	20	Herod's Temple
AD	30	Jesus' Ministry and Death
	70	Destruction by Rome
	135	Aelia Capitolina
	335	Holy Sepulchre
	687	Dome of the Rock
	1099	Crusader Kings of Jerusalem
	1516	Turkish Walls
	1920	British Mandate
	1948	State of Israel
		Divided Jerusalem
	1967	United Jerusalem

At times of religious festivals above all, Jerusalem displays an infinite variety, which age cannot wither nor custom stale. When Latin and Orthodox Easters coincide, Holy Sepulchre can scarcely contain all the colourful ceremonies that take place. When they differ by a week, one can take part in the Palm Sunday celebrations of one and the Easter of the other in the same morning, and perhaps share a Jewish Passover *seder* the same evening.

The walls were constructed to be walked upon, and the fine wall-walk which encircles most of the city has recently been reopened to the public. It affords those with a head for heights, and a heart for steps, an extensive bird's eye view of Jerusalem, and of the 600 acres of landscaped green belt with which it is being enhanced outside. Since the walk passes through some of the city's less frequented areas, ladies would do well not to travel alone.

Taxis, for those who wish to travel further afield, or even simply from one gate to another, are available at the Jaffa Gate, and outside the Damascus and Herod Gate. Here also may be found the 'sherut' taxis which travel to fixed destinations when they are full, the cost being shared by the occupants.

ANTONIA   see p. 34

ARMENIAN MOSAIC   see p. 71

ASCENSION   see p. 55

BETHESDA (fig. 2)

Between the Ecce Homo Convent on the Via Dolorosa and St Stephen's gate is the Greek Catholic seminary directed by the White Fathers. It stands most probably on the site of the pool of Bethesda spoken of in the story of the paralytic in John 5. Closed 11.45 - 14.00 and Sundays. Small slide shop.

The vast pool, 13m. deep (1), was dug in 200 BC to collect the local rainwater and form a reservoir for the nearby Temple. It was divided into two basins by a dike (2), which may account for the 'five' porticoes mentioned in the gospel story. Bowls and medicinal baths cut into the rock have been discovered in the area, indicating that it

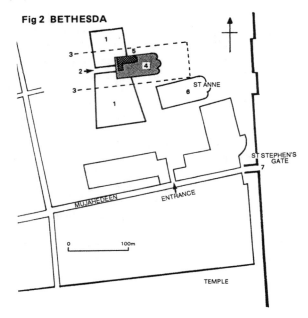

Fig 2 BETHESDA

became (before Christ or after?) a shrine of the Greek-Roman healing god Aesculapius.

Only the area around the dike intersecting the two basins has been excavated (3), to reveal the remains of a Byzantine church (4) built in the 5th c. AD, curiously spreadeagled over the pool on part of the intersection. It was dedicated to Mary, whom a 2nd c. apocryphal writing described as born near the Temple. This church was destroyed by the Persians. The 12th c. Crusader reconstruction was far smaller, and occupied only one nave of the Byzantine church (5). The Crusader ruins still exist, and a stone staircase still gives access to the water of which John's story speaks. A small museum in the seminary houses exhibits from the excavations and may be viewed by private arrangement.

The Crusaders used the rest of the stones from the Byzantine ruins to build the sober and lovely church of **St Anne** (6), one of the finest buildings in Jerusalem. Its delightful acoustics tend to make pilgrims burst into song. It once served as the chapel for a large community of nuns. Baldwin I's wife found them so delightful that she joined them. A crypt on the right shows the house considered to be that of Mary's reputed parents Anne and Joachim.

28

The church is French property, a gift from Turkey after the Crimean War, and is so jealously guarded that General De Gaulle refused the Israeli offer to repair it when a shell tore a hole in it during the Six Day War of 1967, and preferred to repair it himself.

In the road outside, a fine new assembly point for the Stations of the Cross (p. 195) has been set up. It incorporates some paving stones from New Testament times.

The city gate 50m. further east is known as **St Stephen's Gate** (7). The name originally belonged to the present Damascus Gate, near the church of St Stephen (see p. 73), but the name was moved here when Christians were no longer allowed to use the Damascus Gate. Its Hebrew name is Lion's Gate after its decorative motif. Arabs call it the Gate of the Virgin Mary (Bab Sitti Mariam) after the spring in the Kidron valley to which it leads (see p. 49).

A gospel story links the Bethesda Pool with a 'Sheep gate'. This was presumably connected with a sheep market held in this part of the city. It is interesting that until quite recently a Bedouin sheep market operated outside this north-east corner of the city, though the northern wall has now moved further north, and the colourful market further north still.

John 5$^{2-17}$: There is in Jerusalem by the Sheep Gate a pool, in Hebrew called Bethesda, which has five porticoes. In these lay a multitude of invalids, blind, lame, paralysed. One man was there, who had been ill for thirty-eight years. When Jesus saw him and knew that he had been lying there a long time, he said to him, 'Do you want to be healed?' The sick man answered him, 'Sir, I have no man to put me into the pool when the water is troubled, and while I am going another steps down before me.' Jesus said to him, 'Rise, take up your pallet, and walk.' And at once the man was healed, and he took up his pallet and walked.

Now that day was the sabbath. So the Jews said to the man who was cured, 'It is the sabbath, it is not lawful for you to carry your pallet.' But he answered them, 'The man who healed me said to me, "Take up your pallet, and walk".' ... This was why the Jews persecuted Jesus, because he did this on the sabbath. But Jesus answered them, 'My Father is working still, and I am working.'

BPB p. 30: Father, today our hearts turn to those who are sick.
We are all limbs of Christ's body
so that if one limb suffers, all suffer together...
Christ himself was devoted to the sick...
and many were healed because they trusted him.
Jesus was willing, against bitter opposition,
to heal even on the Sabbath day.
The honest needs of the sick, he claimed,
took priority over the Jewish holy day.
'The Sabbath was made for man, not man for the Sabbath.'
Father, I thank you
for the gentle healing hands of Christ
who came as Physician to a sick world.
And I pray with him for all who have to endure
loneliness and pain
envy of those healthier than themselves
the agonizing difficulties of prayer.
And if from time to time they lose heart,
strengthen them, Father, with Christ's Holy Spirit
so that they know no one has failed too much
if he is still trying not to fail.

CALVARY see p. 43

CARDO MAXIMUS See p. 42, 69, 75

CENACLE see p. 59

CITADEL (TOWER OF DAVID) (fig. 3)

Citadel is the name given to the fortress which dominates Jerusalem's western wall (1) and guards its vulnerable gate. The Byzan-

tines mistakenly thought David's palace stood here (see Mt Zion, p. 58), and its largest tower is still known as the **Tower of David** (2). But towers to fortify the city were not built here until a thousand years later, by Herod the Great. He curiously dedicated them to his wife Mariamne, his brother Phasael and his favourite general Hippicus. They formed the entrance to a vast palace which Josephus described as indescribable, stretching south from here for 400m. If the Roman governor or praetor lived here when visiting Jerusalem in New Testament times, then this imposing building was the 'praetorium' in which Jesus was sentenced to death, (but see also p. 34).

Only the lower courses of Herod's stones remain. The rest of what one sees today is a Crusader reconstruction (their 'kings of Jerusalem' ruled from here), later modified by the Turks who built the present walls. The Citadel has recently been turned into a fine and comprehensive museum of the 3,000 year history of Jerusalem. Breathtaking views from the three towers. Buffet and toilets. Entrance fee. 10.00 - 17.00 (Fridays and Saturdays 14.00). In the open courtyard a fine 40 minute *Son et Lumière* is presented in English most evenings in the tourist season (bring a blanket).

Adjoining the Citadel is the **Jaffa Gate** (3), the intervening wall having been demolished to accommodate the entry of Kaiser Wilhelm II into the city in 1898. Twenty years later General Allenby marked the end of Turkish rule (and the beginning of the end of the Great War) in equally dramatic fashion: he dismounted

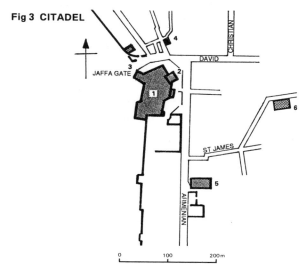

Fig 3 CITADEL

31

and entered Jerusalem on foot. Inside the gate, the road which goes up to the left (after the arcaded alley) leads within 100m. to the doorway of the **Greek Catholic Patriarchate** (on the right) (4). Most Catholic pilgrims to the Holy Land associate so exclusively with the Franciscans, Dominicans and Benedictines from the West that they remain unaware of the existence of an indigenous community of fellow-Catholics. They are called 'Greek' because they follow the Greek liturgical tradition, but the language of their services is their own — Arabic. The White Fathers from Bethesda and the Little Sisters of Jesus regularly sing in their choir. Times of services are posted on the door (they are exceptionally colourful in Holy Week), but the church is worth a visit even outside those times, having recently been decorated from ceiling to floor with brilliant murals, the work of two Romanian brothers anxious to forge back beyond Burns Oates and St Sulpice to the true ikon tradition.

The area of the walled city south of here, once occupied by Herod's palace, is now the quarter of the Armenian Christians, a persecuted people who in this century alone have suffered the massacre of two million, and who have put down firm roots in this land of their exile. Their **Cathedral of St James** (5) is on the left of the main road going south. It is a medieval building refurbished throughout with brilliant tiles in the 17th c. (access during daily service at 15.00 only, or by appointment). The Cathedral is surrounded by the Armenian 'Monastery', a small village housing two or three hundred families. In the grounds a stone is shown as the one which would have praised God if Jesus' disciples had not.

Just north of the Cathedral, St James Rd and Ararat Rd lead to the medieval **Church of St Mark** (6), the headquarters of Jerusalem's small community of Syrian Christians. It claims to be the house of the Last Supper, and the house where Peter found refuge after escaping from prison. Closed 12.00 - 14.00.

Act 4[27]: Truly in this city there were gathered together against thy holy servant Jesus, whom thou didst anoint, both Herod and Pontius Pilate, with the Gentiles and the People of Israel.

Acts 12[1–3]: About that time Herod (Agrippa I) the king laid violent hands on some who belonged to the church. He killed James the brother of John with the sword; and when he saw that it pleased the Jews, he proceeded to arrest Peter also.

Luke 19[37–40]: As Jesus was drawing near ... the whole multitude of the disciples began to rejoice and praise God with a loud voice for all the mighty works that they had seen.... And some of the Pharisees in the multitude said to him, 'Teacher, rebuke your disciples'. He answered, 'I tell you, if these were silent, the very stones would cry out.'

Acts 12[12-17]: (Peter) went to the house of Mary, the mother of John whose other name was Mark, where many were gathered together and were praying. And when he knocked at the door of the gateway, a maid named Rhoda came to answer. Recognising Peter's voice, in her joy she did not open the gate but ran in and told them that Peter was standing at the gate. They said to her, 'You are mad.' But she insisted that it was so. They said, 'It is his angel!' But Peter continued knocking; and when they opened, they saw him and were amazed. But motioning to them with his hand to be silent, he described to them how the Lord had brought him out of the prison.

A Greek Catholic Bishop: I came to the Holy Land to give. And behold I was overwhelmed by what I received. I came to enrich and purify. And behold I was the one to be enriched and purified. I loved the family of the Lord. His family are both the Jews and the Arabs. I held the Muslim, the Druze, the Jew, the Christian, everyone, believer and unbeliever, in the same embrace.... They can live together, love together, and see the radiance of God in each other's face.

Was that not the vision of Christ in the Gospel?...

The divine beauty in each race had to have only the occasion to mingle, embrace, and dance together.... These occasions had only to multiply to become permanent. Christ was not wrong: 'If you love as I have loved' the world will be a heaven. The Holy Land of Israel will, some day, be that heaven....

So I tried to identify with Jews and Arabs. It is possible!... Anyone who opens his heart to them can see in each other's face the face of God.... They have the warmth of a mother's womb.... If only we could create a little more understanding. Understanding wipes out suspicion. Love will flower and bloom.

Archbishop Joseph Raya, 1974

DAMASCUS GATE   see p. 69

DAVID'S TOMB   see p. 60

DAVID'S TOWER   see p. 31

DOMINUS FLEVIT   see p. 53

DORMITION See p. 58

ECCE HOMO On the Via Dolorosa, 400m. from St Stephen's
Gate. Closed 12.30–14.00 and Sundays (fig. 4). Toilets.

The Ecce Homo Convent of the Sisters of Sion probably attracts
more pilgrims than any other private site in Jerusalem. It is built on
part of the **Antonia** fortress, the massive Roman garrison guarding
the Temple which Herod the Great dedicated to Mark Antony.

Fig 4 ECCE HOMO

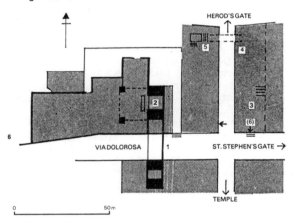

It is one of the two places where the Roman governor or praetor
could reside when he visited Jerusalem from his headquarters at
Caesarea-on-sea (the other being Herod's palace at the Citadel, see
p. 31). If Pilate held court here during Jesus' last Passover, then this
was the 'praetorium' where he was condemned to a Roman death.
Certainly popular devotion from the 16th c. onward identified the
arch (1) spanning the road outside as the one on which Pilate
exhibited his scourged prisoner to the crowds below with the words
'Behold the Man' (Ecce Homo). And certainly the trial which Paul
had to undergo in the footsteps of his master twenty years later took
place in these barracks.

The archway is in fact later than the time of Christ. It was either
the eastern city gate built by Herod Agrippa I in 40 AD, or a triumph-
al arch erected by Hadrian to celebrate the end of the Jewish Revolt
in 135 AD. One bay of the triple arch has been skilfully used as the
reredos of the sisters' chapel (2). Downstairs a magnificent pavement

of beautifully cut red stones has been unearthed (3). This certainly formed part of the market-place which Hadrian built in this area, and may have been the courtyard of the earlier Antonia. This would give point to the word **Lithostrotos** or Pavement where John says Pilate and Jesus passed judgment on each other. Letters and figures scratched into some of the stones suggest that a corner was used by the guards to play the game of 'King', which may be connected with the mockery of Jesus mentioned in the gospels.

The pavement, which extends into the adjoining Franciscan property of the Flagellation, serves as the lid of an enormous cistern, 52m. by 18m., dug here to collect local rainwater for the fortress. It can be viewed from a wellhead at the entrance to the pavement (4), or better still from a doorway leading to it from under the stairs (5). When Jerusalem is short of water, this cistern sill provides the convent with water for washing. All the excavations are well displayed and easily accessible. The sisters provide a very fine shop for slides, books and souvenirs at the street-level exit (6).

From the shop, a visit may be paid on request to the terraces on top of the convent. They provide a fine aerial view of the Temple area opposite, and of the rest of the Old City.

The Greek Church commemorates Pilate's **Praetorium** (Christ's Prison) a little further down the road (6) where a number of chambers cut into the rock may be seen.

John 18²⁸—19¹⁶: They led Jesus from the house of Caiaphas to the praetorium. It was early ... Pilate took Jesus and scourged him. And the soldiers plaited a crown of thorns, and put it on his head, and arrayed him in a purple robe; they came up to him saying, 'Hail, King of the Jews!' and struck him with their hands. Pilate went out again, and said to them, 'See, I am bringing him out to you, that you may know that I find no crime in him.' So Jesus came out, wearing the crown of thorns and the purple robe. Pilate said to them, 'Behold the man!' ...

Pilate brought Jesus out and sat [him?] down on the judgment seat at a place called The Pavement, and in Hebrew, Gabbatha.... He said to the Jews, 'Behold your King!' They cried out, 'Away with him, away with him, crucify him!' ... Then he handed him over to them to be crucified.

Acts 21³⁰⁻³⁶: All the city was aroused, and the people ran together; they seized Paul and dragged him out of the temple, and at once the gates were shut. And as they were trying to kill him ... the tribune came up and arrested him, and ordered him to be bound with two chains. He inquired who he was and what he had done. Some in the crowd shouted one thing, some another; and as he could not learn the facts because of the uproar, he ordered him to be brought into the barracks. And when he came to the steps, he was actually carried by the soldiers because of the violence of the crowd; for the mob of the people followed, crying, 'Away with him!'

DH: Do not lose your crown of thorns, Lord Jesus Christ.
Hold fast the mocking robe of purple,
for these are symbols of true kingship.

Your humility has won us over.
Meeting evil with goodness you have given us hope.
Your defeat has led us to victory,
and we are clothed by your nakedness.
Your weakness is the strength by which the world is conquered,
and brings us to our knees in willing service.

Do not lose your crown of thorns.
Hold fast the mocking robe of purple.
We have beheld our King.

DH: Lord Jesus Christ,
when the force of might has trampled the land,
your gentleness still rules,
hard-pressed but not defeated.
When anger and hatred have done their worst,
your kindness takes up the broken pieces,
and remakes love.
When an unseeing regime turns blind eyes
to human needs,
you give new sight and hope.
When evil and oppression
seem to have won the day,
your love can rise again
with a new dawn.
You are the king
whose yoke is easy,
whose burdens are light with love,
and whose strength is matched with mercy.

BPB p. 51: Father, when Jesus was nailed to his cross,
the crowd below kept mocking him and saying,
'Come down from that cross and we will believe.'
There are times, Father, when I say to him,
'Come down from that cross, Jesus,
so I can have permission to get down from mine.'
In my heart, Lord, I know there was no way
for him to come down from his cross.
Though he is risen now, there is a sense
in which he is so attached to that cross
he will lie on it as long as time lasts.

He is hungry, thirsty, naked, abandoned, crucified,
wherever any follower of his is
hungry, thirsty, naked, abandoned, crucified.
I know that if Jesus had come down from his cross
belief would never have been possible.
He would have proven he was not the Christ
but only a ghost dressed up in the body of a man.
Now there is no mistaking Jesus is a man like us:
when soldiers beat him he was bruised;
when they nailed him to the cross,
he stayed there and bled.
Since Jesus wanted so much to be like us,
we too should want to be like him.
If any man will be my disciple, he said,
let him take up his cross and follow me.
Father, I see in every age and every place
a cheerful army of quiet people,
each shouldering a wooden beam
and following the Carpenter from Galilee.

ECOLE BIBLIQUE   see p. 73

EL AKSA MOSQUE   see p. 79

EN KAREM   see p. 66

GARDEN TOMB   see p. 71

GEHENNA   see p. 50

GETHSEMANE   In the Kidron valley, east of Jerusalem. Access to the church is from a side entrance, where the street vendors are. Closed 12.00 - 14.30 (fig. 5).

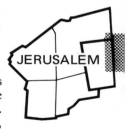

JERUSALEM

The agonising decision which Jesus had to make before his arrest is placed by the gospels 'in a garden called Gethsemane, on the far side of the Kidron'. This spot, as likely as any, was chosen in the 4th c. for a church, and parts of its mosaic floor are still visible under glass, neatly continued in the floor of the present noble and prayerful

church (1924). The countries which contributed to the building of this 'Church of All Nations' (1) have received their reward: their coat of arms displayed in the ceiling.

Before the main altar a piece of rock (the 'Rock of the Agony') has been cut square and isolated from its surroundings — a Byzantine arrangement to ensure that it should remain accessible to everyone.

The grounds outside (2), lovingly tended by the Franciscans, give a better image of the garden commemorated by this spot. The railings help to dissuade over-enthusiastic souvenir hunters, but small groups are sometimes given permission to walk the paths beneath the trees, or to sit in a newly ordered garden on the other side of the road (5). Olives as ancient as these are known locally as *Rumi* (Roman) but they are more likely to be the great great grandsons of the ones Jesus knew.

Outside the exit and a little down the road, steps to the right lead down into a courtyard. From there an alleyway to the right leads to a cave (3), thought by the Byzantines to be the place where the disciples slept while Jesus prayed in the garden higher up. Traces of 5th c. mosaics are still visible. Gutters and runnels beneath suggest

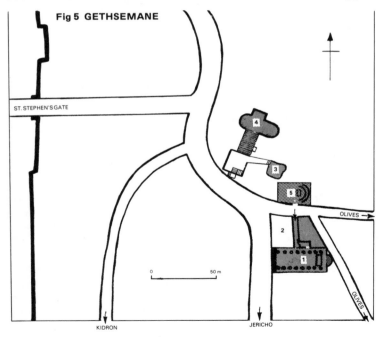

Fig 5 GETHSEMANE

ST. STEPHEN'S GATE

OLIVES →

OLIVES

0   50 m

KIDRON

JERICHO

that olives may once have been pressed here, and given the area the name of Gethsemane or Oilpress.

The courtyard itself is dominated by the Crusader façade of the **Tomb of the Virgin** (4). Its position here is due partly to the status of the Kidron valley as a burial ground (see p. 48), and partly to a tradition that Mary 'rested' here on her journey from Nazareth to Bethlehem. The church itself is a Byzantine construction and is approached down 40 steps. (Closed 12.00 - 14.00). To the left and right of the steps are two funerary chapels of Crusader wives. Down at the bottom, the 'tomb' is in the right-hand apse. It has been isolated from the solid rock in imitation of the tomb in Holy Sepulchre. An indentation in the rock wall to the right marks the direction of Mecca for Muslims, who also venerate Mary, called by Muhammad 'my sister'.

Luke 22$^{39-48}$: Jesus came out, and went, as was his custom, to the Mount of Olives; and the disciples followed him. And when he came to the place he said to them, 'Pray that you may not enter into temptation.' And he withdrew from them about a stone's throw, and knelt down and prayed, 'Father, if thou art willing, remove this cup from me; nevertheless not my will, but thine, be done.' And when he rose from prayer, he came to the disciples and found them sleeping for sorrow, and he said to them, 'Why do you sleep? Rise and pray that you may not enter into temptation.'
   While he was still speaking, there came a crowd, and the man called Judas, one of the twelve, was leading them. He drew near to Jesus to kiss him; but Jesus said to him, 'Judas, would you betray the Son of man with a kiss?'

Hebrews 5$^{7-8}$: In the days of his flesh, Jesus offered up prayers and supplications, with loud cries and tears, to him who was able to save him from death, and he was heard for his godly fear. Although he was a Son, he learned obedience through what he suffered.

DH: The sufferings of the world are yours, eternal Christ. You bear the sins and shame of mankind as though they were your own.
   The agony of rejection is yours, eternal Christ. You faced man's rejection throughout your life. Your friends slept in the hour of need, and on the cross you felt yourself forsaken even by God.
   Out of your dereliction comes our hope. You descended to the depths to raise us to the heights. The glory is yours and the victory, and you offer both to us as though they were our own.
   Come, Lord Jesus, that we who walk this holy place may sense the mystery of your suffering, and glimpse the wonder of your victory in weakness.

39

DH: Father, the sleep of Peter falls also on our unwilling eyes:
the hungry suffer and we sleep,
the lonely cry out in despair and we sleep,
the homeless grieve,
the workless are discounted,
the dying lose hope,
cities are burnt, communities destroyed,
and children die before they live,
and we sleep.
'Could you not stay awake with me one hour?'
Father, the kiss of Judas is on our lips:
our words adore you but our lives deny,
our worship honours you but has no root in love,
we make the gesture of love,
but only to serve our selfish purpose.
'Would you betray the Son of man with a kiss?'
Father forgive.

Jeremy Robson: I can only stare over the cradled city
And watch the rocks, the trees, and the silent streams
dream on.
I can only hear the urgent voices in the air
And the beautiful breathing of a million stars,
And sense the love and music everywhere.
And nobody sees, and nobody hears my tears
Trickle on the sand — and disappear.

Salve Regina, mater misericordiae
Vita, dulcedo, et spes nostra, salve.
Ad te clamamus, exsules filii Hevae;
Ad te suspiramus, gementes et flentes
In hac lacrimarum valle.
Eia ergo, advocata nostra
Illos tuos misericordes oculos ad nos converte.
Et Jesum, benedictum fructum ventris tui,
Nobis post hoc exsilium ostende.
O clemens, o pia, a dulcis Virgo Maria.

GIHON See p. 49

GOLDEN GATE see p. 80

GREEK CATHOLIC PATRIARCHATE see p. 32

HADASSAH HOSPITAL see p. 67

HARAM ESH SHARIF see p. 77

HELENA CHAPEL see p. 43

HEROD'S FAMILY TOMB see p. 62

HEZEKIAH'S TUNNEL see p. 50

HINNOM see p. 50

HOLY SEPULCHRE Open to the public daily 4.30 till 20.00, unless (e.g. in Holy Week) special services are being held. Long sleeves. No shorts (figs. 6 and 7).

No site in the Holy Land is more yearned for by the Christian pilgrim than the spot where Jesus died and was raised to a new life by the power of God. No site is more likely initially to disappoint him, hemmed in as it is now by a constantly expanding city, and reverberating with the shouts of excited visitors, rival worshippers and diligent workmen. Yet no site, if he revisits it often enough, will eventually endear itself to him more. It has little to do with the 'green hill far away' of his dreams. But its power to evoke the centuries of history it enshrines, to bring together Christians of all shades and persuasions, and to inspire the patent devotion of its pilgrims, especially the poor — these will eventually overcome the surprise the pilgrim first experiences here, and move him to find a deep peace within these walls.

The site dates back to the 4th c., when Queen Helena decided to mark the adoption of Christianity as the official religion of her son Constantine's empire by embodying the gospel in a number of magnificent shrines (see Bethlehem, p. 98, Mount of Olives, p. 54). Here, outside the original city walls, local Christians told her that Jesus died and was buried, though the Roman emperor Hadrian had later incorporated the spot into his forum. Constantine's engineers

41

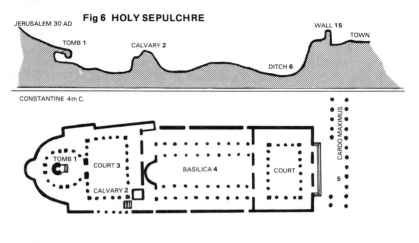

Fig 6 HOLY SEPULCHRE

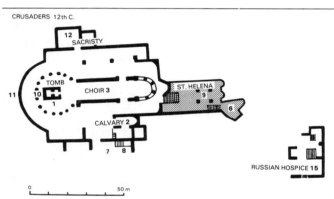

dug the traditional tomb (1) clear of its surrounding rock (in the manner of the tombs in the Kidron Valley, see p. 48) and covered it with a rotunda 40m. wide. Only another 40m. away was the knoll known as Calvary (2). This he squared off, and to it attached an open courtyard (3). Finally he added a noble five-naved basilica (4) opening on to the *Cardo Maximus*, Jerusalem's main north-south thoroughfare (5). The whole complex was 160m. long, about the size of the average English cathedral.

This complex was totally destroyed by the Arabs in the 11th c., and much of the area it covered occupied by new buildings. When the Crusaders decided to rebuild in the 12th c. therefore, it was on only half the scale. The rotunda now became the main building, and the adjoining courtyard was roofed over to provide the nave of their Romanesque church (3). Off it they still had access to the crypt in which Helena believed she found the remains of the discarded cross (6). It is basically this Crusader building which the visitor now sees. It suffered much through the centuries from fires and earthquakes, and the bricking up of collapsing arches tended to turn it into a series of isolated rooms. When sheer neglect threatened total collapse during the British Mandate, the Royal Engineers shored it up with ugly but efficient steel girders. An Italian plan of the 1950s to tear down the whole building and the area around it and to construct something entirely new was fortunately rejected, and in the 1960s sufficient agreement was reached by the occupying Christians (Latin Catholics, Greek Orthodox, Armenians, Syrians, Copts and Ethiopians) to allow the sad Crusader building to be restored, though local masons had to be taught the skills of the 12th c. This work is still in progress. In 1981 a Cambridge firm won the contract for constructing the new dome.

The façade and belfry dominating the square (7) are entirely the work of the Crusaders. The steps to the right (8) provided their access to the hill of Calvary. Inside, a marble plaque in the floor ahead, festooned with lamps, marks the spot where Greek pilgrims remember the preparation of Jesus' body for burial.

Two flights of steep stone steps to the right lead up to **Calvary** (2), its floor being level with the cube of rock which Constantine left standing here. The right hand chapel belongs to the Latins, and has a fine medieval mosaic in the ceiling. The Greek chapel on the left has a hole in the paving under the altar, where those who wish may touch the groundrock in which the cross is thought to have been set. From a balcony one can get a good view of the whole basilica, and appreciate the restoration work in progress.

Downstairs, under Calvary, the 'Chapel of Adam' enshrines the legend that Jesus' cross was planted on Adam's grave — it is in fact his skull which lies at the foot of the cross in many representations of the crucifixion. The legend beautifully expresses the belief that Jesus died, not just for an élite, but for Adam — Mankind. The original rock may be seen behind glass. The Crusader knights Godfrey de Bouillon and Baldwin I were buried in this chapel.

A right turn outside this chapel leads round an ambulatory. Halfway round, steps to the right descend to the chapel of **St Helena** (9), the walls on the way down covered with the carved crosses with which past pilgrims expressed their devotion. The fine Crusader chapel, with capitals borrowed from the el-Aksa mosque, is

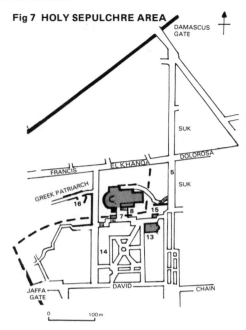

Fig 7 HOLY SEPULCHRE AREA

now served by the Armenian Christians. The Ethiopian Christians live on their roof. Further steps lead down to the crypt where Helena is said to have discovered the cross (6). The rock walls would have been part of the city ramparts in New Testament times.

Upstairs again, the ambulatory continues to circle the simple and dignified choir now served by the Greek Orthodox (3), and leads to the focal point of the whole church, under the dome. Here a little stone house, rather like a kiosk, no more than a hundred years old, covers the tomb which Constantine was at pains to isolate from the surrounding rock (1). Access is through a low doorway, and since there is no exit at the other end, only half a dozen pilgrims can enter at a time. A simple stone slab marks the empty tomb. There is better access to the original rock at the back of the shrine (10), where the Copts make a precarious living sprinkling the pilgrims with scented water. Beyond their domain, by a doorway through the rotunda wall, the Syrians have installed themselves at the original rock face, where a 1st c. tomb (Joseph of Arimathea?) can still be seen (11).

Beyond the kiosk lies the Latin area — a fine Blessed Sacrament chapel (ideal for Roman Catholic group services, (12)) and a sacristy displaying Godfrey de Bouillon's sword, spurs and distinctive

Jerusalem cross. Pilgrims who want devotional articles blessed should bring them here.

Outside the lower exit of Holy Sepulchre Square stands the modern Lutheran church of the Redeemer (13). (Closed 13.00—14.00 and Friday p.m.) Its distinctive white tower affords a fine view of the Old City. Alongside the church runs the area still known as **Mauristan** or Hospice, where the Knights of St John of Jerusalem once offered hospitality. It is now a rather quiet shopping area (14).

Opposite the Redeemer church and a little further back towards the market, the **Russian hospice** (15) (open Monday to Thursday, 9.00—15.00, small entrance fee) displays in its crypt a fine arch which once formed part of the forum Hadrian built here in 135 AD. To its right are some of the columns which lined the *Cardo Maximus* leading to it. In the floor beyond, protected with glass, is the worn sill of what a hundred years earlier could have been the Ephraim Gate leading out of the city to Calvary. If the identification is correct, these stones provide a vivid visual aid for those who need reassuring that Holy Sepulchre church, though now firmly within the city, was once outside the walls.

For those who can find their way to it (out of the stepped upper exit of Holy Sepulchre Square, turn right through the arcaded street, and shortly turn left), a monastery on the left in Greek Orthodox Patriarchate Road (16) affords access to the roof and belfry of Holy Sepulchre church, and a fine view of the square from above. The porter's permission to enter is important.

Mark 15 and 16: They brought Jesus to the place called Golgotha (which means the place of the skull) ... And they crucified him, and divided his garments among them, casting lots for them, to decide what each should take. And it was the third hour, when they crucified him.

And when the sixth hour had come, there was darkness over the whole land until the ninth hour. And at the ninth hour Jesus cried with a loud voice, 'Eloi, Eloi, lama sabachthani?' which means, 'My God, my God, why hast thou forsaken me?' ... And Jesus uttered a loud cry, and breathed his last ... And when the centurion, who stood facing him, saw that he thus breathed his last, he said, 'Truly this man was the Son of God!'

And Joseph of Arimathea bought a linen shroud, and taking him down, wrapped him in the linen shroud, and laid him in a tomb which had been hewn out of the rock; and he rolled a stone against the door of the tomb ...

And when the sabbath was past, Mary Magdalene, and Mary the mother of James, and Salome, bought spices, so that they might go and anoint him. And very early on the first day of the week they went to the tomb when the sun had risen. And they were saying to one another, 'Who will roll away the stone for us from the door of the tomb?' And looking up, they saw that the stone was rolled back — it was very large. And entering the tomb, they saw a young man sitting on the right side, dressed in a white robe; and they were amazed. And he said to them, 'Do not be amazed; you seek Jesus of Nazareth, who was crucified. He has risen, he is not here; see the place where they laid him.'

Psalm 130: Out of the depths I cry to thee, O Lord!
Lord, hear my voice!
Let thy ears be attentive
to the voice of my supplications!...
I wait for the Lord, my soul waits,
and in his word I hope;
my soul waits for the Lord
more than watchmen for the morning.
O Israel, hope in the Lord!

John Donne: We thinke that Paradise and Calvarie,
Christ's Crosse, and Adam's tree, stood in one place;
Looke, Lord, and finde both Adams met in me;
As the first Adam's sweat surrounds my face,
May the last Adam's blood my soule embrace.

Philippians 2$^{5-11}$: Like Adam, he was the image of God;
but unlike Adam, did not presume
that being like God meant to domineer.

He knew it meant to renounce all claims,
except the claim to be servant of all.

So he lived the life of a man among men,
and accepted the lot of men, which is death,
even the shameful death of a slave.

That is why God has raised him up,
and bestowed a title beyond compare:

Every creature, living and dead,
will kneel to him, and give glory to God,
and echo the cry, 'Jesus is Lord'.

(Tr. H.J. Richards)

Venantius Fortunatus: Faithful cross! above all other,
one and only noble tree!
None in foliage, none in blossom,
none in fruit thy peer may be;
sweetest wood and sweetest iron!
Sweetest weight is hung on thee.

(Tr. J.M. Neale)

St Richard: Thanks be to thee, Lord Jesus Christ,
for all the benefits and blessings which thou hast given to me,
for all the pains and insults which thou hast borne for me.
O most merciful Friend, Brother, and Redeemer;
may I know thee more clearly,
love thee more dearly,
and follow thee more nearly.

Isaac Watts: When I survey the wondrous Cross
on which the Prince of Glory died,
my richest gain I count but loss,
and pour contempt on all my pride.

Charles Wesley: Lamb of God, whose dying love
we now recall to mind,
send the answer from above,
and let us mercy find;
think on us who think on thee;
and every struggling soul release;
O remember Calvary,
and bid us go in peace.

Clare Richards: Christ on the cross,
not crushed by death,
but broken by his love too deep for knowing.
Christ on the cross,
not crushed by death,
but living on in love too deep for crushing.

Christ on the cross,
not slain for sin,
but broken by his love too great for giving.
Christ on the cross,
not crushed by death,
but living on in love too great for slaying.

Christ on the cross,
not killed by man,
but broken by his love too strong for holding.
Christ on the cross,
not crushed by death,
but living on in love too strong for killing.

DH: Suffering Lord,
Now you know it all:
the pain that grips the body in untimely death,
the agony of bloody wounds,
the tortured limbs,
and that deep sense of frail humanity.

Forsaken Lord,
You know it all:
  rejection at the hands of men,
  the fleeing footsteps of once-close friends,
  the callous glance of soldiers' eyes, committed to cold duty,
  neglect in the hour of need,
  and a devastating loss of God.

Lord in loneliness,
You know it all:
  the scapegoat's banishment,
  the visionary's isolation,
  the curt dismissal of an alien world,
  and the misunderstanding of those called friends.

Suffering, forsaken Lord in loneliness, bear well the hurt, the pain,
the loss. The world must have one man obedient to the end.
Thanks be to God.

ISRAEL MUSEUM see p. 63

JAFFA GATE see p. 31

JAMES, ST, CATHEDRAL see p. 32

KENNEDY MEMORIAL see p. 69

KIDRON VALLEY (fig. 8)

The Kidron is the valley running to the east of Jerusalem, dividing it from the Mount of Olives. It becomes most distinctive south of **Gethsemane** (see p. 37) from where the following description starts.

Tombs are its dominant feature at this point. First (1) that of Mary near Gethsemane (see p. 39). Then those of countless thousands on the slopes to left and right (Jews mostly on the Olives side, Christians on the valley floor, and Muslims on the slopes reaching up to the city walls) (2). And finally (taking the right fork shortly after Gethsemane) the monumental tombs cut out of the rock face on the left, popularly known as those of Absalom, Zechariah and James (3). In fact these are the tombs of rich citizens in the last centuries BC, and they would have been a familiar sight to Jesus and his disciples. The hope that the last judgment and the general resurrection would take place here under the Temple walls gave this terrain a certain prestige as a cemetery (see Joel 3, p. 55).

The steep slopes to the right topped by the Temple corner (4) (the **'Pinnacle'**, see p. 79) give some idea of why King David chose this site for his capital. With the methods of war then current, these slopes made the City of David invulnerable, at least from this side. The original inhabitants boasted it could be defended by blind cripples. The terracing to be seen on the hillside is partly the work of archaeologists like Kathleen Kenyon who have discovered some of the walls of David's time. Jerusalem would then have looked rather like the present village of Silwan on the slopes of the hill to the left (5).

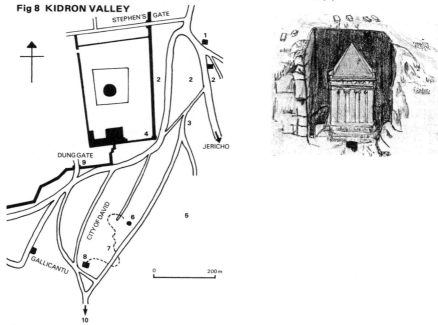

Fig 8 KIDRON VALLEY

A wire-fenced playground to the right gives access down steps to the spring of **Gihon** (6), known locally as the Ain Sitti Mariam — the Spring of the Virgin Mary, Jerusalem's original water-supply. This source of life was so highly regarded that kings were anointed here (the acclamation 'God Save the King' originated here). To allow easier access to the water, especially in times of siege, steps were dug about 1200 BC from the city above to a shaft down which buckets could be sent. It seems as if David knew of this shaft and sent a troop

49

of commandos up it to capture the city from inside. Five hundred years later king **Hezekiah** made even more certain of his water-supply by having a 530m. tunnel dug through the rock (7) to channel the water to a reservoir within the walls further south. Those who wish to experience this tunnel at first foot should wear beach shoes and bathing costumes, since the water can reach waist high after rain. A torch would be useful, though the gatekeeper (who expects an offering) will provide candles. Shortly after entering the tunnel at the bottom of the steps, it swings left. Here a low wall to the right marks the entrance to the original shaft up into the city. The narrow tunnel winds considerably, presumably because the miners avoided the hardest rock. It is low at the north end, but the roof rises towards the south where a second team of miners started too high, and had to dig deeper to allow the water to flow. At the point where the two teams met they placed an inscription on the wall. It was not discovered till 1850, and is now in the Istanbul Museum. Those tracing the path of the tunnel above ground will need to look for a narrow lane to the right about 250m. past Gihon. This leads up shortly to the Pool of Siloam (8).

The **Pool of Siloam** — the word means 'sent' (we speak of 'ducting' or leading water, the Hebrews of sending it) — marks the end of the tunnel. The importance of this reservoir for the life of the Jews was marked at the feast of Tabernacles, when water from here was carried up to the Temple and poured out as a prayer for the rain needed for the coming year. This gives point to the humorous yet profound story in John 9, which designates Jesus as the one 'sent' from above to bring light and life to those who are blind and dead. The Byzantines built a splendid basilica to celebrate the story, 'suspended over the pool' say those who saw it. Only traces of it remain beneath the 9th c. mosque now on the same site. At the exit, turn right and right again for the steep road (actually the Tyropoeon valley) leading back to the Dung Gate of the Old City (9).

A left turn takes one back to the Kidron valley. This shortly joins a valley running west — the valley of Hinnom or **Ge-Henna** —the rubbish tip of ancient Jerusalem, whose perpetual bonfires once provided a potent symbol of hell (10).

The Kidron continues south east, and becomes an impressive gorge before emptying itself into the Dead Sea near the monastery of Mar Saba (see p. 101).

2 Samuel 5[6-7]: David and his men went to Jerusalem against the Jebusites, the inhabitants of the land, who said to David, 'You will not come in here, but the blind and the lame will ward you off' —thinking, 'David cannot come in here.' Nevertheless David took the stronghold of Zion, that is, the city of David.

1 Kings 1^{38–40}: Zadok the priest, Nathan the prophet, and Benaiah the son of Jehoiada, and the Cherethites and the Pelethites, went down and caused Solomon to ride on King David's mule, and brought him to Gihon. There Zadok the priest took the horn of oil from the tent, and anointed Solomon. Then they blew the trumpet; and all the people said, 'Long live King Solomon! [AV God save the King]' And all the people went up after him, playing on pipes, and rejoicing with great joy, so that the earth was split by their noise.

2 Chronicles 32^{2–30}: When Hezekiah saw that Sennacherib had come and intended to fight against Jerusalem, he planned with his officers and his mighty men to stop the waters of the springs that were outside the city ... and closed the upper outlet of the waters of Gihon and directed them down to the west side of the city of David.

*Ecclesiasticus 48*¹⁷: Hezekiah fortified his city,
and brought water into the midst of it;
he tunnelled the sheer rock with iron
and built pools for water.

Siloam Tunnel Inscription: Completion of the Tunnel. Account of the cutting: The [two teams of] miners worked with picks in opposite directions, facing each other. When there were only one and a half more metres to cut, one team was able to hear the other because of reverberations in the rock to the right and left. The final breakthrough was made when the miners struck against each other and pick hit pick. Water began to flow from the Spring to the Pool, 500 metres. Height of the rock above the miners, 50 metres.

*John 7*³⁷ — *9*³⁸: On the last day of the feast [of Tabernacles], Jesus stood up and proclaimed. 'If any one thirst let him come to me, and let him who believes in me drink. As the scripture has said, "Out of his heart shall flow rivers of living water" ' ...

Again Jesus spoke to them, saying, 'I am the light of the world; he who follows me will not walk in darkness, but will have the light of life.'

As he passed by, he saw a man blind from his birth ... He spat on the ground and made clay of the spittle and anointed the man's eyes with the clay, saying to him, 'Go, wash in the pool of Siloam' (which means Sent). So he went and washed and came back seeing ...

They brought to the Pharisees the man who had formerly been blind ... They asked him how he had received his sight. And he said to them, 'He put clay on my eyes, and I washed, and I see.' Some of the Pharisees said, 'This man is not from God ...' But others said, 'How can a man who is a sinner do such signs?' There was a division among them. So they again said to the blind man, 'What do you say about him, since he has opened your eyes?' He said, 'He is a prophet ... Do you too want to become his disciples?' ... They cast him out.

Jesus heard that they had cast him out, and having found him he said, 'Do you believe in the Son of man?' He answered, 'And who is he, sir, that I may believe in him?' Jesus said to him, 'You have seen him, and it is he who speaks to you.' He said, 'Lord, I believe'; and he worshipped him.

BPB p. 23: Father, I believe that you are Light
    and in you there is no darkness at all.
I believe that you are Love
    and in you there is no hatred or revenge.
Your love was shown to us
    when you made us your children in Jesus Christ.
When his face shines on us
    we know the darkness is passing away
      and the light is already shining.
Father, whoever says he is in light and hates his brother
    is, for all his eloquence, still in darkness.

KNESSET   see p. 64

LITHOSTROTOS   see p. 35

MARK, CHURCH   see p. 30

MARY MAGDALENE, CHURCH   see p. 53

MAURISTAN   see p. 45

MEA SHEARIM   see p. 74

MODEL OF JERUSALEM   see p. 64

MONASTERY OF THE CROSS   see p. 64

MOSQUE OF OMAR see p. 77

MOUNT OF OLIVES (fig. 9)

The Mount of Olives, or Bull Mountain as the Arabs call it (Jebel et Tor) rises 100m. above Jerusalem to the east. As with Bethlehem, Christians tend to associate it so exclusively with Jesus that they forget its previous association with David, Jesus' forefather and prototype.

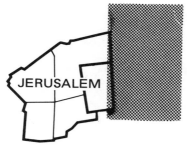

There are two ways up the mountain, by vehicle or on foot. The motor road (1) crosses the Kidron valley close to the north-east corner of the Old City, and climbs up past the trim villa of the Apostolic Delegate, and close to the imposing Victoria Augusta Hospital (2), before turning right to the main square (3).

The footpath is steeper but more delightful. It crosses the Kidron by Gethsemane (4) and then climbs sharply. Immediately above the Church of All Nations the path divides. The left hand continuation is the steeper (5), but illustrates richly why the hill is named after olives, and makes direct for the summit.

The right hand continuation (6) passes:

a. the entrance (left) to the Russian Orthodox convent of **St Mary Magdalene** (7), its onion domes forming one of the distinctive features of the Mount of Olives. Small entrance fee. Vespers and Liturgy well worth a visit: Otherwise open Tuesday and Thursday 10.00 - 11.30 only;

b. the entrance (right) to the devoutly restored **Jewish cemetery** (8) which occupies most of the hillside, a ringside seat for the Last Judgment which the prophet Joel expected to take place in the Kidron valley of 'God's Judgment' (Jeho-shaphat) below;

c. higher, the entrance (left) to the church of **Dominus Flevit** (The Lord Wept) (9). The chapel was built in 1955 on Byzantine

Fig 9 MT. OF OLIVES

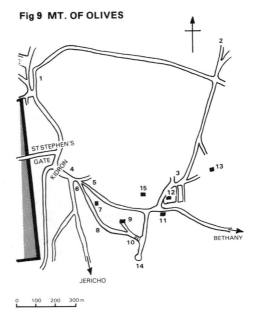

foundation (mosaics outside and inside the chapel entrance). Its famous 'chalice' window frames a fine view of the Old City, especially in the morning sun. The balcony outside is ideal for a group photograph; closed 12.00 - 14.30; toilets;

d. the reputed **Tombs** (right) **of the Prophets** Haggai, Zechariah and Malachi (10). Archeologists say that in fact the tombs are AD rather than BC. Take a torch if you go in;

e. turning left after the final flight of steps and continuing uphill, the entrance (right) to **Paternoster Church** (11) (closed 12.00 - 15.00 and Sundays). In the 19th c. a Carmelite convent was built here on the site of the cave with which Queen Helena in the 4th c. associated Jesus' discourse foretelling the Fall of Jerusalem. The memorial she built — Eleona (Olives) — is now in ruins, and attempts to reconstruct it have been abandoned, though the cave is still visible under the convent chapel. Since the gospel of Luke quotes the Lord's Prayer, not in Jesus' Galilean ministry, but after his story of nearby Bethany, the church was eventually associated with this prayer, which has now been displayed in coloured tiles round the cloister in 72 languages. A sung Paternoster (from those who still remember it) would not be inappropriate here;

f. a little higher up the hill, next to the Mount of Olives Hotel, the stepped entrance to the traditional site of the **Ascension** (12) (small entrance fee). The 4th c. Byzantines built a small circular chapel here, deliberately and symbolically open to the sky. The 12th c. Crusaders reconstructed it as an octagon, and added the surrounding fortification walls. When Saladin captured it he added the roof and made it into the mosque it has been ever since — the Muslims also venerate the Ascension of Jesus. 'Footprints' in the rock, marked with a small stone surround, are meant to remind pilgrims of Christ's 'ascendancy';

g. behind the mosque, the dominant tower of the **Russian church of the Ascension** (13) (entrance by special arrangement only), commanding a superb view of the whole of Jerusalem to the west, and the Jordan valley and Dead Sea to the east. For a small offering a similar view may be had from the balcony of the mosque;

h. outside in the street there are camel rides to be had from Muhammad's obliging Shushu, drinks in a shady garden opposite, and a few metres further up the road (north) (3) the local bus back to Damascus Gate. The camel outside the Intercontinental Hotel (south) (14) is less housetrained and more expensive.

i. in the block opposite the mosque, the Beit Gaudia Dei convent (15) of the **Darmstadt Sisters** (see p. 22), who welcome visitors (including charismatics) to tea on Sundays.

*2 Samuel 15*¹³⁻³⁰: A messenger came to David, saying, 'The hearts of the men of Israel have gone after Absalom.' Then David said to all his servants who were with him in Jerusalem, 'Arise, and let us flee; or else there will be no escape for us.... And all the country wept aloud as all the people passed by, and the king crossed the brook Kidron.... But David went up the ascent of the Mount of Olives, weeping as he went, barefoot and with his head covered; and all the people who were with him covered their heads, and they went up, weeping as they went.

*Joel 3*¹⁻¹⁷: For behold, in those days and at that time,
    when I restore the fortunes of Judah and Jerusalem,
    I will gather all the nations
    and bring them down to the valley of Jehoshaphat,
    and I will enter into judgment with them there....
    Let the nations bestir themselves
    and come up to the valley of Jehoshaphat;
    for there I will sit to judge
    all the nations round about....
    Multitudes, multitudes,
    in the valley of decision!

For the day of the Lord is near
in the valley of decision....
And the Lord roars from Zion,
and utters his voice from Jerusalem....
So you shall know that I am the Lord your God,
who dwell in Zion, my holy mountain.
And Jerusalem shall be holy
and strangers shall never again pass through it.

Jewish Prayer at a Funeral: Everlasting God, help us to realise more and more that time and space are not the measure of all things. Though our eyes do not see, teach us to understand the souls of our dear ones are not cut off. Love does not die, and the truth is stronger than the grave. Just as our affection and memory of the good they did unite us with them at this time, so may our trust in you lift us to the vision of the life that knows no death.

God of our strength, in our weakness help us; in our sorrow comfort us; in our confusion guide us. Without you our lives are nothing; with you there is fullness of life for evermore. May the words of my mouth and the meditation of my heart be acceptable to you, O Lord, my rock and my redeemer.

Luke 19[41–44]: When Jesus drew near and saw the city he wept over it, saying, 'Would that even today you knew the things that make for peace! But now they are hid from your eyes. For the days shall come upon you, when your enemies will cast up a bank about you and surround you, and hem you in on every side, and dash you to the ground, you and your children within you, and they will not leave one stone upon another within you; because you did not know the time of your visitation.'

Mark 13[1–37]: As Jesus came out of the temple, one of his disciples said to him, 'Look, Teacher, what wonderful stones and what wonderful buildings!' And Jesus said to him, 'Do you see these great buildings? There will not be left here one stone upon another, that will not be thrown down.'

And as he sat on the Mount of Olives opposite the temple, Peter and James and John and Andrew asked him privately, 'Tell us, when will this be, and what will be the sign when these things are all to be accomplished?' And Jesus began to say to them ... 'Of that day or that hour no one knows, not even the angels in heaven, nor the Son, but only the Father.... What I say to you I say to all: Watch.'

Luke 10[38–11⁴]: As they went on their way, Jesus entered a village; and a woman named Martha received him into her house.... He was praying in a certain place, and when he ceased, one of his disciples said to him, 'Lord, teach us to pray, as John taught his disciples.' And he said to them, 'When you pray, say:
Father, hallowed be thy name.
Thy kingdom come.
Give us each day our daily bread;

and forgive us our sins,
for we ourselves forgive every one who is indebted to us;
and lead us not into temptation.'

DH: Lord Jesus Christ,
today we share your tears for the cities of the world;
— still we have not loved the things that make for peace.

We weep for the divided cities:
where brother fights with brother,
where anger feeds on hatred,
where prejudice blinds the eyes of compassion,
and even religion divides,
where children are taught to hate,
and old men relish ancient wrongs.

We weep for the cities of oppression:
where iron law imprisons freedom,
where thought is curbed and conscience stifled,
where the questioning spirit is called a traitor,
where art and civilising truth grow barren,
and each must think in manner as his neighbour.

We weep for the cities of poverty:
where children live, but die too soon,
where eager hands can find no work,
where hunger rules and aid is short,
where mothers clutch uncomprehending young,
and where the little we could do, we fail to do.

We weep for our cities, and for ourselves;
We have not learned the things that make for peace.

Lord,
turn tears to love,
and love to work.
Turn work to justice,
and all that makes for peace.

Acts 1[6–12]: When they had come together, the apostles asked Jesus, 'Lord, will you at this time restore the kingdom of Israel?' He said to them ... 'You shall receive power when the Holy Spirit has come upon you; and you shall be my witnesses in Jerusalem and in all Judea and Samaria and to the end of the earth.' And when he had said this, as they were looking on, he was lifted up, and a cloud took him out of their sight. And while they were gazing into heaven as he went, behold, two men stood by them in white robes, and said, 'Men of Galilee, why do you stand looking into heaven? This Jesus, who was taken up from you into heaven, will come in the same way as you saw him go into heaven.' Then they returned to Jerusalem from the mount called Olivet, which is near Jerusalem, a sabbath day's journey away.

DH: Once, Lord Jesus Christ, you lived in one place, bound by time, and limited in ministry by human weakness and the constraints of sound and sight. But now you are the eternal Lord, powerful over all creation, seeing the universe in its grandeur, the nations in their innocence and selfishness, and sensing the life of every man and woman.

Universal Lord, ascended King,
unlimited by time,
constraints released,
with love supreme —
speak your word of love for all to hear,
guide us to justice in all lands,
grant us power to proclaim your reign,
bridge the gaps that divide and unsettle us,
and let your kingdom come.

MOUNT ZION (fig. 10)

Mount Zion is the name given by the Byzantines to the hill outside the south-west corner of the Old City. It is a misnomer. David's 'Zion' never extended beyond the eastern hillock running south of the Temple. But the Byzantine name has stuck. The area offers a number of sites of interest to the Christian pilgrim.

Just outside the Zion Gate (1), the road straight ahead leads by an alley to the right to the **Dormition Church** (2), its conical roof and tall tower forming one of Jerusalem's landmarks (closed 12.00 - 14.00 and Sundays). It is built on part of a Byzantine church which was called 'Holy Sion, Mother of All the Churches'. Mary's death (or falling asleep, *dormitio*) was associated with this site in the 6th c., in spite of the older tradition linking that event with Gethsemane (see p. 39). The present church dates from 1900 and reflects the liturgical and artistic renewal then being initiated by the German Benedictines, who were given this site by their Turkish allies. The crypt has a fine Beuronesque recumbent statue of Mary, surrounded by mosaics of her Old Testament prototypes (Eve, Ruth, Esther, Judith, etc.). The church and tower are still pockmarked with the bullet holes which serve as a reminder that for twenty years it stood in the no-man's land between the embattled Israelis and Arabs. Group leaders should be warned that the souvenir shop at the exit is an excellent one. Refreshments and toilets.

Ave Maria, gratia plena, Dominus tecum,
Benedicta tu in mulieribus,
Et benedictus fructus ventris tui, Jesus.
Sancta Maria, mater Dei,

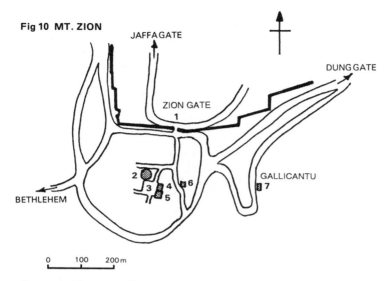

Fig 10 MT. ZION

Ora pro nobis peccatoribus,
Nunc et in hora mortis nostrae, Amen.

The alley outside the Dormition church leads back into a courtyard
(3). Through an archway on the left, a staircase leads up and through
a room into what is now known as the **Cenacle** (4). It formed part of
the Byzantine church mentioned above, built to commemorate the
first Christian community gathered in an 'upper room' at Pentecost.
The later association with the 'upper room' of the Last Supper was
inevitable. The empty vaulted room which is all that the visitor can
see is not older than the 14th c. (closed 16.30 and Friday p.m.)

Acts 1[12]−2[4]: The apostles returned to Jerusalem from the mount called
Olivet, which is near Jerusalem, a sabbath day's journey away; and when
they had entered, they went up to the upper room, where they were staying
... and with one accord devoted themselves to prayer, together with the
women and Mary the mother of Jesus, and with his brothers ...
    When the day of Pentecost had come, they were all together in one place.
And suddenly a sound came from heaven like the rush of a mighty wind, and
it filled all the house where they were sitting. And there appeared to them
tongues as of fire, distributed and resting on each one of them. And they
were all filled with the Holy Spirit.

Mark 14[12−24]: On the first day of Unleavened Bread, when they sacrificed
the passover lamb, Jesus' disciples said to him, 'Where will you have us go

59

and prepare for you to eat the passover?' And he sent two of his disciples, and said to them, 'Go into the city, and a man carrying a jar of water will meet you; follow him, and wherever he enters, say to the householder, "The Teacher says, Where is my guest room, where I am to eat the passover with my disciples?" And he will show you a large upper room furnished and ready; there prepare for us.' ...

And as they were eating, he took bread, and blessed, and broke it, and gave it to them, and said, 'Take; this is my body.' And he took a cup, and when he had given thanks he gave it to them, and they all drank of it. And he said to them, 'This is my blood of the covenant, which is poured out for many.'

The shrine known as **David's Tomb** (5) lies directly beneath the Cenacle, though access is only from a covered passageway at the end of the courtyard downstairs. In fact David was buried on his eastern hill (1 Kings 2^{10}). It was the Byzantine confusion over the where-abouts of Zion which led the Crusaders to venerate his tomb here. It has since become a Jewish national shrine. The arcaded passages adjoining it are black with the smoke of candles burnt in memory of the Jews who died in the Nazi holocaust. A small museum across the lane outside (6) keeps their memory alive with a number of exhibits, including a bar of soap made from the bones of concentration camp internees.

Acts 2^{29}: 'Men of Judea and all who dwell in Jerusalem, I may say to you confidently of the patriarch David that he both died and was buried, and his tomb is with us to this day.'

Psalm 44^{11-25}: Thou hast made us like sheep for the slaughter,
and hast scattered us among the nations.
Thou hast sold thy people for a trifle,
demanding no high price for them.
Thou hast made us the taunt of our neighbours,
the derision and scorn of those about us ...
Why dost thou hide thy face?
Why dost thou forget our affliction and oppression?
For our soul is bowed down to the dust;
our body cleaves to the ground.

From David's Tomb and its museum the road winds downhill in hairpin bends towards the Dung Gate. Halfway there, on the right, is the Assumptionist church of **St Peter in Gallicantu** (7). The name means 'Cockcrow', and suggests that it was here that Peter denied Jesus during his trial before the high priest Caiaphas. In fact the Byzantine church on which this modern church has been built commemorated the tears Peter shed later in memory of his betrayal, and it is more likely that the gospel story of the betrayal at cockcrow is to be located higher up the hill, where the high priest would have had his residence among the gentry around the present Dormition abbey.

The church (closed 12.00-14.00 and Sundays; refreshments, small shop and toilets opposite) is worth a visit for the extensive excavations underneath dating back to New Testament times. There is a stable with tying posts (which *could* have been a torture chamber), and a cistern cut out of the rock (which *could* have been used as a prison — the Byzantines painted red crosses on the walls). The balcony of the church offers a fine view of the eastern hillock which formed the original city of David, and of a long stretch of a Roman stepped street which descends this hillside to the Kidron valley and Gethsemane.

John 18[1]: When Jesus had spoken these words, he went forth with his disciples across the Kidron valley, where there was a garden which he and his disciples entered.

Mark 14[66-72]: As Peter was below in the courtyard, one of the maids of the high priest came; and seeing Peter warming himself, she looked at him, and said, 'You also were with the Nazarene, Jesus.' But he denied it, saying, 'I neither know nor understand what you mean.' And he went out into the gateway and the cock crowed. And the maid saw him, and began again to say to the bystanders, 'This man is one of them.' But again he denied it. And after a little while again the bystanders said to Peter, 'Certainly you are one of them; for you are a Galilean.' And he began to invoke a curse on himself and to swear, 'I do not know this man of whom you speak.' And immediately the cock crowed a second time. And Peter remembered how Jesus had said to him, 'Before the cock crows twice, you will deny me three times.' And he broke down and wept.

BPB p. 48: Father, when Jesus sensed his hour was at hand,
   he went with his disciples to Mount Olivet.
   'You will all fall away,' he said, 'for it is written:

61

"I will strike the shepherd
  and the sheep will be scattered".'
Peter said, 'The rest may fall away but I will not.'
And Jesus replied:
  'Peter this very night before cockcrow,
  three times you will deny me.'
'No, Lord,' cried Peter, 'I would die with you
  but I will not deny you.'
Then he who had lifted his head and boasted like a cock
  nodded and slept three times in Gethsemane ...
Soon afterwards, in the courtyard,
  Peter denied his Master three times
  at the taunt of a serving maid,...
    and he went out and wept bitterly.
Father, teach me, through Peter's humiliation,
  to realise I am always weaker than I think.
Give me the light and strength of your Spirit
  to resist temptation
  to repent like Peter immediately I fall
and to know that Christ whom I repeatedly deny
  is always looking at me
  ready to forgive me
    unto seventy times seven.

NEW CITY

Throughout its history, Jerusalem has expanded to the north and the west, where it is least hemmed in by the lie of the land. This to the extent that the original south-east hill which David first made his capital is no longer part of the walled city. The expansion has been most dramatic since the creation of the State of Israel in 1948, when housing had to be provided for Jewish refugees from Europe, Russia and the Arab countries. New Jerusalem now covers an area at least  ten times the size of the walled Old City, and continues to grow as older villages are included within its boundaries and new ones erected. It has the air, naturally enough, of any other modern European city, with some fine shopping facilities, especially in Jaffa St and Ben Yehuda St.

Of special interest to the Christian pilgrim are the following:

A. West (fig. 11)

Nearest to the Old City, in a side road to the left off King David St, opposite the YMCA, lies the complex of tombs which **Herod the Great** excavated out of the rock for his family (1). Tomb robbers have long since emptied it, but a fine mill-stone rolled back from the

Fig 11 NEW CITY (A) WEST

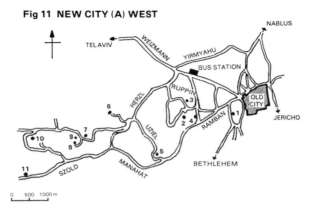

entrance gives a good idea of the way in which the dead of the time were protected from animals.

Matthew 28[2–6]: An angel of the Lord descended from heaven and came and rolled back the stone, and sat upon it ... The angel said to the women, 'Do not be afraid; for I know that you seek Jesus who was crucified. He is not here; for he has risen, as he said.'

The **Israel Museum** (2) adjoins the Hebrew University campus in Ruppin St, opposite the Knesset (Parliament). Open 10.00 - 17.00, except Tuesdays (16.00 - 22.00) and Fridays and Saturdays (10.00 - 14.00). Entrance fee. Refreshments.

This new and expanding museum complements Jerusalem's Rockefeller Museum (see p. 71), and is set in the finely landscaped **Billy Rose Garden**, which has some striking modern outdoor sculpture including pieces by Rodin, Maillol, Epstein and Henry Moore, well worth a visit. The museum is in two sections. The Bronfman Archeological Museum illustrates the whole prehistory and history of the Holy Land (including the finds from Masada, see p. 138) up to the Byzantine age. The Bezalel Museum illustrates Jewish life through the ages, and incorporates a whole 17th c. synagogue from Italy.

Attached to the Museum is the **Shrine of the Book** (nearest the entrance to the grounds) especially built to display the documents discovered in and around Qumran (see p. 162). The eye-catching dome is in the shape of the cover of the jars in which many of the manuscripts were found, and the brilliant tiling symbolises their theme — the war constantly being waged between the Sons of Light and the Sons of Darkness. Downstairs, the tunnel-like corridor into

63

the shrine evokes the caves in which many of their exhibits here displayed were found. They include letters to and from Bar Kokhba, the leader of the Jewish revolt against Rome in 132 AD.

In the centre of the shrine, under the dome, stands a vast roller on which is displayed a complete scroll of the book of Isaiah, made up of 17 pieces of skin sewn together. Beautifully and quite legibly written, the scroll dates from the first century BC, and is one of the most important of the Qumran finds. The original is not always on display, only a lifesize photograph.

In the showcases around are other texts found at Qumran, including a section of the War of the Sons of Light. Downstairs are more showcases exhibiting objects from caves in the vicinity. At the exit, slides, cards, books and toilets.

The Israeli Parliament building or **Knesset** (3), opposite the entrance to the museum, has a fine Chagall tapestry which is on view to the public on Sunday and Thursday mornings. Bring your passport. Outside in a lay-by stands the bronze candelabrum which was Britain's gift to the new State of Israel.

In the valley below the museum, on the Ben Zvi dual carriageway, is the remarkably well-preserved 11th c. **Monastery of the Cross** (4), named after the legend that the tree of which Jesus' cross was made grew here. Originally Russian, the monastery is now served by the Greek Orthodox.

A short journey through some of Jerusalem's new suburbs leads to Uziel St. Here part of the grounds of the Holyland Hotel have been made over to accommodate a 1 in 50 **Model of Jerusalem** (5) as it existed before its destruction in the Jewish War of 70 AD. The model is a memorial to the dead son of the owner of the hotel, and has been constructed under the direction of the archeologist Professor Avi-Yonah. Some aspects of it (e.g. the line of the northern wall) are hypothetical, the sources being vague or ambiguous. But most of it is very soundly based on contemporary sources, and a leisurely stroll round this lilliput after trudging round the actual streets and hills of Jerusalem is a delightful way of recalling the sites one has visited, and getting them in perspective. The exhibit is open 8.00 - 21.00 (18.00 on Fridays). Saturdays by previously purchased tickets only. Souvenirs, refreshments and toilets.

At the top of Uziel St is the T junction of Herzl Ave. A left turn and immediately right leads to the **Yad Vashem Memorial** (6). The name means 'Hand and Name' or 'Monument and Memorial'. The 'hand' is a black pillar 24m. high, and the 'name' a museum which has meticulously documented the Nazi persecution of Jews in the 1930s and 1940s. The approach is lined with an avenue of 400 trees bearing the names of the non-Jewish 'just men' who gave succour to Jews in this unprecedented pogrom.

The museum is a model of clarity and directs the visitor (painlessly is the wrong word) through the harrowing story of Hitler's 'final solution'. Maps, plans, charts, models, photographs and official documents tell their own story. (Closed Friday p.m. and Saturday.)

In the oppressive stone bunker which adjoins the museum, its doors decorated with iron thorns, a permanent flame flickers amid the names of the 21 concentration camps (Dachau, Belsen, Auschwitz, etc) where six million Jews died in the 1940s, a million of them children. It is a place where Christians might say a prayer of repentance and reflect on their complicity in this almost successful genocide. Israel's hawkish stance in Middle Eastern politics cannot be understood without reference to the history of which this place speaks. As well ask them to let bygones be bygones as ask Christians to forget the crucifixion.

Isaiah 56[5]: Thus says the Lord:
> I will give in my house and within my walls
> a Monument and a Name
> better than sons and daughters;
> I will give them an everlasting name
> which shall not be cut off.

Psalm 79[2–10]: How long, O Lord? Wilt thou be angry for ever? ...
> Let thy compassion come speedily to meet us,
> for we are brought very low ...
> The heathen have given the bodies of thy servants
> to the birds of the air for food,
> the flesh of thy saints to the beasts of the earth ...
> Help us, O God of our salvation,
> for the glory of thy name;
> deliver us, and forgive us our sins,
> for thy name's sake!
> Why should the nations say,
> 'Where is their God?'

DH: The sin of the world touches us, each one.
> We cannot escape it.
> We share its shame.
> We share its ill-gotten gains.
> We share its guilt.

I am sorry, Lord;
sorry to the point where sorrow hurts,
sorry to the depths of my life,
sorry to the place where renewal is my only hope.
I am truly sorry, Lord.

Lamb of God, you take away the sin of the world:
have mercy on us.

Requiem aeternam dona eis Domine
Et lux perpetua luceat eis.

Back on the Herzl Ave, a right fork goes downhill to the village of
En Karem. Byzantine piety identified a cave in this very old village
as the place where St Elizabeth and her son John the Baptist took
refuge from Herod's massacre of the Innocents. By the 10th c. this
had become the 'house' of Elizabeth and the stories of Luke's
opening chapters were associated with it. A second church was built
to celebrate the visit paid to Elizabeth by Mary.

The church of St John the Baptist (7) lies nearest the main road
(leave cars in the square and walk up). Closed 12.00 - 14.30. The
church is a Crusader building. The cool blue tiles which decorate the
interior date from 1495 - only three years after America was discovered - the work of the Spanish Franciscans. The cave is ahead on the
left - a good place to say (or sing!) the *Magnificat*.

A lane on the other side of the main road leads to the restored
Crusader church of the Visitation (8). The hillside beyond is dotted
with the hermitages of Russian nuns, now mostly abandoned.

A sharp right turn up a narrow alleyway at the beginning of this
lane (just negotiable by coaches) leads to the walled Sion Convent on
the summit of the hill (9). Shrewd groups book lunch here. The
founder of the Sion order, Theodore Ratisbonne, is buried in the
cool gardens.

Luke 1[39-45]: In those days Mary arose and went with haste into the hill
country, to a city of Judah, and she entered the house of Zechariah and
greeted Elizabeth. And when Elizabeth heard the greeting of Mary, the babe
leaped in her womb; and Elizabeth was filled with the Holy Spirit and she
exclaimed with a loud cry, 'Blessed are you among women, and blessed is the
fruit of your womb! And why is this granted me, that the mother of my Lord
should come to me? For behold, when the voice of your greeting came to my
ears, the babe in my womb leaped for joy. And blessed is she who believed
that there would be a fulfilment of what was spoken to her from the Lord.'

Luke 1[46–55]: My soul magnifies the Lord,
My spirit rejoices in God, my Saviour.
He looks on his servant in her nothingness;
henceforth all ages will call me blessed.
The Almighty works marvels for me.
Holy his name!
His mercy is from age to age
on those who fear him.
He puts forth his arm in strength
and scatters the proud-hearted.
He casts the mighty from their thrones
and raises the lowly.
He fills the starving with good things,
sends the rich away empty.
He protects Israel, his servant
remembering his mercy,
the mercy promised to our fathers,
for Abraham and his sons for ever.   *(Grail)*

Prepare ye the way of the Lord!
Prepare ye the way of the Lord!

Beyond En Karem the road climbs up to the left to the **Hadassah Hospital** (10) which crowns the hill opposite. When the cease-fire lines of 1946 cut Jews off from the Hebrew University which was then being built north-east of the Old City on Mt Scopus, a new medical centre was begun here. Over the years this has become so established that it now forms the medical faculty of Hebrew University. Hadassah (Esther) is the name of the American women's

organization which has provided funds for this project from the beginning. The twelve windows of its freestanding synagogue, to the left of the main entrance, are the work of Marc Chagall. They represent in symbolic form the deathbed promises made to the twelve tribes of Israel by Jacob and by Moses. They are astonishingly moving. Closed 13.00 - 14.00 and Saturdays.

Genesis 49$^{1-27}$ and *Deuteronomy 33*$^{1-25}$:

Reuben (light blue)
    Reuben, you are my first-born,
    my might, and the first fruits of my strength ...
    Unstable as water, you shall not have pre-eminence.

Simeon (dark blue)
    Simeon and Levi are brothers;
    weapons of violence are their swords ...
    Cursed be their anger, for it is fierce;
    and their wrath, for it is cruel!

Levi (gold)
    They observed thy word,
    and kept thy covenant.
    They shall teach Jacob thy ordinances,
    and Israel thy law.

Judah (dark red)
    Judah, your brothers shall praise you;
    your hands shall be on the neck of your enemies ...
    Judah is a lion's whelp ...
    The sceptre shall not depart from Judah.

Zebulun (light red)
    Zebulun shall dwell at the shore of the sea;
    he shall become a haven for ships.

Issachar (green)
    Issachar is a strong ass,
    crouching between the sheepfolds;
    he saw that a resting place was good,
    and that the land was pleasant;
    so he bowed his shoulder to bear.

Dan (blue)
    Dan shall judge his people ...
    Dan shall be a serpent in the way,
    a viper by the path,
    that bites the horse's heels.

Gad (dark green)
  Raiders shall raid Gad,
  but he shall raid at their heels.

Asher (olive)
  Asher's food shall be rich,
  and he shall yield royal dainties ...
  Blessed above sons be Asher ...
  and let him dip his foot in oil.

Naphtali (yellow)
  Naphtali is a hind let loose,
  that bears comely fawns.

Joseph (orange)
  Joseph is a fruitful bough,
  a fruitful bough by a spring;
  his branches run over the wall ...
  Blessed by the Lord be his land.

Benjamin (blue)
  Benjamin is a ravenous wolf,
  in the morning devouring the prey ...
  The beloved of the Lord,
  he dwells in safety by him.

From Hadassah it is possible to go a few km. further into the Judean hills to the monument erected in memory of the American president **John F. Kennedy** (11), a great friend of Israel, assassinated in his prime in 1963. The memorial has been built in the form of a powerful tree cut in half. The windows bear the emblems of the confederated states of America.

B. North (fig. 12)

The following sites of interest to the Christian pilgrim in the area north of the Old City are all within striking distance of each other:

The **Damascus Gate** (1) is known to Jews as the Shechem Gate, and to Arabs as the Column Gate (Bab el Amud), since it once boasted an enormous column, and gave access to the colonnaded street *(Cardo Maximus)* which once ran due south from here as Jerusalem's principal thoroughfare. The present gate is of the same date as the walls — 16th c. Turkish — but recent excavations, beautifully displayed by means of a new bridge, show it to stand on foundations going back to Roman times, perhaps Herod Agrippa (40 AD), perhaps even Herod the Great (BC), as the stones suggest. But the

69

Fig 12 NEW CITY (B) NORTH

northern wall would here have stepped back to the south, leaving the site of Holy Sepulchre outside the city (see p. 44). St Paul knew this Roman gate, and presumably rode through it on the 'road to Damascus'. Toilets and moneychangers at the gate.

Inside the fortified L-shaped entrance there is access to the excavations (a Roman watch-tower 11m. high was unearthed in 1985), and to a walkway on which it is possible to see most of the Old City from the top of the walls (National Parks card). West goes to Jaffa Gate, east to St Stephen's Gate. Open 9.00 - 16.00

Acts 9[1-5]: Saul, still breathing murder and threats against the disciples of the Lord, went to the high priest and asked him for letters to the synagogues at Damascus, so that if he found any belonging to the Way, men or women, he might bring them bound to Jerusalem. Now as he journeyed he approached Damascus, and suddenly a light from heaven flashed about him. And he fell to the ground and heard a voice saying to him, 'Saul, Saul, why do you persecute me?' And he said, 'Who are you, Lord?' And he said, 'I am Jesus, whom you are persecuting.'

Just to the right, outside Damascus Gate, in a newly landscaped rose garden, is the entrance to **Solomon's Quarries** (2) (open 8.00 - 17.00. Small entrance fee. Tickets for Saturdays in advance). No one knows who first quarried here, but the amount of stone it yielded could have built the whole of ancient Jerusalem, including perhaps Solomon's Temple, which is spoken of as built of stones quarried where the workman could not be heard. The limestone shows signs of having been removed from the rockface with wood wedges.

The cave, which runs for 300m. under the Old City, was thought in medieval times to extend as far as Jericho, and to be the means by which King Zedekiah escaped the besieging Babylonian army (2 Kings 25$^{4-5}$). Its existence was forgotten until 1854 when an American doctor's dog found its way in. Exploration revealed a dead body dumped at the far end by someone who got there before the dog.

1 Kings 5^{15}—*6*^{7}: Solomon had seventy thousand burden-bearers and eighty thousand hewers of stone in the hill country ... At the king's command they quarried out great, costly stones in order to lay the foundation of the house with dressed stones ... When the house was built, it was with stone prepared at the quarry; so that neither hammer nor axe nor any tool of iron was heard in the temple, while it was being built.

The towered stone building on an eminence outside the north-east corner of the Old City is the **Rockefeller Museum of Archaeology** (3). Entrance is from the rear of the building. Open 10.00 - 17.00, Fridays and Saturdays 10.00 - 14.00. Entrance fee.

The exhibits are arranged chronologically, from the Stone Age (500,000 BC) to the 16th c. AD. In each of the two main galleries, catalogues listing the exhibits in different languages are available to the public. The most important items in each showcase have red stars.

The left hand fork north of the Damascus Gate is Prophets Street. In a courtyard just before the first right-hand turn stands the **Armenian chapel of St Polyeuctus** (4), which has recently put on public display a beautifully preserved mosaic floor of the 5th c., a memorial to the Armenian dead. The mosaic is one of the finest in the Holy Land, and is well worth a visit. Closed 17.30.

The road directly north of Damascus Gate is Nablus Road. 200m. up on the right is the entrance to the **Garden Tomb** (5). Closed 12.00 - 14.30 and Sundays. Entrance is free.

It was known originally as Gordon's Tomb after General Charles Gordon. Dissatisfied and disedified by Queen Helena's Holy Sepulchre church, so patently within Jerusalem's present walls, he searched for a more sympathetic site outside, and in 1883, from his hotel on the north wall, saw the shape of a skull in the caves which form a backdrop to the present bus station. Golgotha — Calvarium — Skull Hill? Further investigation revealed in the rocks beyond a perfectly preserved 1st c. tomb, complete with groove for a rolling stone. He telegraphed Queen Victoria, 'I have found the site of

71

Calvary'. Victoria graciously thanked him, but added that she intended to persevere in the tradition first established 'by our cousin Helena'.

There is little possibility of the site being authentic. The present skull-like caves in the rock do not even appear in a 17th c. drawing of the place. But there is equally no doubt that it is able to recreate, in a way that Holy Sepulchre no longer can, the kind of garden setting of the tomb in which Jesus was laid. The place has a deserved significance among evangelical Christians. The Resurrection service at sunrise on Easter day is most moving.

John 19[41]—*20*[16]: In the place where he was crucified there was a garden, and in the garden a new tomb where no one had ever been laid ... As the tomb was close at hand, they laid Jesus there.

Now on the first day of the week Mary Magdalene came to the tomb early, while it was still dark, and saw that the stone had been taken away from the tomb ... She stooped to look into the tomb; and she saw two angels in white, sitting where the body of Jesus had lain, one at the head and one at the feet. They said to her, 'Woman, why are you weeping?' She said to them, 'Because they have taken away my Lord, and I do not know where they have laid him.' Saying this, she turned round and saw Jesus standing, but she did not know that it was Jesus. Jesus said to her, 'Woman, why are you weeping? Whom do you seek?' Supposing him to be the gardener, she said to him, 'Sir, if you have carried him away, tell me where you have laid him, and I will take him away.' Jesus said to her, 'Mary.' She turned, and said to him in Hebrew, 'Rabboni!'

Mark 16[5−7]: Entering the tomb, (the women) saw a young man sitting on the right side, dressed in a white robe; and they were amazed. And he said to them, 'Do not be amazed; you seek Jesus of Nazareth, who was crucified. He has risen, he is not here; see the place where they laid him.'

DH: Dead, Lord, they said, dead and buried;
and the new truth of your presence leapt into their lives.
Gone, they said, gone. Gone for ever;
and there you were, present in heart and community.
Finished, they said, finished. Finished and forgotten;
and your friends found you, in a garden, in a room, on a road.
Lost, they said, lost. Lost and gone for ever;
and your Church today proclaims your eternal presence and
abiding love.

Alive, we say, alive and living.
Here, we say, here and always.
Fulfilled we say, fulfilled and completed.
The heartbeat of the world throbs again:
Christ reborn from the grave, and we his friends with him.

Adjoining the Garden Tomb, 50m. further up the road, is the walled enclosure of the **Ecole Biblique** (6) (ring for entrance). The school was founded in 1890 by the French Dominicans, and has been in the vanguard of the Roman Catholic biblical renewal in this century, as the names of its scholars testify: Lagrange, Vincent, de Vaux, Tournay, Benoit. The *Jerusalem Bible* originated here.

The enclosed courtyard gives on to a church which has preserved the plan of the 5th c. building erected by the empress Eudocia to house the relics of the first Christian martyr, **St Stephen**. The original mosaics are still to be seen under the rugs which protect them.

Acts 6⁸—7⁶⁰: Stephen, full of grace and power, did great wonders and signs among the people ... No one could withstand the wisdom and the Spirit with which he spoke ... As they were stoning Stephen he prayed, 'Lord Jesus, receive my spirit.' And he knelt down and cried with a loud voice, 'Lord, do not hold this sin against them.' And when he had said this, he fell asleep.

400m. further up the Nablus Road (past traces in St George's Rd of a northern wall of uncertain date) is the entrance right to **St George's Cathedral** (7), its quiet courtyard, cloister and gardens seemingly transplanted from some English cathedral town. It boasts a font for baptism by immersion. The cathedral is the seat of the Anglican Archbishop of the Near East, and has attached to it a secondary school, a house of studies, and an excellent pilgrims' hospice.

Just beyond St George's, where Saladin Street meets the Nablus Road, is a notice proclaiming 'Tombeaux des Rois', **Tombs of the Kings** (8). It is a misnomer, since no kings of Judah were buried here, as popular tradition had it. But a queen was, as the French archaeologists of 1863 discovered - Helena, queen of Adiabene in Syria, converted to Judaism in the 1st c. A.D.

The approach is down a noble staircase cut into the rock, with gutters and channels directing rainwater into great cisterns at the base. A gateway leads into a disused quarry, which has been turned into a majestic courtyard by decorating the rockface with an ornate façade. A rolling stone gives access to an antechamber, off which there are three further chambers, each with several burial places for the queen's family. All had been emptied by tomb robbers when excavated, except the well-hidden queen, who was carried back to France and laid to rest in the Louvre. The man who provides candles expects a small offering. Closed at 17.00.

The lane opposite St George's leads to St George Street. A left turn on this road leads within 200m. to the intersection which until 1967 served as the **Mandelbaum Gate** (9), the sole point of contact between east and west Jerusalem. 300m. further along, the sharp right turn is Mea Shearim Road. The narrow alleys, lanes and courtyards to the left and right of this road comprise the quarter of **Mea Shearim** or 'Hundred Gates' (10).

Mea Shearim was one of the first areas in Jerusalem to be settled by Jews from eastern Europe. It still bears the air of a 19th c. *stetl* and can give the visitor the impression of wandering on to the set of *Fiddler On The Roof*. Fiercely traditional in its way of life, its boys in ringlets and its married women shaven and forbidden to grow hair (but not to wear wigs), it remains totally opposed to the secularist aims of the Israeli State. Billboards ask visitors not to give offence to this way of life by outrageous dress. Men should cover their heads and women their arms. Christian pilgrims would do well not to display a cross, which Jews of this culture still remember as a rod often used to beat them with.

Beyond Mea Shearim, Prophets Street (Haneviim) will lead back to Damascus Gate, or Strauss and Jaffa Street to the Jaffa Gate.

PATERNOSTER CHURCH   see p. 54

PETER IN GALLICANTU   See p. 60

PINNACLE   see p. 79

PRAETORIUM   see p. 35

ROCKEFELLER MUSEUM   see p. 71

RUSSIAN HOSPICE   see p. 45

SHRINE OF THE BOOK   see p. 63

SILOAM   see p. 50

SION SISTERS   see p. 34

SOLOMON'S QUARRIES   see p. 70

SOLOMON'S STABLES   see p. 79

STEPHEN'S CHURCH   see p. 73

STEPHEN'S GATE   see p. 29

SUK (fig. 13)

The word 'suk' means market. Old Jerusalem is full of them, but the title is generally used of the principal north-south thoroughfare from Damascus Gate (1), now called Suk Khan ez-Zeit. This was once the *Cardo Maximus* or Main Pivot of Hadrian's Jerusalem (135 AD), and even through Byzantine times was lined with a colonnade on either side. One broken column is still to be seen a third of the way down, marking the 7th Station of the Cross (2).

The joy of the suk is that it is designed not for the tourist but for the ordinary Jerusalem shopper. Groceries, household goods, vege-

tables, meat, clothes, bread — all are available in tiny lockups, outside which the Bedouin women display the wares they have brought in from the country. Donkeys ply to and fro in this traffic-

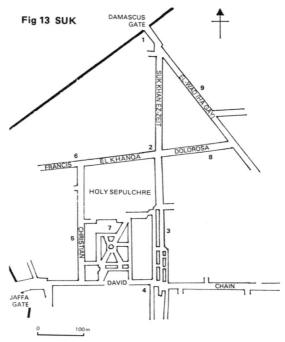

Fig 13 SUK

free zone, and the air is filled with the aroma of spices, coffee and frying *felafel*. Many of the shops are owned by Muslims, and are therefore closed on Fridays.

Beyond Holy Sepulchre the suk divides into two, and then into three, each arcaded avenue with its distinctive trade (3). It ends at the principal west-east thoroughfare (David and Chain Street) (4), running from the Jaffa Gate to the Temple. These two roads cater more for the tourist and the pilgrim, as do the other roads (Christian (5), El Khanqa (6), Mauristan (7)) surrounding Holy Sepulchre Church. There are some very fine dealers in antiquities in the Via Dolorosa (8) and Wad Street (9).

TEMPLE AREA (fig. 14)

The Temple Area is the name given to the splendid esplanade which occupies a fifth of the walled city. It is the work of Herod the Great, but on the site chosen for a Temple by king David and his son Solomon. The building at its centre is generally referred to as the **Dome of the Rock** from its main feature, or (mistakenly) as the

Mosque of Omar (it is neither a mosque nor the work of Omar). Muslims refer to the whole area more fittingly as the Noble Sanctuary — **Haram esh-Sharif**.

The story of the Temple begins with King David in 1000 BC, whose capture of Jerusalem prompted him to make the city not only the capital of a newly confederated Israel but also its religious centre. He rescued the abandoned Ark of the Covenant, symbol of God's protection since Exodus times, had it solemnly installed in Jerusalem, and marked out a high point just north of his city, till then apparently used as a windswept threshing floor, as a permanent 'House of God'. Here his son Solomon, aided by his new Phoenician allies, put the plan into operation. The Book of Kings enthuses on the countless sheep and oxen slaughtered to mark the dedication.

This First Temple was totally destroyed in the Babylonian invasion of 586 BC, and the Second Temple with which the returning exiles replaced it 70 years later was never regarded as containing God's Presence *(Shekinah)* or Glory *(Kabhod)* in the way that Solomon's had. Yet it became what the First Temple had never been, the focal point of Israel's life, and the goal of all its pilgrimages. All the psalms were written for use in this Temple, and every pious Jew hoped to be buried in its shadow.

Twenty years before Christ, Herod the Great ingratiated himself with his Jewish subjects by embarking upon a rebuilding project so spectacular that it transformed this Second Temple, whose bulk would have been about twice that of the present Dome of the Rock. But it was in the area surrounding the Temple that Herod displayed his magnificence. Using massive retaining walls and arched supports, he extended the platform on which the Temple stood to its present imposing size of 30 acres, and lined the whole area with splendid colonnades. On the north he guarded it with a fortress (**Antonia**, see p. 34), and dug two vast reservoirs to ensure its water supply. Notices at each gate warned non-Jews (like Herod himself) not to encroach on the sacred area. The excavations currently in progress (see below) have revealed the splendour of Herod's project.

The project was still in course of realisation in New Testament times, when Jesus was teaching in the Temple precincts. Jesus' own attitude to the Temple echoed the reserve expressed by many of the Old Testament prophets, for whom the true Temple of God was in the hearts of men. He worshipped there with the rest of his Jewish countrymen, but he did not hesitate to suggest that he himself and his body of disciples could replace it as the dwelling place of God among men. For this apparently blasphemous claim he was put to death.

77

Herod's Temple was not finished till the year 64 AD, and stood for only six years more before it was again totally destroyed, this time never to be rebuilt. The Byzantines were not interested in restoring it and used it as a rubbish tip. The 7th c. Caliphs built the present Dome and the el-Aksa mosque, which the 12th c. Crusaders turned into a church and a palace. The buildings reverted to Arab use after the defeat of the Crusaders, and have remained Muslim holy places ever since.

Fig 14 TEMPLE AREA

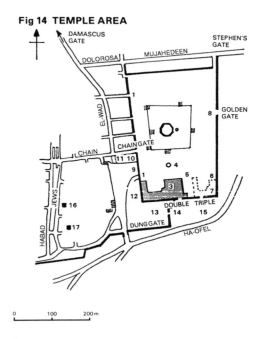

Entrance to the Temple Area is free, via any of the five main gates on the west side. Entrance to the Dome and the el-Aksa mosque is by ticket, obtainable at the ticket offices near the extreme gates (1). Closed for midday prayers, after 15.00, and all Friday.

The **Dome of the Rock** (2) remains essentially the beautiful octagonal monument erected in the 7th c. AD, though it has been restored many times, most extensively in 1963/4 when much of the external tiling was refurbished, and the 200-ton lead dome replaced with a more elegant one in aluminium and bronze weighing only 35 tons. Inside, the heart is uplifted by the perfect proportions, the eyes by the gentle light filtering through the stained glass, the ears by the hushed atmosphere of reverence, and the unshod feet by the soft and magnificent carpets, the gift of Egypt's President Nasser. Under the elaborately carved dome, surrounded by a balustrade, is the bare rock which gives the building its name. Later tradition identified this as the Mount Moriah where Abraham was willing to sacrifice his only son Isaac — hence the Muslim interest in it. Certainly it is the hilltop chosen by David for the worship of his heavenly God, for whom a Holy of Holies was built in the Temple which lay beyond. The rock remained in the open, and served as an altar for the sacrifice of animals. From the cave beneath it (stairs) a hole can be seen in the ceiling, presumably cut to drain away the blood of these lambs of God.

The **el-Aksa** building to the south (3) is more properly a Muslim mosque or house of prayer. It was built shortly after the Dome to commemorate the 'distant' journey made by Muhammad on his winged horse before ascending to heaven. It similarly provides a fine sense of proportion and beautiful carpets for unshod feet. The Crusaders used it for a few years as a residence for the armed monks known as the Knights Templar, and it has suffered many times from earthquakes and fires, of which the most recent was started by an Australian messianic pretender in 1969. This did considerable damage to the painted ceiling recently donated by King Farouk of Egypt, though the marble columns given by Mussolini were not harmed.

Outside the mosque a sunken area contains a delightful fountain (4) for worshippers to wash their feet (ritually or non-ritually) before entering. A little to the right (5) are the stairs which lead down to the stepped tunnel, now blocked, which once gave access to Herod's Temple from the south (entrance by special arrangement only, since the Australian affair). A similar flight of steps over by the wall to the east (6) leads down to the so-called **Solomon's Stables** — actually the subterranean arched vault which Herod built over this eastern cliff in order to extend his esplanade. The Crusaders kept their horses in these vast cellars, which give access to another Herodian tunneled ramp into the south wall. Here too entrance is by special arrangement.

It is possible from here to walk up on to the wall and along the battlements, though one needs a head for heights. There is a spectacular view from the south-east corner (7) of the Kidron valley below and of the Mount of Olives beyond. Since the Herodian wall here drops a sheer 47m. to bedrock (the Dome itself is only 43m. high), the corner has become known as the **Pinnacle of the Temple**, though it is more likely that the pinnacle referred to in

79

Jesus' Temptations was one of the towers of the Temple building itself.

To the north of this viewpoint, halfway along the eastern retaining wall, is the **Golden Gate** (8), a Latin misunderstanding *(aurea)* of its Greek name, Beautiful Gate *(horaia)*. It is a Byzantine construction on Herodian foundations, and once gave access to the Temple from the Kidron valley. It has been walled up since Crusader times, and given rise to the legend that it will only be opened again for the Coming of the Messiah.

The Jewish tradition also patiently marks time for the Messiah, and forbids orthodox Jews to set foot on the Temple mount until that happy time arrives. A notice to that effect is posted on the ramp leading from the southerly ticket office (1) to the **Western Wall** below (9). This area, which until recently was hemmed in with buildings to within four metres of the Wall, has since 1967 been cleared to reveal the beauty of Herod's stones, some up to 23m. long. The area now provides a vast open-air synagogue, where the devotion of praying Jews (no longer 'wailing') mingles easily with the songs of the birds nesting in the timeworn crevices. Men who wish to join the worshippers at the Wall must cover their heads (paper hats provided free). Particularly impressive on Friday nights and Saturdays, when photography is forbidden.

The clearing of the area was followed up, immediately after the end of the Six Day War, with digs which have brought to light the magnificence of Herod's Temple project. The arch already discovered by the British army engineer Wilson (10) is now known to have supported a viaduct, 15m. wide, connecting the Temple with the city to the west. Shafts dug under the arch (similarly a synagogue area, closed Saturdays) reveal the depth from which Herod began his building. Close by, an ancient arcaded road has been re-excavated to allow direct access from el-Wad Street (11). The arch springing out of the Temple Wall further south, first discovered by the American geographer Robinson (12) is now known to have supported a staircase which turned at right angles to meet the elegant paved shopping street running along the base of the Wall. All around there is plenty of evidence of the violence with which the Romans destroyed these buildings in 70 AD.

Excavations have also been made along the southern end of the Temple Area, where the Arab rulers of the 7th c. AD built their palaces (as Solomon had done) and a hospice for pilgrims (13). Beyond the Turkish fortifying wall, and easily visible from the road outside the Dung Gate, Herod's paved street can be seen to terminate in three great flights of steps leading up to two tunnels (14 and 15) (one for entry and one for exit) into the Temple Area. Some of the steps have been restored. Those which survived the Roman destruction were perfectly smooth, reflecting the few years they were in use. Access to the whole excavated area is from a ticket-office (entrance fee) inside the Dung Gate.

Because of its association with the Jewish Temple, the district immediately to the west has traditionally been the **Jewish Quarter**. Long inhabited by Jews who lived on easy terms with their neighbours, it was abandoned in 1948 and suffered neglect, deliberate damage and looting. Since 1967 its complex network of streets has been sensitively restored on a scale and in a style Jerusalem has not known for centuries. The accompanying archaeological study has made available a better understanding of the biblical, Byzantine and Crusader history of this part of the Old City. Worthy of note are the restored synagogues of the 13th and 17th c. (16 and 17).

2 Samuel 24[18–24]: Gad came that day to David, and said to him, 'Go up, rear an altar to the Lord on the threshing floor of Araunah the Jebusite.' ... And Araunah said, 'Why has my Lord the king come to his servant?' David said, 'To buy the threshing floor of you, in order to build an altar to the Lord.' ... Araunah said to David, 'Let my lord the king take and offer up what seems good to him.' ... But the king said to Araunah, 'No, but I will buy it of you for a price; I will not offer burnt offerings to the Lord my God which cost me nothing.' So David bought the threshing floor and the oxen for fifty shekels of silver.

2 Samuel 6[1–15]: David gathered all the chosen men of Israel, thirty thousand ... And they carried the ark of God upon a new cart ... And David and all the house of Israel were making merry before the Lord with all their might, with songs and lyres and harps and tambourines and castanets and cymbals ... And David danced before the Lord with all his might; and David was girded with a linen ephod. So David and all the house of Israel brought up the ark of the Lord with shouting, and with the sound of the horn.

1 Kings 5²—8⁶: Solomon sent word to Hiram king of Tyre ... 'I purpose to build a house for the name of the Lord my God ... Now therefore command that cedars of Lebanon be cut for me; and my servants will join your servants, and I will pay you for your servants such wages as you set; for you know that there is no one among us who knows how to cut timber like the Sidonians' ...

So Hiram supplied Solomon with all the timber of cedar and cypress that he desired, while Solomon gave Hiram twenty thousand cors of wheat as food for his household, and twenty thousand cors of beaten oil. Solomon gave this to Hiram year by year ... So Solomon's builders and Hiram's builders and the men of Gebal did the hewing and prepared the timber and the stone to build the House ...

All the elders of Israel came, and the priests took up the ark. And they brought up the ark of the Lord, the tent of meeting, and all the holy vessels that were in the tent; the priests and the Levites brought them up. And King Solomon and all the congregation of Israel, who had assembled before him, were with him before the ark, sacrificing so many sheep and oxen that they could not be counted or numbered. Then the priests brought the ark of the covenant of the Lord to its place, in the inner sanctuary of the House, in the most holy place, underneath the wings of the cherubim.

Jeremiah 7²⁻⁴: Hear the word of the Lord, all you men of Judah who enter these gates to worship the Lord. Thus says the Lord of hosts, the God of Israel, amend your ways and your doings, and I will let you dwell in this place. Do not trust in these deceptive words: 'This is the temple of the Lord, the temple of the Lord.'

Ezra 3⁸⁻¹³: In the second year of their coming to the House of God at Jerusalem, Zerubbabel ... made a beginning ... And when the builders laid the foundation of the Temple of the Lord, the priests in their vestments came forward ... and they sang responsively, praising and giving thanks to the Lord,

'For he is good,
for his steadfast love endures for ever towards Israel.'

And all the people shouted with a great shout, when they praised the Lord, because the foundation of the House of the Lord was laid. But many of the priests and Levites and heads of fathers' houses, old men who had seen the first House, wept with a loud voice when they saw the foundation of this House being laid, though many shouted aloud for joy; so that the people could not distinguish the sound of the joyful shout from the sound of the people's weeping, for the people shouted with a great shout, and the sound was heard afar.

Psalm 84: How lovely is your dwelling place,
Lord, God of hosts.
My soul is longing and yearning,
is yearning for the courts of the Lord.
My heart and my soul ring out their joy
to God, the living God.
The sparrow herself finds a home
and the swallow a nest for her brood;
she lays her young by your altars,
Lord of hosts, my king and my God.
They are happy, who dwell in your house,
for ever singing your praise.
They are happy, whose strength is in you,
in whose hearts are the roads to Sion.   *(Grail)*

Haggai 2³⁻⁹: Who is left among you that saw this House in its former glory? How do you see it now? Is it not in your sight as nothing? Yet now take courage ... My Spirit abides among you; fear not: Once again, in a little while, I will shake the heavens and the earth and the sea and the dry land ... and I will fill this House with glory, says the Lord of hosts . . . The latter glory of this House shall be greater than the former.

Luke 1⁵—2⁴⁶: In the days of Herod, king of Judea, there was a priest named Zechariah ... Now while he was serving as priest before God ... it fell to him by lot to enter the temple of the Lord and burn incense ... And there appeared to him an angel of the Lord ... And the people were waiting for Zechariah, and they wondered at his delay in the temple ...

When the time came for the purification, according to the law of Moses, Mary and Joseph brought Jesus up to Jerusalem to present him to the Lord ...

His parents went to Jerusalem every year at the Passover. And when he was twelve years old, they went up according to custom; and when the feast was ended, as they were returning, the boy Jesus stayed behind in Jerusalem ... After three days they found him in the temple, sitting among the teachers.

Mark 11⁹—13²: Those who went before Jesus and those who followed cried out, 'Hosanna! Blessed is he who comes in the name of the Lord! Blessed is the kingdom of our father David that is coming! Hosanna in the highest!'

And he entered Jerusalem, and went into the temple ... and began to drive out those who sold and those who bought in the temple and he overturned the tables of the moneychangers and the seats of those who sold pigeons; and he would not allow anyone to carry anything through the temple. And he taught, and said to them, 'Is it not written, "My house shall be called a house of prayer for all the nations"?'...

As he came out of the temple, one of his disciples said to him, 'Look, Teacher, what wonderful stones and what wonderful buildings!' And Jesus said to him, 'Do you see these great buildings? There will not be left here one stone upon another, that will not be thrown down.'

John 2[19-21]: Jesus said to the Jews, 'Destroy this temple, and in three days I will raise it up.' The Jews then said, 'It has taken forty-six years to build this temple, and will you raise it up in three days?' But he spoke of the temple of his body.

1 Corinthians 3[16-17]: Do you not know that you are God's temple and that God's Spirit dwells in you? If anyone destroys God's temple, God will destroy him. For God's temple is holy, and that temple you are.

Ephesians 2[19-22]: You are no longer strangers and sojourners, but you are fellow citizens with the saints and members of the household of God, built upon the foundation of the apostles and prophets, Christ Jesus himself being the cornerstone, in whom the whole structure is joined together and grows into a holy temple in the Lord; in whom you also are built into it for a dwelling place of God in the Spirit.

Acts 3[1-8]: Peter and John were going up to the temple at the hour of prayer, the ninth hour. And a man lame from birth was being carried, whom they laid daily at that gate of the temple which is called Beautiful to ask alms of those who entered the temple ... Peter said, 'I have no silver and gold, but I give you what I have; in the name of Jesus Christ of Nazareth, walk.' And he took him by the right hand and raised him up ... And leaping up he stood and walked and entered the temple with them, walking and leaping and praising God.

BPB p. 97: Father, of all the gospels' tales of generosity
    I am challenged most by the one about a poor widow.
Jesus had been sitting opposite the temple treasury.
He had watched many rich people, as they filed by,
    putting in considerable sums.
Then along came this poor widow.
She put in a couple of copper coins, a mere penny.
Jesus was so excited by this he called his disciples:
'Listen carefully,' he said.
'This poor widow has put in the treasury more than anyone.
The rest gave out of their abundance.
She, out of her poverty, gave everything she had.'
I have often wondered, Father,
    whether that widow was wise in parting with her money.
Her action seems to have been proud and improvident,
    leaving her a penniless nuisance
        and dependent on charity.
But Jesus generously praised her generosity.
Was it, Father, because she was a kindred soul to him
    who was improvident enough to give his all on the cross,
even though it seemed small enough at the time,
    and hardly likely to make
        any difference to the world?

Prayer of Solomon (1 Kings 8²⁷⁻³⁰):

Will God indeed dwell on the earth?
Behold, heaven and the highest heaven cannot contain thee:
how much less this House which I have built!
Yet have regard to the prayer of thy servant
and to his supplication, O Lord my God,
hearkening to the cry and to the prayer
which thy servant prays before thee this day;
that thy eyes may be open
night and day towards this House,
the place of which thou hast said,
'My name shall be there',
that thou mayest hearken to the prayer
which thy servant offers towards this place.
And hearken thou to the supplication
of thy servant and of thy people Israel,
when they pray towards this place;
yea, hear thou in heaven thy dwelling place;
and when thou hearest, forgive.

TOMB OF THE VIRGIN   see p. 39

TOMBS OF THE KINGS   see p. 73

TOWER OF DAVID   see p. 30

WESTERN WALL   see p. 80

YAD VASHEM   See p. 64

A SONG FOR JERUSALEM
(N. Shemer, 1967. Tr. by H.J. Richards and N. Brummer)

Awir harim salul kayyayin, vereach oranim
Nissa beruach ha'arbayim'im qol pa'amonim.
Ubetardemath ilan va'eben shevuyah bachalomah;
Ha'ir asher badad yoshevet, ubelibbah chomah.
  Yerushalayim shel zahav veshel nechoshet veshel 'or,
  Halo lekol shirayik ani kinnor?

Chazarnu el borot hammayim, lashuq velakikkar;
Shofar qore' behar habayyit ba'ir ha'atiqah.
Ubammearot asher bassela', alphey shmashot zor'chot;
Nashuv, nered el Yam Hammelach bederek Yericho.
  Yerushalayim shel zahav veshel nechoshet veshel 'or,
  Halo lekol shirayik ani kinnor?

Ak bebo'i hayyom lashir lak, velak liqshor k'tharim,
Qatonti misse'ir banayik, umeacharon ham'shorerim;
Ki shmek sorev et-hashfatayim kineshiqat saraf.
Im eshkachek Yerushalayim ... asher kullah zahav.
  Yerushalayim shel zahav veshel nechoshet veshel 'or,
  Halo lekol shirayik ani kinnor?

The evening breeze upon the hillside, the sweet perfume of pine,
The bells which chime out in the distance intoxicate like wine;
And in a dream of towers and treetops, walled in by sleeping stone,
Jerusalem, the waiting city, lies silent and alone.
  Yerushalayim bathed in light, bathed in bronze and bathed in gold,
  What am I but the harp on which your songs are told?

We greet again the streets and fountains, we walk the old bazaar,
And from the top of Temple Mountain the trumpet sounds afar,
And from a thousand rocky caverns a thousand windows gleam;
Jerusalem the golden city is spellbound in her dream.
  Yerushalayim bathed in light, bathed in bronze and bathed in gold,
  What am I but the harp on which your songs are told?

But when I come to sing your praises with words fit for a king,
I am a child who cannot speak yet, a poet who cannot sing.
For your name needs a choir of angels, your glory to unfold;
Jerusalem, if I forget you ... city of purest gold.
  Yerushalayim bathed in light, bathed in bronze and bathed in gold,
  What am I but the harp on which your songs are told?

THE HOLY LAND

He who walks only six yards in the land of Israel
has a share in the everlasting life.

Sayings of the Rabbis

ABU GHOSH   15km. from Jerusalem, just off the Tel Aviv road.

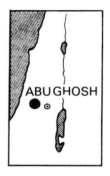

Abu Ghosh was the name of a 19th c. brigand who operated a highly
successful tollgate on this approach to Jerusalem, and bequeathed his
name to the village. In biblical times it was better known as **Qiryat
Yearim**, where the Ark of the Covenant was stranded for twenty
years before David realised its potential and transported it to his new
capital of Jerusalem. St Luke's allusive identification of Mary as the
new Ark, bringing the presence of God (Jesus) into the midst of men,
has inspired the modern church on the hill (on Byzantine foundations), whose tower is formed by a gigantic statue of the Madonna
and child.

Down in the village itself, the Crusaders built a far finer church,
one of the most elegant in the country, to commemorate Luke's
Emmaus story (closed 11.00 - 14.30, and Sundays and Thursdays).
Though it roughly fits the distance from Jerusalem specified in the
gospel (60 stadia = 11km.) it has no other claim to authenticity (see
Qubeiba, p. 119).

1 Samuel 6²¹—2 Samuel 6¹⁶: The men of Bethshemesh sent messengers to
the inhabitants of Kiriath-jearim, saying, 'The Philistines have returned the
ark of the Lord. Come down and take it up to you'. And the men of Kiriath-
jearim came and took up the ark of the Lord, and brought it to the house of
Abinadab on the hill; and they consecrated his son, Eleazar, to have charge
of the ark of the Lord. From the day that the ark was lodged at Kiriath-
jearim, a long time passed, some twenty years, and all the house of Israel
lamented after the Lord ...

David gathered all the chosen men of Israel, thirty thousand ... And they
carried the ark of God upon a new cart, and brought it out of the house of
Abinadab which was on the hill ... And David said, 'How can the ark of the
Lord come to me? ... And the ark of the Lord remained in the house of
Obed-edom the Gittite three months ... And David danced before the Lord
with all his might ... So David and all the house of Israel brought up the ark
of the Lord with shouting, and with the sound of the horn.

Psalm 132[1-8]: O Lord, remember David
and all the hardships he endured,
the oath he swore to the Lord,
his vow to the Strong One of Jacob ...
'I will give no sleep to my eyes
to my eyelids will give no slumber
till I find a place for the Lord,
a dwelling for the Strong One of Jacob.'
At Ephrata we heard of the ark;
we found it in the plains of Yearim.
'Let us go to the place of his dwelling;
let us go to kneel at his footstool.'
Go up, Lord, to the place of your rest,
you and the ark of your strength.   *(Grail)*

Luke 1[26-56]: The angel Gabriel was sent from God ... to a virgin ... whose name was Mary. And he came to her and said, 'Hail, O favoured one, the Lord is with you ... The Holy Spirit will come upon you, and the power of the Most High will overshadow you....'

Mary arose and went with haste into the hill country, to a city of Judah ... and she greeted Elizabeth. And when Elizabeth heard the greeting of Mary, the babe leaped in her womb. ... And Elizabeth exclaimed, 'Why is this granted to me, that the mother of my Lord should come to me?' ... And Mary remained with her about three months.

ACRE—AKKO   22km. from Haifa, 44km. from Nazareth (fig. 15).

Though it has an Old Testament history as venerable as many other cities in this land, Acre has been so stamped by its Crusader history that one thinks of it as a Crusader town. Baldwin I made it his headquarters and lifeline to Europe at the beginning of the 12th c. Saladin captured it in 1187, but four years later Richard the Lionheart put it back into Crusader hands for another hundred years. During that century, under the Knights of St John, it became a trading centre between east and west. Abandoned for 400 years, it was magnificently rebuilt as an Arab capital in the 18th c. Under the British Mandate it lost much of its importance to Haifa, but Jewish Resistance fighters jailed here kept Acre in the headlines until Israel's independence was achieved in 1948.

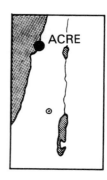

Visitors will be mainly interested in the walled city, where parking is allowed at (1) and (2). The two principal attractions are the el-Jazzar Mosque and the Crusader Crypt. The Mosque (3) was built in the 18th c. with marble from the ruins of Caesarea, and rests on the foundations of the medieval church of St. John. The Crusader Crypt (4) once formed part of the same complex of Knights' buildings. Entrance (fee, closed 18.00, Fridays 13.00) is across the road from the mosque. The vast vaulted and pillared halls transport one back immediately to the 12th c. A tunnel is shown which once gave underground access to the sea 150m. away.

Further downtown are the great enclosed courtyards or khans which served as camel loading bays in the days of the European

Fig 15 ACRE

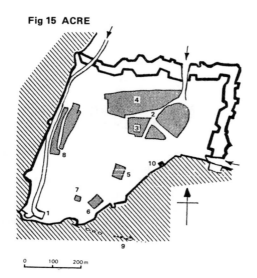

merchants. The merchants of Venice had their centre at the Khan el Faranj (Inn of the Franks) (5), those of Genoa at the Khan el-Umdan (6), and those of Pisa at the Khan esh-Shuna (7). Crusader buildings are to be seen all over the city, perhaps the best preserved being in a narrow street at (8). The ramparts surrounding the city provide an exceptional wall-walk, with fine views of the bay, of the Crusader mole built on the islands to the south (9), and of the only remaining Crusader tower at (10).

AMWAS = IMWAS   see p. 137

ANATHOTH   see p. 120

ARMAGEDDON   see p. 141

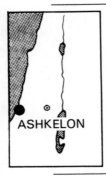

ASHKELON   73km. from Jerusalem, 63km. from Tel Aviv.

Ashkelon, famous in the Old Testament and in Crusader times as a coastal stronghold, is now a National Park (closed 17.00, Fridays 16.00) (National Parks card). The medieval walls are still visible, but too little is left of the Byzantine and Crusader churches to be worth exploring. The beach, with its swimming facilities, is excellent.

AYYALON   see p. 136

BANYAS—DAN   70km. from Tiberias, in the foothills of Mt Hermon. Restaurant and toilets.

Banyas still keeps the Greek name Paneas, the Town of Pan. The car park gives immediate access to the cave dedicated to this god of nature, whose generative powers are evidenced in the great spout of water gushing forth from within. It is one of the sources of the river Jordan. In Jesus' lifetime Banyas was chosen by Herod's son Philip as the capital of the region he inherited. Ever his father's son, he dedicated it to Caesar, but ensured that history would remember his name too by calling it **Caesarea Philippi**. The gospel remembers it as the scene of Peter's crucial profession of faith in Jesus.

3km. further west, a vast nature reserve and picnic area embellishes a second source of the Jordan. Entrance to the reserve is free (toilets, refreshments), and a 45-minute nature trail is clearly marked out. Near Station Nine it is possible to visit the archaeological mound which is all that remains of the ancient town of **Dan** (closed 16.00, Fridays 15.00), traditionally regarded as the northern limit of the territory of Israel.

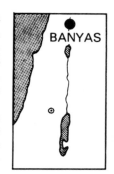

Forming as it does the northern doorway into the country, the town attracted inhabitants from Stone Age times. When the Israelite tribes split into two kingdoms in the 10th c. BC, Dan was turned into a holy place in the hope it would act as a counter-attraction to Jerusalem. Excavations on the northern part of the mound have brought to light a noble flight of steps leading up to a high place dating from this time.

Judges 19[27-30]: The Danites came to Laish, to a people quiet and unsuspecting, and smote them with the edge of the sword, and burned the city with fire. And there was no deliverer because it was far from Sidon, and they had no dealings with anyone ... And they rebuilt the city, and dwelt in it. And they named the city Dan, after the name of Dan their ancestor, who was born to Israel (Jacob); but the name of the city was Laish at the first. And the Danites set up a graven image for themselves . . . as long as the House of God was at Shiloh.

1 Kings 12[26-29]: Jeroboam said in his heart, 'Now the kingdom will turn back to the house of David; if this people go up to offer sacrifices in the House of the Lord at Jerusalem, then the heart of this people will turn again to their lord, to Rehoboam king of Judah.' So the king took counsel, and made two calves of gold. And he said to the people, 'You have gone up to Jerusalem long enough. Behold your gods, O Israel, who brought you up out of the land of Egypt.' And he set one in Bethel, and the other he put in Dan.

Matthew 16[13-19]: When Jesus came to the district of Caesarea Philippi, he asked his disciples, 'Who do men say that the Son of man is?' And they said, 'Some say John the Baptist, others say Elijah, and others Jeremiah or one of the prophets.' He said to them, 'But who do you say I am?' Simon Peter replied, 'You are the Christ, the Son of the living God.' And Jesus answered him, 'Blessed are you, Simon Bar-Jona! For flesh and blood has not revealed this to you, but my Father who is in heaven. And I tell you, you are Peter, and on this rock [petra] I will build my church, and the powers of death shall not prevail against it. I will give you the keys of the kingdom of heaven, and whatever you bind on earth shall be bound in heaven, and whatever you loose on earth shall be loosed in heaven.'

BEATITUDES   see p. 144

BEERSHEBA   90km. from Jerusalem via Hebron.

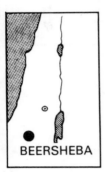

Beersheba is today a busy and expanding town of several thousand inhabitants, the powerhouse of Israel's successful attempt to make the desert bloom. Its importance as a crossroads in the southern Negev desert is marked by evidence of settlement from 3500 BC. It figures in the stories of Abraham, Isaac and Jacob as a watering centre to which their flocks had right of access by treaty (the name means Vow-well), and ever after as the southern limit of the land to which Israel lay claim, from Dan to Beersheba.

An 'Abraham's Well' is shown in the old part of the town, but the city the patriarchs knew lies some km. to the east, at Tel Sheva, where excavations have continued since 1951. The finds are exhibited in the Negev Museum, housed in a mosque in the older part of new Beersheba.

Near the 'Well' the desert Bedouins hold a lively and colourful weekly market on Thursdays. Camels and sheep tend to be sold off very early in the day, and the market does not operate on the Thursday of Passover week.

Genesis 21[25–31]: When Abraham complained to Abimelech about a well of water which Abimelech's servants had seized, Abimelech said, 'I do not

know who has done this thing; you did not tell me, and I have not heard of it until today.' So Abraham took sheep and oxen and gave them to Abimelech, and the two men made a covenant ... Abraham said, 'These seven ewe lambs you will take from my hand, that you may be a witness for me that I dug this well.' Therefore that place was called Beersheba; because there both of them swore an oath.

Genesis 26[18-33]: Isaac dug again the wells of water which had been dug in the days of Abraham his father; for the Philistines had stopped them after the death of Abraham; and he gave them the names which his father had given them ...

He went up to Beersheba. And the Lord appeared to him the same night and said, 'I am the God of Abraham your father; fear not, for I am with you and will bless you and multiply your descendants for my servant Abraham's sake.' So he built an altar there and called upon the name of the Lord, and pitched his tent there. And there Isaac's servants dug a well ... and said to him, 'We have found water.' He called it Shibah; therefore the name of the city is Beersheba to this day.

BEIT SAHOUR   see p. 100

BELVOIR   see p. 106

BET ALFA   see p. 106

BETHANY   4km. from Jerusalem on the Jericho road.

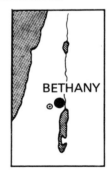

Bethany, the home of Jesus' friends Martha, Mary and Lazarus, is still known locally as El Azariyeh or Lazarus' Place. It lies on the far side (east) of the Mount of Olives, and can easily be reached by car, coach or bus from Jerusalem, the road skirting the base of the hill. Jesus' own journeys between Jerusalem and Bethany are better felt by doing the distance (at least one way) on foot. It means climbing and/or descending the Mount of Olives, but only heavily incapacitated or rushed pilgrims will find this beyond their powers.

To walk there, get to the Mount of Olives and make for Bethphage (see p. 104). Past the church, turn left on a descending path. At the fork keep to the rougher path right. The buildings of Bethany shortly come into view. As the path finally meets the village, the tower on the right marks the Greek Orthodox church. On the Saturday morning preceding their Palm Sunday this will be choc-abloc with Orthodox pilgrims and Boy Scout bands. A stirring scene, but public transport back to Jerusalem will be a problem.

Lower on the right, opposite the souvenir shop, is the entrance to **Lazarus' Tomb**. A narrow flight of uneven stone steps (so only ten pilgrims at a time) leads down to a rock chamber. This used to be accessible from the Latin church, but when a mosque was built over the Tomb (Muslims also venerate Lazarus) this new access had to be made for Christians in the 16th c. The woman at the entrance expects a small offering.

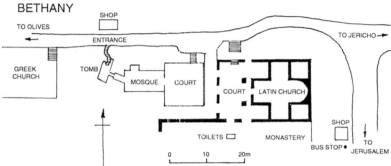

Lower on the right, steps lead down into the Latin church (closed 11.15 - 14.00). The pillars in the courtyard bear traces of the 5th c. Byzantine and 12th c. Crusader churches on this site. One bears a Darmstadt inscription which may raise eyebrows, not of the same quality as the one in the Tomb itself (see below). The present church dates from 1954, and portrays in bright mosaics the stories related in Luke 10 and John 11. There are toilets off the courtyard. The flower garden skirting the church leads to the bus stop, where souvenirs and refreshments can be had. A frequent bus service goes to Stephen's, Herod's or Damascus Gate.

For the return journey on foot, go up the path on the right side of the Latin church, past the Tomb of Lazarus. The path turns sharp right and continues to ascend to the Bethphage church. Continue uphill on the paved road to the main square of the Mount of Olives. A frequent local bus service goes to Damascus Gate.

Psalm 126: Those who sow in tears and sorrow
One day will reap with joy.

Luke 10[38-42]: As they went on their way, Jesus entered a village; and a woman named Martha received him into her house. And she had a sister called Mary, who sat at the Lord's feet and listened to his teaching. But

Martha was distracted with too much serving; and she went to him and said, 'Lord, do you not care that my sister has left me to serve alone? Tell her then to help me.' But the Lord answered her, 'Martha, Martha, you are troubled about many things; one thing is needful. Mary has chosen the good portion, which shall not be taken away from her.'

John 11[1–44]: A certain man was ill, Lazarus of Bethany, the village of Mary and her sister Martha ... So the sisters sent to him, saying, 'Lord, he whom you love is ill.' ... Jesus said to his disciples, 'Our friend Lazarus is dead; and for your sake I am glad that I was not there, so that you may believe.' ...

Now when Jesus came, he found that Lazarus had already been in the tomb four days. Bethany was near Jerusalem, about two miles off, and many of the Jews had come to Martha and Mary to console them concerning their brother. When Martha heard that Jesus was coming, she went and met him while Mary sat in the house. Martha said to Jesus, 'Lord, if you had been here, my brother would not have died. And even now I know that whatever you ask from God, God will give you.' Jesus said to her, 'Your brother will rise again.' Martha said to him, 'I know that he will rise again in the resurrection at the last day.' Jesus said to her, 'I am the resurrection and the life; he who believes in me, though he die, yet shall he live, and whoever lives and believes in me shall never die. Do you believe this?' She said to him, 'Yes, Lord; I believe that you are the Christ, the Son of God, he who is coming into the world.' ...

Mary, when she came where Jesus was and saw him, fell at his feet, saying to him, 'Lord, if you had been here, my brother would not have died.' When Jesus saw her weeping, and the Jews who came with her also weeping, he was deeply moved in spirit and troubled; and he said, 'Where have you laid him?' They said to him, 'Lord, come and see.' ...

Then Jesus, deeply moved again, came to the tomb; it was a cave, and a stone lay upon it. Jesus said, 'Take away the stone.' Martha, the sister of the dead man, said to him, 'Lord by this time there will be an odour, for he has been dead four days.' Jesus said to her, 'Did I not tell you that if you would believe you would see the glory of God?' So they took away the stone ... And Jesus cried with a loud voice, 'Lazarus, come out.' The dead man came out, his hands and feet bound with bandages, and his face wrapped with a cloth. Jesus said to him, 'Unbind him, and let him go.'

John 12[1–8]: Six days before the Passover, Jesus came to Bethany, where Lazarus was, whom Jesus had raised from the dead. There they made him a supper; Martha served, and Lazarus was one of those at table with him. Mary took a pound of costly ointment of pure nard and anointed the feet of Jesus and wiped his feet with her hair; and the house was filled with the fragrance of the ointment. But Judas Iscariot, one of the disciples (he who was to betray him), said, 'Why was this ointment not sold for a year's wages and given to the poor?' ... Jesus said, 'Let her alone, let her keep it for the day of my burial. The poor you always have with you, but you do not always have me.'

BPB p. 95: Father ... when Martha said to Jesus,
    'Lord, if only you had been here,
    my brother would not have died',
he answered her,
    'Your brother will rise again.'
Martha said,
    'I know he will rise again
    in the resurrection at the last day.'
Jesus replied:
    'I am the Resurrection and the Life.
    He who believes in me, though he is dead,
      yet shall he live.
    And whoever lives and believes in me,
      shall never die.'
Father, I believe your Christ is Light inextinguishable
    and Life unquenchable.
How can I thank you enough
    for the miracle of letting me hear his voice
    and see the light of his face?
For I was dead and buried, Father,
    and my name is Lazarus.

DH: Life eternal, replenish our tired lives.
Light eternal, shine into our darkness.
Eternal Word, speak to our deafness.
Eternal Christ, Resurrection and Life,
break into our earthbound lives with gifts eternal,
for we believe;
and being dead
we yet shall live.

Darmstadt: The glory of God shall be seen by those who put their faith in
Jesus in times of greatest distress and hopelessness; they are
certain that he is greater than any distress, even greater than
death itself.

BETHEL   18km. north of Jerusalem. Shortly after Ramallah and
Bireh, take the right fork — a minor road going to
Jericho.

The village of Beitin lies on the first crest. Archaeologists dug here
between 1934 and 1960, and found traces of a high-place of worship
dating back to 2500 BC. All their digs were filled in again, and there
is nothing to be seen. Enthusiastic pilgrims would do well to fork
right in the village. About a km. along on the left, the ruins of a

Turkish fort afford a good high-place to recall the importance of Bethel.

Bethel figures prominently in the Old Testament story as one of the high-places where people who worshipped a God located in the heavens rather than on earth felt nearest to him. Abraham and Jacob worshipped there, and when the Israelites returned from Egypt intent on recapturing the land of their fathers, it was for Bethel they made immediately after taking Jericho. When the tribes later split into northerners and southerners, Bethel became the first capital of the north, its shrine rivalling the southern high-place of Jerusalem. The prophets Amos and Hosea expressed considerable reserve about worshipping God at this shrine. It was wiped out in the Assyrian invasion of the 8th c. BC.

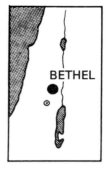

Genesis 28[10–19]: Jacob left Beersheba, and went towards Haran in Syria. And he came to a certain place, and stayed there that night, because the sun had set. Taking one of the stones of the place, he put it under his head and lay down in that place to sleep. And he dreamed that there was a ladder [stairway] set up on the earth, and the top of it reached to heaven; and behold, the angels of God were ascending and descending on it! And behold, the Lord stood above it and said, 'I am the Lord, the God of Abraham your father and the God of Isaac; the land on which you lie I will give to you and to your descendants' ... Then Jacob awoke from his sleep and said, 'Surely the Lord is in this place; and I did not know it.' And he was afraid, and said, 'How awesome is this place! This is none other than the house of God, and this is the gate of heaven.'

So Jacob rose early in the morning, and he took the stone which he had put under his head and set it up for a pillar and poured oil on the top of it. He called the name of that place Bethel, the House of God. (The hymn *Nearer my God to thee*, p. 230 below, is a meditation on this reading.)

John 1[45–51]: Philip found Nathanael, and said to him, 'We have found him of whom Moses in the law and also the prophets wrote, Jesus of Nazareth, the son of Joseph.' Nathanael said to him, 'Can anything good come out of Nazareth?' Philip said to him, 'Come and see.' Jesus saw Nathanael coming to him, and said of him, 'Behold, an Israelite indeed [another Jacob], in whom is no guile!' Nathanael said to him, 'How do you know me?' Jesus answered him, 'Before Philip called you, when you were under the fig tree, I saw you.' Nathanael answered him, 'Rabbi, you are the Son of God! You are the King of Israel!' Jesus answered him, 'Because I said to you, I saw you under the fig tree, do you believe? You shall see greater things than these... You will see heaven opened, and the angels of God ascending and descending upon the Son of man.'

Hosea 4[15–16]: Enter not into Gilgal
nor go up to Bethaven (Bethel)

and swear not, "As the Lord lives."
Like a stubborn heifer,
Israel is stubborn;
Can the Lord now feed them
like a lamb in a broad pasture?

Amos 5$^{4-5}$: Thus says the Lord to the house of Israel:
'Seek me and live;
but do not seek Bethel,
and do not enter into Gilgal
or cross over to Beersheba;
for Gilgal shall surely go into exile,
and Bethel shall come to naught.'

BETHLEHEM   8km. south of Jerusalem, on the Hebron road. Halfway on the right lies the new Ecumenical Institute of **Tantur**, where Christians of all denominations are seconded for study and research on church unity. The main road bypasses Bethlehem, which is reached by a left fork at Rachel's Tomb.

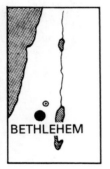

BETHLEHEM

At the entrance to the 'little town of Bethlehem' (and many other towns in Israel) is a banner proclaiming 'Blessed is he who comes' — the traditional Hebrew way of saying 'Welcome'. A gracious greeting to the place where Christians go to remember their origins. St Jerome called it 'The most sacred spot in the world for us, indeed for the whole world.'

Christians associate Bethlehem so strongly with the story of Jesus that they are apt to forget it had a long history beforehand. In fact its association with Jesus only came about because his first followers saw him as another David, who was born and brought up in Bethlehem (like his great-grandparents Ruth and Boaz). David's love for his birthplace is tenderly illustrated in the story preserved in the appendix to the books of Samuel.

Bethlehem's biblical roots go back even further than David. On the main road just outside the town stands a monument known as **Rachel's Tomb**. The tombs of the other Israelite forefathers and foremothers (Abraham and Sarah, Isaac and Rebekah, Jacob and Leah) are shown in Hebron (see p. 127). Rachel's has been placed here by an ancient but mistaken tradition because of a confusion about the 'Ephrathah' where she was buried. This is actually north of Jerusalem near the Babylonian concentration camp of Ramah from where the Rachel tribes were led into exile (see Jeremiah 31[15], p. 122). Matthew found the tradition useful for his story of the Holy Innocents, which he illustrates with the Jeremiah text.

Bethlehem provides perhaps as good an example as any of the relative unimportance of authenticity. Who could ever guarantee the exact location of the 'inn' or of the 'manger' in Luke's story of Jesus' birth? Did he even have an exact location in mind? Does it matter? All that matters is that eventually this spot was chosen to embody the story, and that in coming here one joins the millions of pilgrims — English, French, German, Spanish, Italian, Greek, Russian, Armenian, African, American, Australian — who have here pondered on the mystery of the incarnation — and here understood that God is no longer to be thought of as distant or inaccessible. For Christians, God is as near (and as vulnerable) as a child in swaddling clothes.

Coaches and cars park in the recently reorganised 'Manger Square' (fig. 16) (1). The basilica of the Nativity (closed 18.00), a rather forbidding and fortress-like building on the east side of the square, has a Crusader façade. Baldwin I and II were consecrated here, unlike their successors who insisted on being crowned in Jerusalem like Jesus. One enters the basilica, now, through a door (2) so low that one has to stoop - a device meant to deter looters driving wagons into the church. The original lintels can be seen above. The low entrance could remind the pilgrim to humble himself here where he remembers God's condescension.

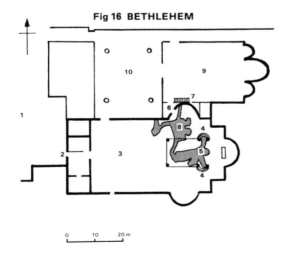

Fig 16 BETHLEHEM

0   10   20 m

Inside, the basilica has not basically altered since it was built by Queen Helena in the 4th c., though the oak roof is more recent — a gift from Edward III of England. The marble with which Helena clad the walls was later appropriated to decorate the Dome of the Rock in Jerusalem. Trapdoors in the floor (3) reveal the fine Byzantine mosaics 60cm. below the present level. The pillars bear Crusader paintings of patron saints (including Canute and Cathal), and the walls above them the remains of the mosaics with which they commemorated the early Councils of the Church.

Either side of the sanctuary (4), Crusader steps lead down to the grotto which is venerated as Jesus' birthplace. Pilgrims usually kiss a star in the floor (5) whose inscription claims that 'Here, of the Virgin Mary, was born Jesus Christ'. The furnishings are only a hundred years old.

Returning upstairs to the basilica, the ikons on the raised sanctuary (Greek Orthodox) are worth inspecting. A narrow door in the north transept (6) leads to the adjoining Franciscan church of St Catherine (also only a hundred years old) (closed 12.00 - 15.00), where steps (7) lead down to the complex of caves associated with the nativity grotto. Here St Jerome founded a 4th c. version of the Religious Life, and in the congenial company of St Paula and her daughter Eustochium spent 36 years translating the Hebrew Bible into Latin (Vulgate). The first cave (St Joseph) (8) is ideal for a group service. Very large groups may need to use the church upstairs (9), or the elegantly restored courtyard outside (10). Back in Manger Square (1) there are souvenir shops enough to delight the soul of the most enthusiastic. They continue to stretch the length of the road linking Bethlehem with the Jerusalem highway. There are public toilets a little way down this road.

Before leaving Bethlehem (or better still before visiting the basilica) it is worth travelling a further 2km. east to **Beit Sahour** (fig. 17) (1) where both the Orthodox and the Latins have a site known as **Shepherds' Field**. In the Franciscan enclosure (closed 11.30 - 14.00), a large cave is shown, of the kind which poor families in the area still use as homes for themselves and animals, and above it a chapel built in the shape of a star in 1954.

10km. south east of Bethlehem lies the perfectly proportioned conical hillock of **Herodium** (2), one of a dozen fortified and centrally-heated palaces which the neurotic Herod the Great built as bolt-holes. All of them served as refuges for the Jewish partisans in 70 AD (see Masada, p. 138). Herodium was excavated in 1962, but no

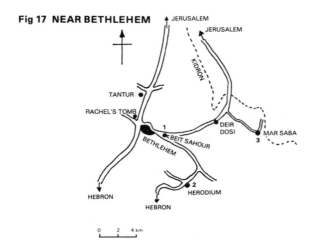

Fig 17 NEAR BETHLEHEM

trace of Herod has been found, though Josephus says he was buried there. Entrance fee (National Parks card). Closed 17.00.

From Bethlehem it is also possible to reach **Mar Saba** (3), one of the finest of the two dozen Byzantine monasteries in the Judean desert. Follow the road through Beit Sahour and past the monastery of Theodosius (Deir Dosi) for 7km. As the road dips into the Kidron valley, turn right along the ridge. The final piece of road is pretty rough (1980). The situation of the monastery, suspended as it were on a cliff, is spectacular. Closed 16.00. Women not admitted.

2 Samuel 23[14-17]: David was in the stronghold of Adullam; and the garrison of the Philistines was then at Bethlehem. And David said longingly, 'O that someone would give me water to drink from the well of Bethlehem which is by the gate!' Then his three mighty men broke through the camp of the Philistines, and drew water out of the well of Bethlehem which was by the gate, and took and brought it to David. But he would not drink of it; he poured it out to the Lord, and said, 'Far be it from me, O Lord, that I should do this. Shall I drink the blood of the men who went at the risk of their lives?'

Micah 5[2-4]: But you, O Bethlehem Ephrathah,
   who are little to be among the clans of Judah,
   from you shall come forth for me
   one who is to be ruler in Israel,
   whose origin is from old, from ancient days.
   Therefore he shall give them up until the time
   when she who is in travail has brought forth ...
   and he shall stand and feed his flock
   in the strength of the Lord.

Hebrews 2^{5-18}: It was not to angels that God subjected the world to come ... For it was fitting that he, for whom and by whom all things exist, in bringing many sons of glory, should make the pioneer of salvation perfect through suffering. For he who sanctifies and those who are sanctified have all one origin. That is why he is not ashamed to call them brethren, saying, 'I will proclaim thy name to my brethren.' ... Since therefore the children share in flesh and blood, he himself likewise partook of the same nature ... He had to be made like his brethren in every respect, so that he might become a merciful and faithful high priest in the service of God, to make expiation for the sins of the people. For because he himself has suffered and been tempted, he is able to help those who are tempted.

Luke 2^{1-14}: In those days a decree went out from Caesar Augustus that all the world should be enrolled ... And all went to be enrolled, each to his own city. And Joseph also went up from Galilee, from the city of Nazareth, to Judea, to the city of David, which is called Bethlehem, because he was of the house and lineage of David, to be enrolled with Mary, his betrothed, who was with child. And while they were there, the time came for her to be delivered. And she gave birth to her first-born son and wrapped him in swaddling cloths, and laid him in a manger, because there was no place for them in the inn.

And in that region there were shepherds out in the field, keeping watch over their flock by night. And an angel of the Lord appeared to them, and the glory of the Lord shone around them, and they were filled with fear. And the angel said to them, 'Be not afraid; for behold, I bring you good news of a great joy which will come to all the people; for to you is born this day in the city of David a Saviour, who is Christ the Lord. And this will be a sign for you: you will find a babe wrapped in swaddling cloths and lying in a manger.' And suddenly there was with the angel a multitude of the heavenly host praising God and saying, 'Glory to God in the highest, and on earth peace among men with whom he is pleased.'

Matthew 2^{16-18}: Herod, when he saw that he had been tricked by the wise men, was in a furious rage, and he sent and killed all the male children in Bethlehem and in all that region who were two years old or under, according to the time he had ascertained from the wise men. Then was fulfilled what

was spoken by the prophet Jeremiah:
'A voice was heard in Ramah,
wailing and loud lamentation,
Rachel weeping for her children;
she refused to be consoled,
because they were no more.'

DH: Lord Jesus Christ, you came to a stable when men looked in a palace; you were born in poverty when we might have anticipated riches; King of all the earth you were content to visit one nation; Creator of the universe you accepted the hills and plains of Galilee for the scene of your ministry. From beginning to end you upturned our human values and held us in suspense.

Come to us, Lord Jesus. Do not let us take you for granted or pretend that we ever fully understand you. Continue to surprise us so that, kept alert, we are always ready to receive you as Lord and to do your will.

DH: Thanksgiving and praise to God!
Eternal God, the gates of heaven were raised in Bethlehem.
Jesus left the place of glory to live with men.
We rejoice that he came,
    not in military power to subdue us,
    nor yet in glory such as would blind our eyes,
    nor yet in such majesty as would set him apart from us,
but left the gates of heaven as a child in helplessness,
    to be born as we were born,
    suckled by a human mother, watched over by a human father,
    and so recognised by us.

Thanksgiving and praise to God!
Eternal God, you strengthen us in our earthly pilgrimage,
    you give daily bread to body and to spirit,
    you grant us to be one with the fellowship of believers,
    you journey with us in close companionship.
Raise the gates of our hearts, O God,
break down the stubborn doors of our spirits,
and come and reign among us.

Rose Macaulay: I liked the dark cavern glittering with silver lamps and gold and silver and tinsel ornaments and smoky incense fumes and tapestried walls ... Bethlehem was charming and moving and strange, and one does not mind either there or in Jerusalem whether the shrines are rightly identified or not, because the faith of millions of pilgrims down the centuries has given them a mystical kind of reality, and one does not much mind their having been vulgarised, for this had to happen, people being vulgar and liking gaudy uneducated things round them when they pray; and one does not mind the original sites and buildings having been destroyed long ago and others built on their ruins and destroyed in their turn, again and again and again, for this shows the tenacious hold they have had on men's imaginations.

Towers of Trebizond, 1956

BETHPHAGE On the eastern slopes of the Mount of Olives, 1km. from the top.

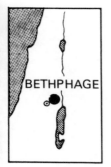

Bethphage is most easily reached on foot from the Mount of Olives. Take the narrow lane alongside the Paternoster church. This descends easily, with fine views of the Judean hills as far as Bethlehem and beyond, to the church on the left (closed 12.00 - 14.00). Ring the bell at the iron gates. Entrance is free, but the gatekeeper accepts an offering. Toilets.

The chapel (1883) has recently been tastefully decorated to fit in with the style of the medieval stone block discovered here. Its purpose is unknown (a symbolic mounting block?), but it is decorated on all four sides with scenes of Jesus at Bethany. Martha holds her nose to give visual expression to John 11^{39} (see p. 95). At the back of the church there is a delightful shady courtyard, readily made available for open-air services.

In spite of the ambiguity of the gospel accounts, the chapel has been traditionally identified with the beginning of Jesus' Palm Sunday journey, and each Palm Sunday the colourful Latin procession still makes this its starting point — no longer, alas, with donkeys.

Mark 11$^{1-10}$: And when they drew near to Jerusalem, to Bethphage and Bethany, at the Mount of Olives, he sent two of his disciples, and said to them, 'Go into the village opposite you, and immediately as you enter it you will find a colt tied, on which no one has ever sat; untie it and bring it. If anyone says to you, "Why are you doing this?" say, "The Lord has need of it and will send it back here immediately."'

And they went away, and found a colt tied at the door out in the open street; and they untied it ... And they brought the colt to Jesus, and threw their garments on it; and he sat upon it. And many spread their garments on the road, and others spread leafy branches which they had cut from the fields. And those who went before and those who followed cried out, 'Hosanna! Blessed is he who comes in the name of the Lord! Blessed is the kingdom of our father David that is coming! Hosanna in the highest!'

Lourdes Benedictus: Benedictus qui venit
in nomine Domini.
Hosanna, Hosanna, Hosanna in excelsis.

DH: A donkey king!
    Were there those who laughed?
    Did some scorn?
    How many turned their heads, embarrassed?
    What of the anger of those who saw a sacred prophecy abused?

But now, O Lord, with the hindsight of the cross,
    it makes sense to us, so we are glad:
    glad of the applause of the crowd
        who trusted their first reactions
        and welcomed the donkey king;
    glad of the shouts of little children
        caught up in a sense of celebration;
    glad that there were those who glimpsed, fleetingly,
        the nature of a king who straddled a donkey.

Donkey King, we join the throng,
    we raise a voice of childlike praise and trust,
    we glimpse the secret of your reign.
Welcome to our Jerusalem!

DH: Blessed is he who comes in the name of the Lord:
    blessed the faithful worshipper with joyous hosanna,
    blessed the priest who leads his people in the name of the Lord,
    blessed the child who, in innocent simplicity,
        reveals the nature of the Kingdom,
    blessed the politician who seeks justice in the name of the Lord,
    blessed the disciple ready to learn and follow.
Blessed is the Lord. He comes in humility to be a servant.

BET SHEAN   In the Jordan valley, 37km. from Nazareth, 120km. from Jerusalem. The site is closed 16.00, Fridays 15.00. Entrance fee (National Parks card).

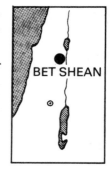

Bet Shean occupies an important crossroads, where the valley of Jezreel finally empties into the Jordan, and links the Mediterranean coast to the east. Not surprisingly it has been occupied since the Stone Age (5000 BC) and the eighteen cities built on top of each other since then have produced an archaeological mound 80m. high. Too well fortified for Joshua's invading army, or even for Saul (whose headless corpse the Philistines displayed on these walls), it did not become part of Israel until the time of Solomon. Under the Greeks it was known as Scythopolis, and under Rome counted more inhabitants than Jerusalem itself. The Byzantines built a fine monastery here in the 6th c. AD, and it finally bowed off the stage of history in the time of the Crusaders.

The Roman theatre, the most well-preserved in the country, is the site's main exhibit. Built in 200 AD, it could seat an audience of 5,000, and had an amplifying system based on tubes and shell-shaped loudspeakers. There is nothing to be seen on the archaeological mound itself, but it gives a fine view of the extensive surrounding fishponds.

The Byzantine monastery (closed 15.00 and Saturdays) lies a kilometre away, and can only be approached through the town's back alleys by someone who knows the way and can acquire the key. The asbestos shack covers a remarkably brilliant circular mosaic of the 6th c. AD, in which a golden sun and redheaded moon are surrounded by figures representing the twelve months of the year. An inscription identifies the builder of the monastery as Lady Mary, wife of a Byzantine official.

Only a few kilometres to the west, on a minor road leading up country, the kibbutz of **Bet Alfa** displays a floor mosaic of the same date and with the same theme, this time done for a Jewish synagogue. It was discovered in 1928 in the course of digging channels for irrigation. The central panel represents the twelve signs of the Zodiac (anticlockwise being in Hebrew). Below there is a charmingly naïve representation of the sacrifice of Isaac. Entrance fee (National Parks card). (Closed 16.00, Fridays 15.00)

13km. to the north of Bet Shean, off the Jordan valley highway, a road to the left rises 500m. in tight hairpins to the well-preserved Crusader castle of **Belvoir**, or Star of the Jordan (Kokhav Hayarden). Here the Crusaders made their last stand to defend the 'Latin Kingdom', and held out for four years after the debacle at Hattin, before similarly yielding to Saladin in 1191. The view from the top is rewarding. Entrance fee (National Parks card). Closed 16.00, Fridays 15.00.

1 Samuel 31[8]—*2 Samuel 1*[20]: When the Philistines came to strip the slain, they found Saul and his three sons fallen on Mount Gilboa. And they cut off his head, and stripped off his armour, and sent messengers throughout the land of the Philistines, to carry the good news to their idols and to the people. They put his armour in the temple of Ashtaroth; and they fastened his body to the walls of Beth-shan ... And David lamented with this lamentation over Saul....
'Thy glory, O Israel, is slain upon thy high places!
How are the mighty fallen!
Tell it not in Gath,
publish it not in the streets of Ashkelon;
lest the daughters of the Philistines rejoice.'

Genesis 22[1–13]: God tested Abraham, and said to him ... 'Take your son, your only son Isaac, whom you love, and go to the land of Moriah, and offer him there as a burnt offering upon one of the mountains of which I shall tell you.' So Abraham rose ... and went to the place of which God had told him ... And Abraham took the wood of the burnt offering, and laid it on Isaac his son; and he took in his hand the fire and the knife. So they went both of them together. And Isaac said to his father, 'My father!' And he said, 'Here am I, my son.' He said, 'Behold the fire and the wood; but where is the lamb for a burnt offering?' Abraham said, 'God will provide' ...

Then Abraham put forth his hand, and took the knife to slay his son. But the angel of the Lord called to him from heaven, and said, 'Do not lay your hand on the lad or do anything to him; for now I know that you fear God, seeing you have not withheld your son, your only son, from me.' And Abraham lifted up his eyes and looked, and behold, behind him was a ram, caught in a thicket by his horns; and Abraham went and took the ram, and offered it up as a burnt offering instead of his son.

BET SHEARIM   18km. from Haifa, 20km. from Nazareth. Turn south at Qiryat Tivon. Closed 16.00, Fridays 15.00. Entrance fee (National Parks card).

These catacombs represent 150 years of Jewish history, from the time that the Sanhedrim was moved here at the end of the 2nd c. AD, until the 4th c. when the town was burnt. At a time when Rome had excluded Jews from Jerusalem, many even from abroad asked to be buried instead in this religious centre of Judaism. 31 catacombs, each with massive freestanding sarcophagi or simpler arched recesses in the rock, were rediscovered in 1936, and the work of restoration has continued since 1957. The more ornate tombs and façades make a surprisingly free use of motifs from Greek mythology, otherwise scrupulously avoided by a people deeply conscious of the danger of images.

CAESAREA   40km. from Haifa, 50km. from Tel Aviv. Entrance fee (National Parks card). Closed 17.00, Fridays 16.00, theatre an hour earlier. Restaurants, shops, toilets, swimming facilities (extra).

Caesarea, 'Caesar's Town', is as fine a monument to the genius of Herod the Great as any of his other bequests to this country (Jerusalem Temple, p. 76, Masada, p. 138, Samaria, p. 165). Until his time, Jaffa had served as the port for what little seafaring was done by the Jews. Herod chose this site 50km. further up the coast, and sunk thousands of cubic metres of stone into the sea to create an artificial harbour. He then erected a palace, theatre, hippodrome and a great temple dedicated to the emperor Augustus to let Rome know how lucky it was to have him as a viceroy. Rome responded by making Caesarea the new capital of Palestine — which it remained for 600 years — and the residence of the governor of Judea once Herod had died.

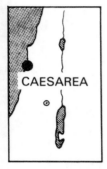

The Christian community's first overtures to the non-Jewish world were made here: the New Testament puts considerable emphasis on the conversion to Christianity of the Roman captain Cornelius who served in the Caesarea garrison. It was this port that Paul used on a number of his missionary journeys, and here that he was imprisoned on his way to trial in Rome. The Jewish War of 66 AD was sparked off by tensions in this Herodian city, and 20,000 of its Jewish citizens died before Titus was able to hold his victory celebrations here.

For the early Christians the town became famous as the home of Origen in the 3rd c., and a century later of the historian Eusebius, whose renowned biblical school was commissioned by Constantine to provide 50 manuscript copies of the bible for distribution round his empire. The 12th c. Crusaders who captured the town 'discovered' here the Holy Grail — the reputed cup of the Last Supper — and began to construct an ambitious cathedral which they never had time to finish. After the Saracens sacked the Crusader fortress in the 13th c., the place remained abandoned until a hundred years ago. Excavations were begun in 1959 and continue.

Visits begin most easily at the theatre (fig. 18) (1), which is the first of the sites one comes across from the main road. Just inside the gate is a copy of an important inscription found here, commemorating the public building which Pontius Pilate dedicated to the emperor Tiberius. The open-air seating of the theatre has been reconstructed so that the magnificent setting facing the sea can still be used for concerts.

Cars and coaches most conveniently drive from here to the main parking area, a km. closer to the main sites (2). Near by, in a sunken area (3), a street of the Byzantine period has been excavated, leading to a square paved in marble. The two massive statues are older, from Roman times.

Caesarea's main exhibit is the moated Crusader fortress, which occupies only a fraction of the town known by Herod and the Byzantines (dotted line). Entrance is over a bridge and through a fortified keep (4). Inside, a well preserved vaulted road leads to the battlements, and down to the remains of the abortive Crusader cathedral (5). Alongside it, on an artificial platform filled with sand, is the podium of the enormous temple which Herod built to be visible for miles out to sea (6).

Shops now occupy the buildings on the sea front, once Herod's warehouses. They are flanked by two restaurants (7 and 8), the second of them perched on what was the Crusader citadel: the cellar is reputed to have been Paul's prison. There is a beach beyond for those who wish to use the bathing facilities (separate entrance fee). As on almost all Mediterranean beaches, there is an amount of oil-tar on the sand to beware of. Those who prefer to wander along the beach to the far breakwater (9) will see in the water a large number of the columns which once graced Herod's harbour.

On leaving Caesarea, an arch on the right of the road offers a view of a field which was once the city's famous racecourse (10), and the

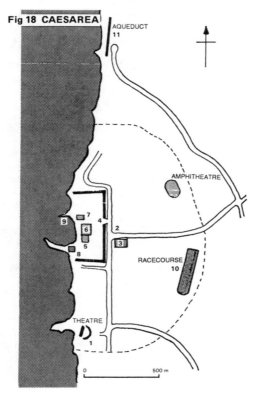

Fig 18 CAESAREA
AQUEDUCT 11
AMPHITHEATRE
THEATRE 1
9 7 4
6 2
5 3
8
RACECOURSE 10
0 500 m

first turning on the left leads to the remains of the beautiful double aqueduct (11) by which Herod (and later Hadrian) piped water to this city from the Carmel hills. Remains of this bold water system have been traced back for 15km.

Acts 10[1-48]: At Caesarea there was a man named Cornelius, a centurion of what was known as the Italian Cohort, a devout man who feared God with all his household, gave alms liberally to the people, and prayed constantly to God ...
Some of the brethren from Jaffa accompanied Peter. And on the following day they entered Caesarea. Cornelius was expecting them and had called together his kinsmen and close friends. When Peter entered, Cornelius met him and fell down at his feet and worshipped him. But Peter lifted him up, saying, 'Stand up; I too am a man ... You know how unlawful it is for a Jew to associate with or to visit any one of another nation; but God has shown me that I should not call any man common or unclean ... God shows no partiality, but in every nation any one who fears him and does what is right is acceptable to him. You know the word which he sent to Israel, preaching good news of peace by Jesus Christ ... To him all the prophets bear witness that every one who believes in him receives forgiveness of sins through his name.'
While Peter was still saying this, the Holy Spirit fell on all who heard the word ... Then Peter declared, 'Can any one forbid water for baptizing these people who have received the Holy Spirit just as we have?' And he commanded them to be baptized in the name of Jesus Christ.

Acts 23[33]—*27*[2]: When the soldiers came to Caesarea and delivered the letter to the governor, they presented Paul also before him ... And he commanded him to be guarded in Herod's praetorium ... He hoped that money would be given him by Paul. So he sent for him often and conversed with him. But when two years had elapsed, Felix was succeeded by Porcius Festus; and desiring to do the Jews a favour, Felix left Paul in prison...
Paul said in his defence, 'Neither against the law of the Jews, nor against the temple, nor against Caesar have I offended at all.' But Festus, wishing to do the Jews a favour, said to Paul, 'Do you wish to go up to Jerusalem, and there be tried on these charges before me?' But Paul said, 'I am standing before Caesar's tribunal, where I ought to be tried ... I appeal to Caesar.' Then Festus, when he had conferred with his council, answered, 'You have appealed to Caesar; to Caesar you shall go.' ...
When some days had passed, Agrippa the king and Bernice arrived at Caesarea to welcome Festus ... Festus laid Paul's case before the king ... Agrippa said to Festus, 'I should like to hear the man myself.' ...
As Paul made his defence, Festus said with a loud voice, 'Paul, you are mad; your great learning is turning you mad.' But Paul said, 'I am not mad, most excellent Festus, but I am speaking the sober truth. For the king knows about these things ... King Agrippa, do you believe the prophets? I know that you believe.' And Agrippa said to Paul. 'In a short time you think to

make me a Christian!' And Paul said, 'Whether short or long, I would to God that not only you but also all who hear me this day might become such as I am — except for these chains.' ... Agrippa said to Festus, 'This man could have been set free if he had not appealed to Caesar.'

And when it was decided that we should sail for Italy, they delivered Paul and some other prisoners to a centurion of the Augustan Cohort, named Julius. And embarking in a ship of Adramyttium, which was about to sail to the ports along the coast of Asia, we put to sea.

CAESAREA PHILIPPI see p. 90

CANA 8km. from Nazareth, on the road to Tiberias.

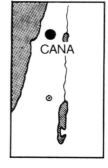

The site of the town in which St John places his heavily symbolic first story about Jesus is disputed. Several places lay claim to being 'Cana of Galilee'. The poor but picturesque village of Kafr Kanna is the only one pilgrims visit. It boasts a number of churches, among them one dedicated to St Nathanael-Bartholomew, identified as a native of Cana in John 21[2]. Pilgrims make for the red-domed Franciscan 'Wedding Church', which is best reached on foot from the lower (northern) entrance to the village. The church is on the left about 200m. up the lane. (Closed 11.45 - 14.30.)

In the main body of the simple church, a wooden panel in the floor lifts up to reveal a 3rd c. mosaic in aramaic. A translation is on the wall to the right. Steps ahead lead down to a crypt where a Roman jar is displayed to evoke the significant story of water changed into wine. Corridors beyond lead to wells from which water was once drawn. To the left the exit back upstairs exhibits some archeological remains.

Out in the lane, opposite the church, a souvenir shop offers samples of the local wine — not the best advertisement for the invigorating 'wine' which Christians claim is provided for them by Jesus.

Psalm 128: O blessed are those who fear the Lord
and walk in his ways!
By the labour of your hands you shall eat.
You will be happy and prosper;
your wife like a fruitful vine
in the heart of your house;
your children like shoots of the olive,
around your table.

Indeed thus shall be blessed
the man who fears the Lord.
May the Lord bless you from Sion
all the days of your life!
May you see your children's children
in a happy Jerusalem!
On Israel, peace!   *(Grail)*

John 2$^{1-12}$: On the third day there was a marriage at Cana in Galilee, and the mother of Jesus was there; Jesus also was invited to the marriage, with his disciples. When the wine gave out, the mother of Jesus said to him, 'They have no wine.' And Jesus said to her. 'O woman, what have you to do with me? My hour has not yet come.' His mother said to the servants. 'Do whatever he tells you.' Now six stone jars were standing there, for the Jewish rites of purification, each holding twenty or thirty gallons. Jesus said to them, 'Fill the jars with water.' And they filled them up to the brim. He said to them, 'Now draw some out, and take it to the steward of the feast.' So they took it. When the steward of the feast tasted the water now become wine, and did not know where it came from (though the servants who had drawn the water knew), the steward of the feast called the bridegroom and said to him. 'Every man serves the good wine first; and when men have drunk freely, then the poor wine; but you have kept the good wine until now.' This, the first of his signs, Jesus did at Cana in Galilee, and manifested his glory; and his disciples believed in him.

After this he went down to Capernaum, with his mother and his brothers and his disciples.

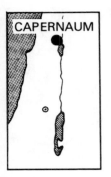

CAPERNAUM   18km. north of Tiberias, on the lakeside. Open 8.30 - 16.30. Small entrance fee. Cards, slides and toilets (fig. 19).

Capernaum (or Capharnaum) lies in a walled compound owned by the Franciscans. In New Testament times it was a frontier town (it still lies close to the Syrian border), and was clearly such a lively place that Jesus chose it as the headquarters of his Galilean ministry, to the extent that it could be called 'his own city'. He called his disciples Peter, Andrew and Matthew here, and its synagogue was the scene of much of his preaching. The familiar words 'Lord, I am not worthy' were first uttered by a centurion from the local Roman garrison (Matthew 8^8), and at least parts of the famous discourse on the Bread of Life were spoken in this setting.

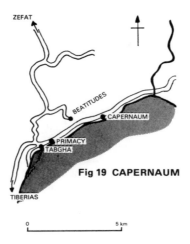

Fig 19 CAPERNAUM

The limestone synagogue, later than the time of Jesus but only by a hundred years or so, has been partially reconstructed at the far end of the site, and its delicate carvings are splendidly displayed on the paths which lead to it. Note especially the decorative date-palm and the symbolic Temple-on-wheels. Other exhibits in the grounds are of grain mills and oilpresses of Roman times, all in the black basalt of the region.

More recent excavations have brought to light remains of a 5th c. basilica with mosaics similar to Tabgha's (see p. 174), reputedly on the site of the house of St Peter.

113

If the gates alongside the monastery are open, it is worth while walking 100m. down to the seashore, where a small jetty has been built for passengers coming from Tiberias and En Gev by steamer.

Matthew 9[1-9]: Getting into a boat, Jesus crossed over and came to his own city. And behold they brought to him a paralytic, lying on his bed; and when Jesus saw their faith he said to the paralytic, 'Take heart, my son; your sins are forgiven.' And behold, some of the scribes said to themselves, 'This man is blaspheming.' But Jesus, knowing their thoughts, said, 'Why do you think evil in your hearts? For which is easier, to say, "Your sins are forgiven," or to say, "Rise and walk"? But that you may know that the Son of man has authority on earth to forgive sins' — he then said to the paralytic — 'Rise, take up your bed and go home.' And he rose and went home. When the crowds saw it, they were afraid, and they glorified God, who had given such authority to men.

As Jesus passed on from there, he saw a man called Matthew sitting at the tax office; and he said to him, 'Follow me.' And he rose and followed him.

John 6[48-59]: Jesus said, 'I am the bread of life ... which came down from heaven; if anyone eats of this bread, he will live for ever; and the bread which I shall give for the life of the world is my flesh.'

The Jews then disputed among themselves, saying, 'How can this man give us his flesh to eat?' So Jesus said to them, 'Truly, truly, I say to you, unless you eat the flesh of the Son of man and drink his blood, you have no life in you; he who eats my flesh and drinks my blood has eternal life, and I will raise him up at the last day. For my flesh is food indeed, and my blood is drink indeed. He who eats my flesh and drinks my blood abides in me, and I in him ...' This he said in the synagogue, as he taught at Capernaum.

DH: Lord Jesus Christ, Bread of Life,
    as vulnerable as bread placed in a man's hand,
      to be accepted with joy or cast aside,
    as satisfying as bread to the hungry,
      and giving life for the future,
    broken like bread that all may share,
      and as necessary as bread to sustain our living.

Lord, give us each day our daily Bread.

BPB p. 21: Father, Jesus never seems to have tired of saying:
    Everyone who exalts himself will be humbled,
    but he who humbles himself will be exalted.
The Pharisee, in his story,
    stood in (this) synagogue in silent prayer.
His whole life was a Lenten exercise.
He thanked you, God, as he supposed,
    for his fasts, his many efforts to be good,
    for his not being a sinner like the rest of men,

and plainly not at all like yonder publican.
The publican, for his part, stood a long way off,
  seeing no one and not knowing he was seen.
He did not even dare to lift his eyes to heaven,
  but only beat his breast and said,
  'O God, be merciful to me a sinner.'
My heart is drawn irresistibly
  to that humble publican
    whom Christ exalted.
My only fear is, Father, I may end up as a Pharisee
  who believes himself to be a publican and says:
'I thank you, God, I am not like the rest of men
  who do not know that they are sinners.
I thank you especially for not being like
  the Pharisees surrounding me.
I do not keep the commandments,
  neither do I pray or fast or give alms;
but I stand far apart in church
  not daring to lift my eyes to heaven.
And I beat my breast continuously and say:
  "O God, be merciful to me a sinner." '
O God of labyrinths,
  be merciful to me
    a Pharisee.

CARMEL   see p. 143

CORAZIN   see p. 170

DAN   see p. 91

DEAD SEA

The Dead Sea is part of the Great Rift Valley extending 6,500km. from the Jordan sources to the lakes of eastern Africa. This great fissure in the earth's crust reaches its deepest point here. The Sea lies 400m. below sea level, and at its northern end its salty waters descend another 400m. It is 80km. long and 18km. at its widest point.

Since the Sea's only source of water is the river Jordan and its tributaries, and since these diminish year by year as more and more water is drawn from them, plans are at present in preparation to dig a 100km. tunnel to bring water from the Mediterranean.

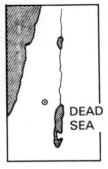

DEAD SEA

There is a rabbinical saying that to be called living one must both receive and give; this Sea is called dead because it only receives — there is no exit for its waters at the southern end. Yet it does give too, partly in the seven billion kg. of water daily evaporated into the air (the mild climate of Jerusalem depends totally on this feature), and partly in the rich mineral deposits produced by this evaporation. The calcium, magnesium, potassium and sodium farmed at the southern end provide Israel with a most profitable export — an unexpected 'fulfilment' of Ezekiel's wild hope that this dead Sea would one day be a source of life. St John saw the wild hope fulfilled in the abundant and lifegiving 'waters' pouring out of the side of the crucified Jesus.

Many of the Sea's interesting features have been described elsewhere in this book. What follows is a full list in geographical order (fig. 20).

The Jordan empties itself into the Dead Sea near **Jericho** (1) (see p. 132). Being part of the Rift, the muddy river is too deeply sunk in its trench to be able to fertilize the land through which it lazily meanders, measuring over 300km. to cover a distance of less than 100km. It is crossed at this point by two bridges which carry a fair amount of traffic to and from Jordan, the Allenby (2) and the Abdullah (3). A third road from Jericho to the river goes to the traditional spot of Jesus' baptism (4), now unfortunately classified as a forbidden military zone.

A finely engineered road hugs the west bank of the Sea, newly constructed to cope with visitors to the monastery of **Qumran** (5) (see p. 162), the swimming resorts of **Ein Fashkha (Enot Zuqim)** (6) (see p. 164) and **En Gedi** (7) (see p. 123), and the mountain fortress of **Masada** (8) (see p. 138). The top of Masada is the best point to appreciate the extent to which the 'tongue' of land here sticking out from the east (**Lisan** or **Lashon**) (9) has recently effectively cut the Sea into two. The water at this point is only 10m. at its deepest, and fordable passes are emerging as Jordan water is siphoned off for irrigation further north.

South of Masada, the luxury hotels of **En Boqeq** (10) illustrate the extent to which the Dead Sea waters are used as a spa, and the noisome complex further down the Elat road the extent to which they are proving commercially profitable. Shortly before this industrial zone lies the glowing white salt mountains of **Sedom** (11), the destruction of whose city is linked by the Genesis saga with Abraham. An eroded salt formation is shown, strangely, as Lot's Daughter and Dog, and a local café bears a notice saying, 'Be careful with the salt; you never know who it's been'. A natural cave, festooned with salt stalactites, leads a kilometre deep into the mountain.

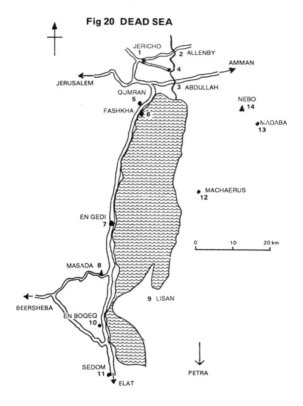

Fig 20 DEAD SEA

On the eastern bank (belonging to Jordan), points of interest to the pilgrim are the Herodian fortress of **Machaerus** (12) where John the Baptist probably met his end, the town of **Madaba** (13) in whose church the famous Byzantine mosaic map of Palestine can be seen and the heights of **Nebo** (14) from which Moses is said to have wistfully surveyed the Promised Land he was not to enter. The road to **Petra**, the 'rose-red city half as old as time', similarly leads through Jordan. The journey, though rewarding, is long and arduous (250km. from Amman, viz. 700km. return from Jerusalem). Those who wish to undertake the project must be prepared to devote

117

at least a 20-hour day to it, and discuss arrangements with one of Jerusalem's accommodating taxi drivers.

Genesis 19[17-28]: The angels said to Lot, 'Flee for your life; do not look back or stop anywhere in the valley; flee to the hills, lest you be consumed' ... Then the Lord rained on Sodom and Gomorrah brimstone and fire from the Lord out of heaven; and he overthrew those cities, and all the valley, and all the inhabitants of the cities, and what grew on the ground. But Lot's wife behind him looked back, and she became a pillar of salt. And Abraham went early in the morning to the place where he had stood before the Lord; and he looked down toward Sodom and Gomorrah and toward all the land of the valley, and beheld, and lo, the smoke of the land went up like the smoke of a furnace.

Deuteronomy 34[1-5]: Moses went up from the plains of Moab to Mount Nebo ... which is opposite Jericho. And the Lord showed him all the land ... and said to him, 'This is the land of which I swore to Abraham, to Isaac, and to Jacob, "I will give it to your descendants." I have let you see it with your eyes, but you shall not go over there.' So Moses the servant of the Lord died there in the land of Moab, according to the word of the Lord.

Mark 6[17-29]: Herod had sent and seized John, and bound him in prison for the sake of Herodias, his brother Philip's wife, because he had married her ... Herod on his birthday gave a banquet for his courtiers and officers and leading men of Galilee. And when Herodias' daughter came in and danced, she pleased Herod and his guests; and the king said to the girl, 'Ask me whatever you wish, and I will grant it.' ... And she went out, and said to her mother, 'What shall I ask?' And she said, 'The head of John the baptizer.' ... And immediately the king sent a soldier of the guard and gave orders to bring his head. He went and beheaded him in the prison, and brought his head on a platter, and gave it to the girl; and the girl gave it to her mother. When his disciples heard of it, they came and took his body and laid it in a tomb.

Ezekiel 47[1-8]: He brought me to the door of the Temple; and behold, water was issuing from below the threshold of the Temple toward the east ... The man measured a thousand cubits, and then led me through the water; and it was ankle deep. Again he measured a thousand and led me through the water; and it was knee-deep. Again he measured a thousand, and led me through the water; and it was up to the loins. Again he measured a thousand, and it was a river that I could not pass through ... And he said to me, 'This water flows toward the eastern region and goes down into the Arabah; and when it enters the stagnant waters of the [Dead] Sea, the water will become fresh.'

John 7[14-19][34]: About the middle of the feast Jesus went up into the Temple and taught ... On the last day of the feast, Jesus stood up and proclaimed, 'If anyone thirst, let him come to me, and let him who believes in me drink. As

the scripture has said, "Out of his heart shall flow rivers of living water." '
Now this he said about the Spirit, which those who believed in him were to
receive ...

When they came to Jesus and saw that he was already dead ... one of the
soldiers pierced his side with a spear, and at once there came out blood and
water.

EIN FASHKHA see p. 164

EMMAUS (Qubeiba)   14km. north west of Jerusalem, off the
Ramallah Road (fig. 21).

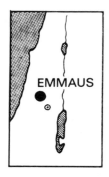

The Ramallah road has two turns to the left that will lead to
Qubeiba. The first is in the suburb of Beit Hanina (1), where a
hillock on the right of the main road crowned with concrete pillars
marks the site of the palace which King Hussein of Jordan began to
build for his occasional visits to Jerusalem before the Six Day War in
1967. It is the same hill of **Gibeah** (2) which King Saul chose for his
capital among his own Benjaminite tribesmen.

The Beit Hanina road passes under a delightful hill topped by a
solitary mosque, a landmark for miles around. It has been mistakenly
known since Byzantine times as the tomb of the prophet Samuel,
Nabi Samwil (3). The Crusaders built a church on the hill and
called it Mountjoy, because of the first view of Jerusalem it gave
them as they came up from the coast.

At Biddu (4), the narrow road ahead leads steeply down to
Qubeiba (5). At least four places lay claim to be the Emmaus of
Luke's evocative resurrection story. Qubeiba has led the field since
about 1500 (though it is a less likely candidate than the others), and
this is where pilgrims continue to read the Emmaus story. Its biggest
day is Easter Monday when the Latins come out from Jerusalem by
the coachload for the blessing of bread by the 'Custodian' of the
Holy Land.

The Franciscan church (closed 11.45 - 14.00) is less than a
hundred years old, though on Crusader foundations. The low wall
running half the length inside is perhaps later. Out in the gardens, a
balcony offers a beautiful view of the foothills running down to the
coast. This was the Roman route to Caesarea.

The alternative and more northerly route to Qubeiba leads past the
village of Jib (6), which keeps the name of biblical **Gibeon**, though
the site has moved a little to the north. The excavated mound, its

Fig 21 EMMAUS

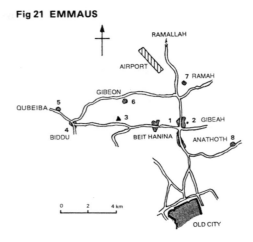

shape clearly visible from the road, has revealed the importance of this city. The invading Israelites accepted it as an ally rather than fight it (Joshua 9), Joshua defended it when 'the sun stood still over Gibeon' (Joshua 10), Solomon chose it as a high-place for worship (1 Kings 3), and it served as a Roman camp for the assault on Jerusalem in 66 AD. Excavations in 1956 brought to light a complex water system of the 12th c. BC involving a cistern 25m. deep approached by a spiral staircase with 79 steps, and a cellar cut two metres deep into the rock to hold at least 100,000 litres of wine. Those who wish to explore need a torch.

Just north of the intersection of the Jib road with the Ramallah road, the village of er-Ram (7) marks Samuel's birthplace **Ramah**. In the 6th c. BC it was the concentration camp where people were herded before deportation to Babylon. Jeremiah's moving description of the scene imagines Rachel, mother of the tribes being deported, arising from her tomb to weep for them.

Jeremiah's birthplace, **Anathoth**, is now called Anata (8), a small village on a turning to the east off the road back to Jerusalem.

1 Samuel 22[6–8]: Saul was sitting at Gibeah, under the tamarisk tree on the height, with his spear in his hand, and all his servants were standing about him. And Saul said to his servants who stood about him, 'Hear now, you

Benjaminites; will the son of Jesse [David] give every one of you fields and vineyards, will he make you all commanders of thousands and commanders of hundreds, that all of you have conspired against me?'

Luke 24[13–35]: On the first day of the week, two of the disciples were going to a village named Emmaus, about seven miles from Jerusalem, and talking with each other about all these things that had happened. While they were talking and discussing together, Jesus himself drew near and went with them. But their eyes were kept from recognising him. And he said to them, 'What is this conversation which you are holding with each other as you walk?' And they stood still, looking sad. Then one of them, named Cleopas, answered him ... 'Concerning Jesus of Nazareth, who was a prophet mighty in deed and word before God and all the people, and how our chief priests and rulers delivered him up to be condemned to death, and crucified him. But we had hoped that he was the one to redeem Israel'... And he said to them, 'O foolish men, and slow of heart to believe all that the prophets have spoken. Was it not necessary that the Christ should suffer these things and enter into his glory?' And beginning with Moses and all the prophets, he interpreted to them in all the scriptures the things concerning himself.

So they drew near to the village to which they were going. He appeared to be going further, but they constrained him, saying, 'Stay with us, for it is toward evening and the day is now far spent.' So he went in to stay with them. When he was at table with them, he took the bread and blessed, and broke it, and gave it to them. And their eyes were opened and they recognised him; and he vanished out of their sight. They said to each other, 'Did not our hearts burn within us while he talked to us on the road, while he opened to us the scriptures?' And they rose that same hour and returned to Jerusalem; and they found the eleven gathered together ... and they told them what had happened on the road, and how he was known to them in the breaking of the bread.

DH: Come to us, Lord Jesus Christ,
     come as we search the Scriptures and see God's hidden purpose,
     come as we walk the lonely road, needing a companion,
     come when life mystifies and perplexes us,
     come into our disappointments and unease,
     come at table where we share our food and hopes,
     and, coming, open our eyes to recognise you.

BPB p. 66: Father, it is strange how often
     the dearest things seem unfamiliar
     the nearest things seem far away.
   On Easter day, Jesus was not recognised
     when he walked with two of his disciples to Emmaus.
   He spoke to them and listened to them;
     and proved to them how necessary it was
     for the Christ to suffer if he was to enter his glory.

He made them see that Calvary
　　was all of a piece with Moses and the prophets.
Inspired by his presence, the disciples pleaded with him,
　　'Stay with us, for night is coming on
　　　　and the day is almost spent.'
Christ incognito agreed and sat down with them at table.
He assumed the role of host:
　　he took the bread, said the blessing, broke it
　　　　and gave them a share of it....
Father, give us this food
　　that will sustain us on life's journey
　　and save us from being frightened
　　　　by the long and lonely night.

Jeremiah 1[1-5]: The words of Jeremiah, the son of Hilkiah, of the priests who were in Anathoth in the land of Benjamin, to whom the word of the Lord came ... saying, 'Before I formed you in the womb I knew you, and before you were born I consecrated you; I appointed you a prophet to the nations.'

Jeremiah 11[21-23]: Thus says the Lord concerning the men of Anathoth, who seek your life, and say, 'Do not prophesy in the name of the Lord, or you will die by our hand' — therefore thus says the Lord of hosts: 'Behold, I will punish them... I will bring evil upon the men of Anathoth.'

Jeremiah 31[15-17]:Thus says the Lord:
　　　　'A voice is heard in Ramah,
　　　　lamentation and bitter weeping.
　　　　Rachel is weeping for her children;
　　　　She refuses to be comforted for her children,
　　　　because they are not ...
　　　　Keep your voice from weeping ...
　　　　they shall come back from the land of the enemy.
　　　　There is hope for your future, says the Lord,
　　　　and your children shall come back to their own country.'

EN BOQEQ see p. 116

EN GEDI 30km. south of Qumran, or 20km. north of Masada, on the Dead Sea. Refreshments and toilets. There is a swimming resort (entrance fee) on the Sea.

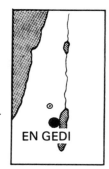

The sudden splash of date palms and vines under a deep cleft in the mountain betrays the 'Spring of David' which has formed this little oasis in an otherwise barren area. The spring gushes out of the rock in the form of a delicious waterfall at the top of the cleft, and forms a number of pools on the way down. Rainfall can affect the depth of these pools, but bathers will always be found in the top one. The path up the cleft through the animal reserve (entrance fee) is steep but worthwhile (30 minutes). Warnings are posted about not feeding the leopards.

Above the spring another 15 minutes trudge leads to a plateau commanding a magnificent view of the Dead Sea. Here the stone foundations of a temple dating from 3000 BC, to which people must have come for worship from miles around, provide a moving tribute to man's perennial religious quest.

Ecclesiasticus 24[13–14]:
 (Wisdom praises herself)
 'I grew tall like a cedar in Lebanon,
 and like a cypress on the heights of Hermon.
 I grew tall like a palm tree in Engedi,
 and like rose plants in Jericho.'

Song of Solomon 1[14–15]:
My beloved is to me a bag of myrrh,
that lies between my breasts.
My beloved is to me a cluster of henna blossoms
in the vineyards of Engedi.

1 Samuel 24[1–7]: Saul was told, 'Behold, David is in the wilderness of Engedi.' Then Saul took three thousand chosen men out of all Israel, and went to seek David and his men in front of the Wildgoats' Rocks. And he came to the sheepfolds by the way, where there was a cave; and Saul went in to relieve himself. Now David and his men were sitting in the innermost parts of the cave. And the men of David said to him, 'Here is the day of which the Lord said to you, "Behold, I will give your enemy into your hand, and you shall do to him as it shall seem good to you." ' Then David arose and stealthily cut off the skirt of Saul's robe. And afterwards David's heart smote him, because he had cut off Saul's skirt. He said to his men, 'The Lord forbid that I should do this thing to my lord, the Lord's anointed, to put forth my hand against him, seeing he is the Lord's anointed.' So David persuaded his men with these words, and did not permit them to attack Saul.

EN GEV see p. 170

EN KAREM see p. 66

GENNESARETH see p. 168

GIBEAH see p. 119

GIBEON see p. 119

GINNOSAR see p. 170

GOOD SAMARITAN INN 18km. from Jerusalem, on the Jericho road. Entrance is free. Closed Fridays.

One can be grateful that the most famous and most challenging story told by Jesus is earthed in this abandoned police post, which even in ruins still dominates the road. Entrance to the compound, which is well signposted, is from a service road behind.

No one imagines it is the actual spot where the 'inn' of the parable stood. Indeed, being in a story, it scarcely needs an actual spot. But it is good to have somewhere in this austere yet beautiful countryside where the story can be read again. The new arterial road has made cuttings through many of the hills en route, and no longer reveals how easy it would once have been for lurking brigands to ambush travellers. In any case the New Testament road ran some distance to the north of the present one.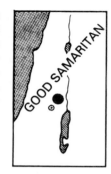

The story, of course, is not a simple lesson in neighbourliness. Jesus' stories always had a far sharper point. In his time Jews were at daggers drawn with Samaritans, who were regarded not only as heretics but as dangerous enemies whom no respectable Jew would fraternise with (see John 4⁹ p. 152). That someone of this ilk should echo God's mercy when the officials of God's chosen people were passing by on the other side, perhaps in the name of ritual cleanliness, is a dig in the ribs for all religious people.

*Luke 10*³⁰⁻³⁷: A man was going down from Jerusalem to Jericho, and he fell among robbers, who stripped him and beat him, and departed, leaving him half dead. Now by chance a priest was going down that road; and when he saw him he passed by on the other side. So likewise a Levite, when he came to the place and saw him, passed by on the other side. But a Samaritan, as he journeyed, came to where he was; and when he saw him, he had compassion, and went to him and bound up his wounds, pouring on oil and wine; then he set him on his own beast and brought him to an inn, and took care of him. And the next day he took out two day's wages, and gave it to the innkeeper, saying, 'Take care of him; and whatever more you spend, I will repay you when I come back.'

Which of these three, do you think, proved neighbour to the man who fell among the robbers? ... Go and do likewise.

¹ *BPB p. 106:* Father, help me during these days ...
to make my religion more sincere.
Too often when I pray, you are forced

to turn your head away from me
 in embarrassment
because I call you 'Father'
 while not treating my fellows
  as my brothers and sisters.
I go upon my knees in prayer
 but seldom is my spirit humbled
  before God or men.
I worship you
 but do not cease from evil
  or learn to do good.
I go to church
 but do not strive after justice,
  nor am I kind to the unhappy
   or generous to the unfortunate.
With a pious granite face,
 I walk on the other side of every road,
  past countless wounded strangers,
   while I pray hard for the needy.
I am in grave danger, Lord,
 of being lost in my prayers eternally.
Send upon me, Father, Christ's Spirit of sincerity
 lest I become
  like an oak whose leaf is withered
  like an unwatered garden without flowers
  like a spark swallowed up by eternal night.

HAIFA see p. 143

HATTIN see p. 168

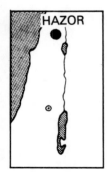

HAZOR 30km. from Tiberias on the main road north. Entrance fee (National Parks card). Closed 16.00.

Hazor controls the northern approach to the country, and inevitably was a theatre of battle throughout its 2,000 years of history. Joshua ensured that it was one of his first conquests. Solomon fortified it along with Megiddo, and his successors dug here, as there, an immense shaft and tunnel through solid rock to ensure the water supply in times of siege. It was nonetheless destroyed in the 8th c. BC by the Assyrians in their advance on Jerusalem. It was never rebuilt.

 The excavations, only recently completed under the direction of Yigael Yadin, are some of the most important in the land, throwing new light on a considerable part of Israel's history. The pity is that they are too confusing for the layman to understand. The site occupies both an upper and a lower level across a span of 190 acres, and there are 14 different excavation areas, bringing to light evidence of occupation at 21 different levels. Those who have the time to explore the excavations would do well to spend a considerable part of it in the museum on the other side of the main road, where some of the finds are exhibited, and where models, plans and photographs give an explanation of the site.

Joshua 11[10–12]: Joshua turned back at that time, and took Hazor, and smote its king with the sword; for Hazor formerly was the head of all those kingdoms. And they put to the sword all who were in it, utterly destroying them; there was none left that breathed, and he burned Hazor with fire. And all the cities of those kings, and all their kings, Joshua took, and smote them with the edge of the sword, utterly destroying them, as Moses the servant of the Lord had commanded.

HEBRON   35km. south of Jerusalem, on the Beersheba road. Toilets.

Hebron is known in Arabic as El Khalil, 'the friend (of God)'. The reference is to Abraham, beloved of God, venerated as their patriarchal ancestor by both Arabs and Jews. The diverting story of his haggling to purchase a piece of land on this spot is presumably meant to mark the transition of his clan from its unlanded nomadic past to a more settled future. Israelite tradition has it that not only he

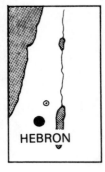

HEBRON

and his wife Sarah, but also his son Isaac and wife, and their son Jacob and wife, are all buried here.

Hebron remained famous through Old Testament times as the capital of the powerful tribe of Judah. David reigned here as king of Judah before moving to Jerusalem as king of all Israel, and when his son Absalom raised a rebellion he too set up his throne in Hebron.

The monument to Abraham — Haram el Khalil (fig. 22) — stands on an elevation at the far end of the ramshackle town, beautifully landscaped since the Israelis took possession in 1967, but at the cost of demolishing the houses which once clustered round it. The building is basically the work of Herod the Great, and its massive bossed stone blocks still inspire wonder in the visitor. The armed soldiers manning the entrance remind the visitor that he is in a war zone, and that the Israeli determination to resettle in this largely Arab town after their shameful expulsion in 1929 does not go unresisted.

Inside (men are required to cover their heads: paper hats on request), one is in a medieval church, the work of the Crusaders. The shrouded memorials which mark the six tombs (there is a 7th to Joseph near the exit) date only from the 10th c., and have never been excavated. The most beautiful item is a carved wood pulpit donated by Saladin in the 12th c. (Closed 11.30 - 13.00; 14.30 - 15.30, and all Friday and Saturday.)

3km. short of Hebron, a turn to the east leads within a hundred metres to an enclosure on the left. This is **Ramat el Khalil** and marks the traditional site of **Mamre**, which is mentioned several times in reference to Abraham's journeys. The well associated with his name is in the corner near the road. The magnificent enclosing walls were probably first put in place by Herod the Great in deference to the importance of the place for his Jewish subjects. Later Constantine's mother-in-law filled the eastern half of the enclosure with a Christian church, of which only the ruins remain. Entrance is free.

4km. further back towards Jerusalem is the village of Halhul, whose abundant spring is reputed to be the place where the deacon Philip baptised the Ethiopian eunuch.

Genesis 13[18]: Abram moved his tent, and came and dwelt by the oaks of Mamre, which are at Hebron; and there he built an altar to the Lord.

Genesis 18[1–15]: The Lord appeared to Abraham by the oaks of Mamre, as he sat at the door of his tent in the heat of the day. He lifted up his eyes and looked, and behold, three men stood in front of him. When he saw them, he ran from the tent door to meet them, and bowed himself to the earth, and

Fig 22 HEBRON

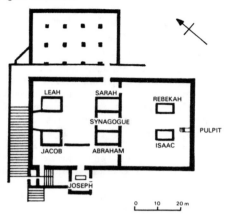

said, 'My lord, if I have found favour in your sight, do not pass by your servant. Let a little water be brought, and wash your feet, and rest yourselves under the tree, while I fetch a morsel of bread, that you may refresh yourselves, and after that you may pass on — since you have come to your servant.' So they said, 'Do as you have said.' And Abraham hastened into the tent to Sarah, and said, 'Make ready quickly three measures of fine meal, knead it and make cakes.' And Abraham ran to the herd, and took a calf, tender and good, and gave it to the servant, who hastened to prepare it. Then he took curds, and milk, and the calf which he had prepared, and set it before them; and he stood by them under the tree while they ate.

They said to him, 'Where is Sarah your wife?' And he said, 'She is in the tent.' The Lord said, 'I will surely return to you in the spring, and Sarah your wife will have a son.' And Sarah was listening at the tent door behind him. Now Abraham and Sarah were old, advanced in age; it had ceased to be with Sarah after the manner of women. So Sarah laughed to herself, saying, 'After I have grown old, and my husband is old, shall I have pleasure?' The Lord said to Abraham, 'Why did Sarah laugh and say, "Shall I indeed bear a child, now that I am old?" Is anything too hard for the Lord? At the appointed time I will return to you, in the spring, and Sarah shall have a son.' But Sarah denied, saying, 'I did not laugh'; for she was afraid. He said, 'No, but you did laugh.' [The Hebrew for 'laugh' is *isaac*.]

Genesis 23: Sarah lived a hundred and twenty-seven years ... and died at Kiriath-arba (that is Hebron); and Abraham went in to mourn for Sarah and to weep for her. And Abraham rose up from before his dead, and said to the Hittites, 'Give me property among you for a burying place.'... The Hittites answered Abraham, 'Hear us, my lord; you are a mighty prince among us. Bury your dead in the choicest of our sepulchres ...' Abraham rose and bowed to the Hittites, the people of the land. And he said to them ... 'Entreat for me Ephron the son of Zohar, that he may give me the cave of Machpelah, which he owns; it is at the end of his field. For the full price let him give it to me in your presence as a possession for a burying place.'... Ephron the Hittite answered Abraham in the hearing ... of all who went in at the gate of his city, 'No, my lord, hear me; I give you the field, and I give you the cave that is in it; in the presence of the sons of my people. I give it to you; bury your dead.' Then Abraham bowed down before the people of the land. And he said to Ephron in the hearing of the people of the land ... 'I will give the price of the field; accept it from me that I may bury my dead there.' Ephron answered Abraham, 'My lord, listen to me; a piece of land worth four hundred shekels of silver, what is that between you and me? Bury your dead.' Abraham agreed with Ephron; and Abraham weighed out for Ephron the silver which he had named in the hearing of the Hittites, four hundred shekels of silver ...

After this Abraham buried Sarah his wife in the cave of the field of Machpelah east of Mamre ... The field and the cave that is in it were made over to Abraham as a possession for a burying place by the Hittites.

2 Samuel 15[7-12]: Absalom said to David, 'Pray let me go and pay my vow, which I have vowed to the Lord, in Hebron ...' The king said to him, 'Go in peace.' So he arose and went to Hebron. But Absalom sent secret messengers throughout all the tribes of Israel, saying, 'As soon as you hear the sound of the trumpet, then say, "Absalom is king at Hebron!" ' With Absalom went two hundred men from Jerusalem ... and the conspiracy grew strong, and the people with Absalom kept increasing.

Galatians 3[6-14]: Abraham 'believed God, and it was reckoned to him as righteousness.' So you see that it is men of faith who are the sons of Abraham. And the scripture, foreseeing that God would justify the Gentiles by faith, preached the gospel beforehand to Abraham, saying, 'In you shall all the nations be blessed.' So then, those who are men of faith are blessed with Abraham who had faith ... In Christ Jesus the blessing of Abraham came upon the Gentiles, that we might receive the promise of the Spirit through faith.

Acts 8[27-38]: An Ethiopian, a eunuch, a minister of the Candace, queen of the Ethiopians, in charge of all her treasure, had come to Jerusalem to worship and was returning ... And the Spirit said to Philip, 'Go up and join this chariot.' So Philip ran to him ... and told him the good news of Jesus. And as they went along the road they came to some water, and the eunuch said, 'See, here is water! What is to prevent my being baptised?' And he commanded the chariot to stop, and they both went down into the river, Philip and the eunuch, and he baptised him.

HERODIUM   see p. 100

HISHAM'S PALACE   see p. 133

IMWAS   see p. 137

JACOB'S WELL   see p. 149

JAFFA-YAFO   61km. from Jerusalem.

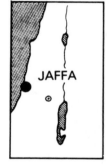

Jaffa is now only a tiny suburb of the sprawling town of Tel Aviv. Being one of the few harbours on the Palestine seaboard, it figured prominently, in history and legend, as the town founded by Noah's son Japhet, as the place where Perseus rescued the naked Andromeda from the sea monster (Lydda, a little further south, is the reputed birthplace of St George), as the port from which Jonah set out to meet his whale, and as the scene of Egypt's infiltration when 200 warriors where hidden in jars and carried Ali Baba fashion into the town. The prosperous port was eventually supplanted by Herod's Caesarea, and made little further mark on history until 1909, when 60 Jewish families moved out to build Tel Aviv on the sand dunes to the north.

Christians will be interested in Jaffa mainly because it was here, according to the New Testament, that Peter first realised during his midday siesta that the gospel message had to be extended beyond the confines of Judaism. The modern church commemorating the story stands above the port, which has some delightful waterfront restaurants.

Jonah 1[1-3]: Now the word of the Lord came to Jonah the son of Amittai, saying, 'Arise, go to Nineveh, that great city, and cry against it; for their wickedness has come up before me.' But Jonah rose to flee to Tarshish from the presence of the Lord. He went down to Jaffa and found a ship going to Tarshish; so he paid the fare, and went on board, to go with them to Tarshish, away from the presence of the Lord.

Acts 9³⁶—10¹⁶: There was at Jaffa a disciple named Tabitha ... In those days she fell sick and died; and when they had washed her, they laid her in an upper room ... The disciples sent two men to Peter entreating him, 'Please come to us without delay' ... When he had come, they took him to the upper room. All the widows stood beside him weeping, and showing tunics and other garments which Tabitha made while she was with them. But Peter put them all outside and knelt down and prayed; then turning to the body he said, 'Tabitha, rise.' And she opened her eyes, and when she saw Peter she sat up ... And he stayed in Jaffa for many days with one Simon, a tanner ...

Peter went up to the housetop to pray, about the sixth hour. And he became hungry and desired something to eat; but while they were preparing it, he fell into a trance and saw the heaven opened, and something descending, like a great sheet, let down by four corners upon the earth. In it were all kinds of animals and reptiles and birds of the air. And there came a voice to him, 'Rise, Peter; kill and eat.' But Peter said, 'No, Lord; for I have never eaten anything that is common or unclean.' And the voice came to him again a second time, 'What God has cleansed, you must not call common.'

JEBEL QURUNTUL see p. 133

JERICHO 39km. north east of Jerusalem, in the Jordan valley.

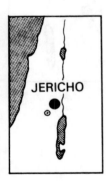

Jericho has moved around over the centuries. The present dusty town dates only from the 12th c. AD, even though one of its ageing sycamore trees is proudly shown as the one on which Zacchaeus rose above his shortcomings. The Jericho which Jesus frequently passed through on his journeys from Galilee was 2km. to the west, close to the extravagant winter palace which Herod the Great built in the wadi descending from the hills. The Old Testament town was 2km. to the north, at the mound of Tel es-Sultan. This is where the visitor makes for. Entrance to the mound is from the fenced car park (Entrance fee. National Parks card.) A number of refreshment and souvenir shops are within striking distance.

The site illustrates the strategic importance of the area. Fed by an abundance of springs which have created a fertile oasis 5km. wide, and enjoying a climate of extraordinary mildness even in winter (at 260m. below sea level it is the lowest inhabited spot on earth) Jericho has attracted settlers from the Stone Age onwards. Anyone invading the country from the east would first have to deal with these settlers; hence the enthusiasm with which the Old Testament describes their defeat by Joshua at the conclusion of the Exodus journey. For the Israelites, the fall of Jericho guaranteed the fall of the rest of the country.

When Joshua took this town in 1200 BC, it was already six or seven thousand years old. Nomadic hunters had first used its copious water supply ('Elisha's Spring') for growing crops which they could harvest from year to year, and then finally downed spears to settle permanently. The first walls date from 7000 BC, and the number of walls which have been successively built on their ruins can be counted in the strata revealed by the archeologist's spade. The walls enclose only five acres and constituted a fortress rather than a town, whose citizens lived in the fields around. The star attraction is the 9,000-year-old tower which came to light in the slice which Kathleen Kenyon took out of the mound. What one looks down upon is actually the top. The bottom is another 8m. down a perfectly preserved stairway in its centre.

The mound provides a view of one of Jericho's two refugee camps (the other lies on the Jerusalem side of the modern town) where 70,000 displaced Palestinians built themselves mud huts while they waited to return to the homes they had abandoned in Haifa and elsewhere in 1948. When Israel extended its borders to this West Bank in 1967, most of them fled even further east into Jordan. Behind the camp, clinging to the rock face of **Jebel Quruntul** (the 'Mountain of the Forty Days'), a Greek monastery commemorates the gospel story which tells of Jesus resisting the temptation to dominate by force. Higher up, a walled surround is all that remains of a 19th c. attempt to dominate the summit with a church.

2km. north of this site it is worth visiting the ruins of the magnificent **Umayyad Palace** (closed 17.00, winter 16.00, earlier on Fridays. Entrance fee. National Parks card). It is attributed to the 8th c. AD caliph **Hisham**, son of the builder of the Dome of the Rock in Jerusalem. Based in Damascus, he clearly appreciated the Jericho climate as much as the Victorians (who also flocked to this valley to escape the English winter), and the numerous negroid Arabs in Jericho still remind one of the African slaves he brought here to serve him. The opulence of the palace, which had its own swimming bath and sauna, is well illustrated in the stucco work which decorated its main entrance (now reconstructed in Jerusalem's Rockefeller Museum, see p. 71), the carved stone window now forming the

133

centrepiece of the courtyard, and particularly the exquisite mosaic floor of one of the reception rooms at the far end of the site. The palace was destroyed by earthquake shortly after completion and never rebuilt. There is a toilet and a small museum adjoining the entrance.

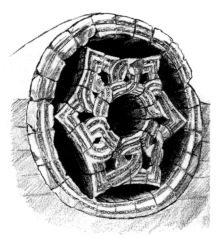

The river Jordan flows 8km. east of Jericho. Since 1967 the roads leading to it have been classified as a military zone. Before then Greek pilgrims would come in great numbers, especially on January 6, to renew their baptism by plunging naked into the fast-flowing stream. A chapel on the banks commemorates Jesus' own baptism by John, who obviously chose this area (as the Qumran community had done before him, see p. 162) to evoke memories of the Exodus, and the need to enter the Holy Land anew before a renewed Kingdom of God could be built. Facilities for renewing baptisms are now provided at the Jordan Bridge in Galilee (see p. 171).

Joshua 1¹—6²¹: After the death of Moses, the servant of the Lord, the Lord said to Joshua the son of Nun, Moses' minister, 'Moses my servant is dead; now therefore arise, go over this Jordan, you and all this people, into the land which I am giving to them.'...
   When the people set out from their tents, to pass over the Jordan with the priests bearing the ark of the covenant before the people, and when those who bore the ark had come to the Jordan, and the feet of the priests bearing the ark were dipped in the brink of the water ... the waters coming down from above stood and rose up in a heap far off ... and those flowing down toward the Salt Sea were wholly cut off; and the people passed over opposite Jericho ...

Jericho was shut up from within and from without because of the people of Israel; none went out and none came in. And the Lord said to Joshua, 'See, I have given into your hand Jericho, with its king and mighty men of valour. You shall march around the city, all the men of war going around the city once. Thus shall you do for six days ... And on the seventh day you shall march around the city seven times, the priests blowing the trumpets ... Then all the people shall shout with a great shout; and the wall of the city will fall down flat, and the people shall go up, every man straight before him.'...

As soon as the people heard the sound of the trumpet, the people raised a great shout, and the wall fell down flat, so that the people went up into the city, every man straight before him, and they took the city. Then they utterly destroyed all in the city, both men and women, young and old, oxen, sheep and asses, with the edge of the sword.

2 Kings 2[19–22]: The men of Jericho said to Elisha, 'Behold, the situation of this city is pleasant, as my lord sees; but the water is bad, and the land is unfruitful.' He said, 'Bring me a new bowl, and put salt in it.' So they brought it to him. Then he went to the spring of water and threw salt in it, and said, 'Thus says the Lord, I have made this water wholesome; henceforth neither death nor miscarriage shall come from it.' So the water has been wholesome to this day.

Matthew 3[1]—*4*[10]: In those days came John the Baptist, preaching in the wilderness of Judea, 'Repent, for the kingdom of heaven is at hand.'... Then went out to him Jerusalem and all Judea and all the region about the Jordan, and they were baptized by him in the river Jordan, confessing their sins ...

Then Jesus came from Galilee to the Jordan to John, to be baptized by him ... And when Jesus was baptized, he went up immediately from the water, and behold, the heavens were opened ...

Then Jesus was led up by the Spirit into the wilderness to be tempted by the devil ... The devil took him to a very high mountain, and showed him all the kingdoms of the world and the glory of them; and he said to him, 'All these I will give you, if you will fall down and worship me.' Then Jesus said to him ... 'You shall worship the Lord your God and him only shall you serve.'

Mark 10[46–52]: As Jesus was leaving Jericho with his disciples and a great multitude, Bartimaeus, a blind beggar ... was sitting by the roadside. And when he heard that it was Jesus of Nazareth, he began to cry out and to say, 'Jesus, Son of David, have mercy on me.'... And throwing off his mantle he sprang up and came to Jesus. And Jesus said to him, 'What do you want me to do for you?' And the blind man said to him, 'Master, let me receive my sight.' And Jesus said to him, 'Go your way; your faith has made you well.' And immediately he received his sight and followed him on the way.

Luke 19[1–10]: Jesus entered Jericho and was passing through. And there was a man named Zacchaeus; he was a chief tax collector, and rich. And he sought to see who Jesus was, but could not, on account of the crowd, because he was small of stature. So he ran on ahead and climbed up into a sycamore tree to see him, for he was to pass that way. And when Jesus came to the place, he looked up and said to him, 'Zacchaeus, make haste and come down; for I must stay at your house today.' So he made haste and came down, and received him joyfully. And when they saw it they all murmured, 'He has gone in to be the guest of a man who is a sinner.' And Zacchaeus stood and said to the Lord, 'Behold, Lord, the half of my goods I give to the poor; and if I have defrauded anyone of anything, I restore it fourfold.' And Jesus said to him, 'Today salvation has come to this house, since he also is a son of Abraham. For the Son of man came to seek and to save the lost.'

JIB   see p. 119

JORDAN BRIDGE   see p. 171

KINNERETH   see p. 168

KURSI   see p. 170

LATRUN   25 km. from Jerusalem, on the Tel Aviv road. Closed 11.30 - 14.30 and at 17.00.

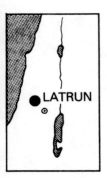

The main highway between Jerusalem and the coast is dominated at its midway point by the Cistercian monastery of Latrun. Visitors to the Holy Land will recognise it as the name of a popular wine made by the monks from the extensive vineyards on the surrounding hills. History knows it better as a strategic crossroads guarding Jerusalem, which has inevitably been the repeated scene of battle. In the 13th c. BC the adjoining valley of **Ayyalon** was the scene of one of Joshua's fiercest struggles for control of the country. In the 2nd c. BC the Maccabees fought unsuccessfully to hold it against the Syrians. In the 1st c. AD it was the camp for the Fifth Legion in the Roman assault on Jerusalem. In the 12th c. the Crusaders built a fortress (curiously in honour of the Good Thief, 'Latro') to guard this approach to Jerusalem. In 1917 it was the scene of bitter fighting between the retreating Turkish army and General Allenby. From 1948 to 1967 it remained the front line between the embattled Arabs and Israelis, and when Israel finally occupied the West Bank the neighbouring village of Imwas was demolished.

Imwas has preserved the biblical name of Emmaus, having discarded its grander 3rd c. Roman name of Nicopolis. Though the Byzantines twice built a basilica there in honour of the Emmaus story, and the Crusaders a smaller one on their ruins, it is unfortunately too far away from Jerusalem to fit Luke's resurrection story of the breaking of the bread (see Qubeiba, p. 119).

Joshua 10[5-13]: The five kings of the Amorites, the king of Jerusalem, the king of Hebron, the king of Jarmuth, the king of Lachish, and the king of Eglon, gathered their forces ... Joshua came upon them suddenly, having marched up all night from Gilgal. And the Lord threw them into a panic before Israel, who slew them with a great slaughter ...
And Joshua said in the sight of Israel,
'Sun stand thou still at Gibeon,
and thou Moon in the valley of Aijalon.'
And the sun stood still, and the moon stayed, until the nation took vengeance on their enemies.

Luke 23[39-43]: One of the criminals who were hanged railed at Jesus, saying, 'Are you not the Christ? Save yourself and us!' But the other rebuked him, saying, '... This man has done nothing wrong.' And he said, 'Jesus, remember me when you come into your kingdom.' And he said to him, 'Truly, I say to you, today you will be with me in Paradise.'

LAZARUS' TOMB see p. 94

LISAN see p. 116

MACHAERUS see p. 117

MADABA see p. 117

MAGDALA see p. 169

MAMRE see p. 128

MAR SABA see p. 101

MASADA 130km. from Jerusalem via Hebron and Arad, or 98km. via Jericho and the Dead Sea. Restaurant and museum on the east. Refreshments on the west. Further generous toilet facilities on the summit. Entrance fee (National Parks card).

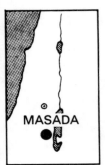

The rock of Masada, detached from the surrounding cliffs, rides like a gigantic ship in the desert along the shores of the Dead Sea. Its story was always known: the Jewish historian Josephus had spoken of it eloquently, and described in detail the final suicidal stand made there by the Zealots in the Jewish war of the 1st c. AD. But nobody knew where it was until British explorers identified it in 1850. Remote and inaccessible, it was not excavated until 1963.

The archaeologists discovered that the mountain was first made into a fortress a hundred years before Christ, but it was Herod the Great who put it on the map. Realising its possibilities, he dug cisterns into the sides of the mountain to hold 170,000 cubic metres of water, and ducted rainwater from the adjacent hills to fill them — enough to allow a spacious stepped swimming pool to be provided on the summit. He built a massive palace in the centre, paved with exquisite mosaics which are still to be seen. On the northern tip, catching the best view and the coolest winds, he built a summer villa in three tiers on the sheer cliff face, and decorated it with the most delicate stucco. An adjoining bath-house provided elegant and spacious sauna rooms for his guests. To support this enormous undertaking, he built fifteen vast storerooms, where hundreds of grain and liquid jars were unearthed. Finally he surrounded the whole hill with a double wall with 37 watch-towers. One needs to be a little mad to erect this kind of 5-star hotel up 400m. of rock in a total desert — but no one can fail to admire the single and prodigal mind which could conceive of it.

Herod died in 4 BC, and the Roman army took over Masada as a garrison. In the rebellion of 66 AD, Jewish partisans captured it, intent on making it the scene of their final resistance. They attracted a thousand refugees from Qumran and other centres from which the Roman army had driven them. They camped out in the palace in haphazard style, and in the walls built a synagogue which remains the oldest in existence. They resisted five years of siege.

In 72 the Roman general Silva was put in charge of 15,000 men of the Tenth Legion with orders to reduce Masada. He surrounded the mountain with eight fortified camps linked with a wall, and laboriously built a ramp up the western rock face. Up this he sent firing towers and battering rams to breach the walls. The Zealots knew it was the end and agreed to die by each other's hands rather than become slaves of Rome. Lots were drawn for ten men to kill the rest and then each other. The sherds with the names were found in the ruins. Josephus says that five children and two women escaped the mass suicide to tell the story to the world. For Israel the story remains a powerful symbol of heroic patriotism, enshrined in their motto, 'Masada shall not fall a second time.'

In two seasons between 1963 and 1965 (an area this size would normally require 26 seasons) Masada was dug out of the rubble of centuries by an army of volunteers working under Yigael Yadin. They excavated 97 per cent of the area down to groundrock, rebuilding parts of what they found to give visitors a better concept of what Masada once was. A black painted line separates what was found from what has been reconstructed. The copious finds (pottery, manuscripts, 4,000 coins, skeletons, clothes, shoes, food) are in the Israel Museum in Jerusalem (see p. 63).

There are two ways up the mountain (fig. 23). From the Arad side one can walk up the 75m. high Roman ramp (1) in twenty minutes. From the much lower eastern side, one can either walk up the steep and sinuous Snake Path (2) (at least 40 minutes) or take the cable car (3) up the 300m. rise. In either case one is back to sea level at the summit. Those who cannot afford at least an hour on the summit would waste their time going up. The last cable down is at 16.00.

Signposts and billboards round the excavated area give a very clear explanation of what is to be seen. The main palace with its mosaics is in the centre (4), closely flanked by a mosaic-paved chapel (5) built by Byzantine monks 400 years later, when Herods were as forgotten as Zealots. To the south lie the swimming pool (6), the 'columbarium' (for funerary urns or for pigeon post?) (7) and the largest water cistern (8). To the north lie the synagogue in the walls (9), the storerooms, the bath-house (10), and the tiered summer villa (30 minutes descent and ascent) (11). Superb views of the Roman camps, of the Moabite mountains to the east, and in general of the Dead Sea, especially of the Lisan peninsular which can be seen from this altitude to cut the Sea into two.

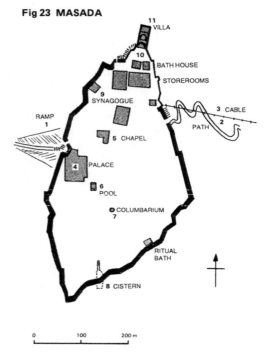

Fig 23 MASADA

The Zealot commandant's last address: My loyal followers, long ago we resolved to serve neither the Romans nor anyone else but only God, who alone is the true and righteous Lord of men: now the time has come that bids us prove our determination by our deeds ... For we were the first of all to revolt, and shall be the last to break off the struggle. And I think it is God who has given us this privilege, that we can die nobly and as free men, unlike others who were unexpectedly defeated. In our case it is evident that day-break will end our resistance, but we are free to chose an honourable death with our loved ones ...

Let our wives die unabused, our children without knowledge of slavery: after that, let us do each other an ungrudging kindness ...

But first let our possessions and the whole fortress go up in flames: it will be a bitter blow to the Romans, that I know, to find our persons beyond their reach and nothing left for them to loot. One thing only let us spare — our store of food: it will bear witness when we are dead to the fact that we perished, not through want but because, as we resolved at the beginning, we chose death rather than slavery.

MEGIDDO   23km. from Nazareth, 100km. from Tel Aviv. Entrance fee (National Parks card). Toilets, refreshments, souvenirs. Closed 17.00.

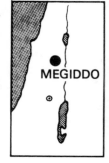

The most outstanding mention of Megiddo in the Bible is in its last book, where it is referred to as **Armageddon**, the 'Mountain of Megiddo', the symbolic site of the final decisive battle between the forces of good and the forces of evil. Its position on the map explains the reference. Megiddo guards the vital pass through the Carmel range of mountains through which all north-south traffic must pass, from Damascus to Egypt. This makes Megiddo a kind of cock-pit of the ancient world. Its history was one of constant battles from the 30th to the 4th c. BC, as twenty times a new city was built on the ruins of the old. The 13th c. BC Canaanite city, vassal to Egypt, was too strong for Joshua to take, and it did not fall into Israelite hands until the time of David. Solomon fortified it, as did King Ahab in magnificent style. In the 7th c. BC the pious King Josiah died here trying to stop Egypt coming to the aid of Assyria. In 1917 the defeat of the Turks at this place accelerated the end of the Great War, and the victorious general was accorded the title Allenby of Megiddo.

Entrance is through the museum (fig. 24) (1) where an excellent mobile model gives a clear overview of the site. Careful photography has kept a record of the many strata which had to be removed to reveal those which lay beneath. A path from the side entrance leads

Fig 24 MEGIDDO

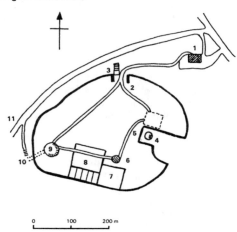

up a ramp to the heavily fortified city gate (2) with its adjoining steep stairway for pedestrians (3). A deep slice cut out of the eastern side of the mound has felicitously brought to light a beautiful stepped altar built of unhewn stones, the city's 'high place' in 2500 BC (4). Behind it stood the Canaanite temple which served it (5).

A little higher up the mound a fine grain silo has been unearthed, with circular stairways to allow two-way traffic (6). Beyond this lay the royal palace (7), and beside it a spacious courtyard flanked by rows of standing pillars (8). The many feeding troughs found in this area suggested to the original excavators that Megiddo was one of the 'chariot cities' which Solomon is said to have built for the 12,000 cavalry he introduced into Israel's army. But it is now clear that the stones are the remains of warehouses from the time of Ahab a century later. Ahab was also responsible for the daring shaft dug through thirty metres of rock close by (9). Steps lead down to a tunnel 70m. long and wide enough for a bus to drive through, and bring one to Megiddo's water supply in the valley outside the city walls (10). This could be blocked off once the tunnel was completed. Those who make their way through the lit tunnel can have their coach meet them at the exit (11) to save the long walk back to the museum car park.

Exodus 20[25]: If you make me an altar of stone, you shall not build it of hewn stones; for if you wield your tool upon it you profane it.

1 Kings 9[15–19]: This is the account of the forced labour which King Solomon levied to build the House of the Lord, and his own house, and the Millo, and the wall of Jerusalem, and Hazor, and Megiddo ... and all the store-cities that Solomon had, and the cities for his chariots, and the cities for his horsemen, and whatever Solomon desired to build ...

2 Kings 23[29–30]: In Josiah's days, Pharaoh Neco king of Egypt went up to the king of Assyria to the river Euphrates. King Josiah went to meet him; and Pharaoh Neco slew him at Megiddo, when he saw him. And his servants carried him dead in a chariot from Megiddo, and brought him to Jerusalem, and buried him in his own tomb.

Revelation 16[12–19]: The sixth angel poured his bowl on the great river Euphrates, and its water was dried up, to prepare the way for the kings from the east ... to assemble them for battle on the great day of God the Almighty ... And they assembled them at the place which is called in Hebrew Armageddon ... And a loud voice came out of the temple, from the throne, saying, 'It is done!' ... And the cities of the nations fell.

MOUNT CARMEL

Mount Carmel is the range of hills which swings the land's central mountain massif to the west and brings it to within 200m. of the sea at Haifa, effectively cutting off Galilee from the rest of the country (hence the importance of Megiddo, see p. 141). The name means Garden of God, the mountain having been regarded as sacred throughout history. Pilgrims will most naturally think of it as the 'high place' where Elijah challenged the prophets of Baal in the 9th c. BC; as the spiritual home of the 13th c. Carmelite order which claims descent from the early Christian hermits who inhabited its caves; and as the resting place of the Persian Muslim Baha who founded the comprehensive Bahai faith at the end of the last century.

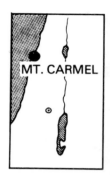

The Carmelite monastery lies next to the lighthouse, on the very western tip of the hill (closed 13.30 to 15.00). It contains a cave reputedly inhabited by Elijah. His stirring competition with Baal is traditionally associated with a spot 18km. further inland and several hundred metres higher up the mountain range. Still called The Sacrifice (el Muhraqa), it is accessible off the road from Yoqneam to Zikhron Yaaqov, and offers a view of the sea and the Jezreel plain which brings the biblical text vividly to life.

From the monastery, the road descending to Haifa affords a number of fine panoramas of the modern town, with its bustling harbour and its sweeping bay. **Haifa** has changed its character considerably since the creation of the State of Israel in 1948. It has lost much of its Arab population, and attracted a great deal of industry. It has expanded astronomically, and the desirable Carmel hillside has inevitably become a honeycomb of apartment buildings.

To the south of Haifa there are a number of swimming resorts along the sandy coast. 17km. along the inner coast road (not the motorway), in the hillside to the left, are the famous caves which brought the 150,000 year old Mount Carmel Man into the limelight in the '30s, because of his obvious links with the neanderthal skeletons found in Europe.

Song of Solomon 7[5–6]: Your head crowns you like Carmel,
and your flowing locks are like purple;
a king is held captive in the tresses.
How fair and pleasant you are,
O loved one, delectable maiden!

1 Kings 18[17–40]: When King Ahab saw Elijah, Ahab said to him, 'Is it you, you Troubler of Israel?' And he answered, 'I have not troubled Israel; but you have, and your father's house, because you have forsaken the command-

143

ments of the Lord and followed the Baals. Now therefore send and gather all Israel to me at Mount Carmel, and the 450 prophets of Baal, and the 400 prophets of Asherah, who eat at Jezebel's table.'

So Ahab sent to all the people of Israel, and gathered the prophets together at Mount Carmel. And Elijah came near to all the people, and said, 'How long will you go limping with two different opinions? If the Lord is God, follow him; but if Baal, then follow him.' And the people did not answer him a word. Then Elijah said to the people. 'I, even I only, am left a prophet of the Lord; but Baal's prophets are 450 men. Let two bulls be given to us, and let them choose one bull for themselves, and cut it in pieces and lay it on the wood, but put no fire to it; and I will prepare the other bull and lay it on the wood, and put no fire to it. And you call on the name of your god, and I will call on the name of the Lord; and the God who answers by fire, he is God.' And all the people answered, 'It is well spoken.'...

The prophets of Baal took the bull which was given them, and they prepared it, and called on the name of Baal from morning until noon, saying, 'O Baal, answer us!' But there was no voice, and no one answered ... Elijah mocked them, saying, 'Cry aloud ... perhaps he is asleep and must be awakened' ... but there was no voice; no one answered, no one heeded.

Then Elijah said to all the people, 'Come near to me'; and all the people came near to him. And he repaired the altar of the Lord that had been thrown down ... and made a trench about the altar ... and he said, 'Fill four jars with water, and pour it on the burnt offering, and on the wood.' And he said, 'Do it a second time'; and they did it a second time. And he said, 'Do it a third time'; and they did it a third time. And the water ran round about the altar, and filled the trench also with water....

Elijah said, 'Answer me, O Lord, answer me, that this people may know that thou, O Lord, art God, and that thou hast turned their hearts back.' Then the fire of the Lord fell, and consumed the burnt offering, and the wood, and the stones, and the dust, and licked up the water that was in the trench. And when all the people saw it, they fell on their faces; and they said, 'The Lord, he is God; the Lord, he is God.' And Elijah said to them, 'Seize the prophets of Baal; let not one of them escape.' And they seized them; and Elijah brought them down to the brook Kishon, and killed them there.

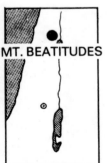

MT. BEATITUDES

MOUNT OF BEATITUDES

16km. north of Tiberias, on a side road to the right after a series of hairpin bends past the turn for Tabgha and Capernaum (see p. 113).

The gospels make no attempt to locate the famous Sermon on the Mount anywhere specific. In fact Matthew's 'mount' may be no more than a literary device to point to Jesus as a new Moses, teaching the law of God from a new Sinai. Luke does not hesitate to locate a similar collection of Jesus' teaching on a 'plain' (6[17]).

Nonetheless this site chosen by the Franciscan Sisters is an ideal spot on which to recall the surprising list of those whom Jesus regarded as 'blessed' — the really lucky people. The chapel was provided by Mussolini. Its engaging colonnade provides an exceptionally fine view of the full extent of the Sea of Galilee. The peaceful gardens (a row of stone seats surround an 'altar' under the trees at the far end) provide as adequate a setting for group prayer as the chapel. The hymn *Dear Lord and Father* is appropriate — the 'hills above' are the Golan heights to the east. Closed 12.00 - 14.30.

Matthew 5^{1-10}: Seeing the crowds, Jesus went up on the mountain, and when he sat down his disciples came to him. And he opened his mouth and taught them, saying:
'Blessed are the poor in spirit, for theirs is the kingdom of heaven.
Blessed are those who mourn, for they shall be comforted.
Blessed are the meek, for they shall inherit the earth.
Blessed are those who hunger and thirst for righteousness, for
    they shall be satisfied.
Blessed are the merciful, for they shall obtain mercy.
Blessed are the pure in heart, for they shall see God.
Blessed are the peacemakers, for they shall be called sons of God.
Blessed are those who are persecuted for righteousness' sake, for
    theirs is the kingdom of heaven.'

BPB p. 12: Father, we know we are too anxious about our life,
    about what we shall eat or drink,
      and what we shall wear.
Your Son assured us that life is more than food,
    and the body more than clothing.
Turning to heaven, he said:
    'Look at the birds of the air;
they neither sow nor reap nor gather into barns
    and yet your heavenly Father feeds them.
Are you of not more value than they?
However anxious you are,
    it will not add one second to your life.'
Turning to the earth, he said:
    'Why are you so anxious about clothing?
Look at the lilies of the field;
    see how they grow.
They do not toil or spin, and yet I tell you,
even Solomon in all his glory
    was not arrayed like one of these.
And if God so clothes the grass of the field
    which is alive today
    and feeds the oven tomorrow,

how much more will he clothe you,
O men of little faith.'
The Man who taught us this
ended his days on a cross,
stranded between heaven and earth,
without clothing and crying vainly for a drink.
And in this way, Lord, he showed you to be
a Father who cares.

MOUNT TABOR   27km. from Nazareth via Afula, 32 km. from
Tiberias.

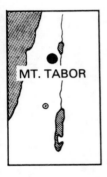

Tabor rises 588m. in solitary splendour from the Plain of Jezreel
(Esdraelon). A natural fortress, the Arabs call it Bull Mountain (Jebel
et Tor), and the sight of it recalled for Jeremiah the threatening
might of Nebuchadnezzar's advance on Egypt in the 6th c. BC. It
figures in the Bible as the thrilling scene of victory by a rarely confederated Israel in the 12th c. BC, when Canaanite pressure could
have exterminated the tribes one by one. It was an important strong-
point in the struggle between Egypt and Syria in the 3rd c. BC. In the
Jewish War of 66 AD it provided Galilee's front line of defence
against Rome, and its fall so shattered its Jewish commander Josephus that he joined the Romans. The Crusaders held it and lost it
several times. Napoleon defeated the Turks here in 1799. And in the
Israeli-Arab conflict of 1948 it played a key role in determining the
future of Galilee.

The gospels speak of Jesus' 'transfiguration' as taking place on
'a high mountain apart', and the description could fit many places in
the land. No one thought of locating the story here until the 3rd c.,
but the identification has stuck, and this is where pilgrims come to
recall the evocative story. The hairpin road will not accommodate
coaches above the village of Dabburiya, from where one must either
walk (40 minutes) or take one of the taxis generally available.

The top of the mountain is divided between Greeks and Latins,
with a wall separating them. The Latin road ends at the Franciscan
hospice (toilets, refreshments, slides), from whose balcony there is a
fine view of the war-torn plain below, and to the right the Gilboa
hills where King Saul died. Beyond the hospice lies the noble
modern basilica, whose open crypt preserves what remains of the
Crusader apse. Pilgrims would normally hold their service here. The
mosaics on the wall evoke the other episodes in the story of Jesus in
which he was 'transfigured' — his birth, eucharist, death and resurrection. Two chapels near the entrance, under the basilica's two
towers, honour the memory of Moses (the Law) and Elijah (the

Prophets) whom the gospel story speaks of as finding their fulfilment in Jesus. Closed 12.00 - 14.00

Outside the basilica, a path along its left side leads to the top of a Saracen tower, from which there is an excellent view of the Galilee hills to the north.

Jeremiah 46[18–19]: As I live, says the King,
whose name is the Lord of hosts,
like Tabor among the mountains . . .
shall one come.
Prepare yourselves baggage for exile,
O inhabitants of Egypt!

Judges 4[6]—*5*[31]: Deborah sent and summoned Barak . . . and said to him, 'The Lord, the God of Israel, commands you, "Go, gather your men at Mount Tabor, taking ten thousand from the tribe of Naphtali and the tribe of Zebulun. And I will draw out Sisera, the general of Jabin's army, to meet you by the river Kishon with his chariots and his troops; and I will give him into your hand." '

When Sisera was told that Barak had gone up to Mount Tabor, Sisera called out all his chariots, nine hundred chariots of iron, and all the men who were with him to the river Kishon. And Deborah said to Barak, 'Up! For this is the day in which the Lord has given Sisera into your hand. Does not the Lord go out before you?' So Barak went down from Mount Tabor with ten thousand men following him. And the Lord routed Sisera and all his chariots and all his army before Barak at the edge of the sword . . . not a man was left . . .

Then sang Deborah and Barak:
'Hear, O kings; give ear, O princes;
to the Lord I will sing,
I will make melody to the Lord,
the God of Israel . . .
Down marched the remnant of the noble . . .
From Ephraim they set out into the valley,
following you, Benjamin, with your kinsmen;
from Machir marched down the commanders,
and from Zebulun those who bear the marshall's staff;
the princes of Issachar came with Deborah . . .
Zebulun is a people that jeoparded their lives to the death;
Naphtali too, on the heights of the field.
The kings came, they fought;
then fought the kings of Canaan,
at Taanach, by the waters of Megiddo;
they got no spoils of silver.
From heaven fought the stars,
from their courses they fought against Sisera.
The torrent Kishon swept them away,

the onrushing torrent, the torrent Kishon.
March on, my soul, with might!
Then loud beat the horses' hoofs
with the galloping, galloping of his steeds ...
So perish all thine enemies, O Lord!
But thy friends be like the sun as he rises in his might.'

Mark 9[2-8]: Jesus took with him Peter and James and John, and led them up a high mountain apart by themselves; and he was transfigured before them, and his garments became glistening, intensely white, as no fuller on earth could bleach them. And there appeared to them Elijah with Moses; and they were talking to Jesus. And Peter said to Jesus, 'Master, it is well that we are here; let us make three booths, one for you and one for Moses and one for Elijah.' For he did not know what to say, for they were exceedingly afraid. And a cloud overshadowed them, and a voice came out of the cloud, 'This is my beloved Son; listen to him.' And suddenly looking around they no longer saw anyone with them but Jesus only.

2 Peter 1[16-19]: We did not follow cleverly devised myths when we made known to you the power and coming of our Lord Jesus Christ, but we were eye-witnesses of his majesty. For when he received honour and glory from God the Father and the voice was borne to him by the Majestic Glory, 'This is my beloved Son, with whom I am well pleased', we heard this voice borne from heaven, for we were with him on the holy mountain. And we have the prophetic word made more sure. You will do well to pay attention to this as to a lamp shining in a dark place, until the day dawns and the morning star rises in your hearts.

DH: Father God, we praise you for our Lord Jesus Christ. He is our Law and yet he comes with such compassion that we willingly obey. He is Prophet to our lives, and yet he speaks his searing truth in such a way that binds us to him in love. His transfigured life illuminates and guides, and gives us new resources for our lives.

Father, may we stand with Christ in glorious light and hope, and then descend to meet him once again in life's routine and agony.

BPB p. 31: Father, I thank you for this gospel story
which illustrates so well Christ's sovereignty.
I believe, Lord, that in everything he says and does
he lights up and fulfils the law and the prophets;
and it is enough now to listen to him.
For Jesus is your Christ,
even though death and dereliction
are waiting for him in Jerusalem.
It will be dark there,
and on another hill, shaped like a skull,
two other men will be beside him.

From his unclothed body no light will radiate;
and even you, Father, will be silent,
except for the one Word you will be saying to us
in the tremendous love of Jesus crucified.

NABI SAMWIL see p. 119

NABLUS — SHECHEM 64km. north of Jerusalem (fig. 25).

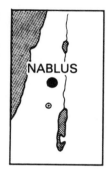

Nablus preserves the name Neapolis or New Town given it when it was built for the Roman veterans of the Jewish War in 72 AD. Guarding the important east-west trade route which passes between Mounts Ebal and Gerizim, it is the natural capital of the hill country of Samaria. And so it was even before the Romans came, when it was called **Shechem**, as Israel now insists on calling it again.

The site was then on the eastern edge of the modern town (1), where excavations have given a good idea of what a walled city state looked like in Bronze Age times. Entrance to the archaeological mound - Tel Balata - is from the lane to its north. This was the town known by Abraham and Jacob, in whose sagas the name frequently crops up. The bones of Joseph are said to have been brought back from Egypt to be buried, by a nice play on words, in 'this same area'. Jacob is even said by the New Testament to have dug a well here, no doubt to ensure his own water supply in an area well served by springs.

The only well lies just to the east of Shechem. It is exceptionally deep (35m.), as the New Testament remarks, and is clearly the scenario John has in mind in his story of the Samaritan woman. **Jacob's Well** (2) is now approached downstairs in the crypt of a Greek Orthodox church, begun in 1914 on the foundations of a Byzantine and Crusader church, and sadly left unfinished when funds from Czarist Russia were no longer forthcoming. (Closed 12.00-14.30 and after 17.00. Toilets rather basic).

It is interesting that the account of Joshua's conquest of the land in 1200 BC, having enthused on the victories in the south (Jericho, Ai, Gibeon) and in the north (Hazor), makes no mention of any fighting in these midlands. It is highly likely that the tribes living in this area became part of the later Israelite confederation by blood relationship rather than by direct involvement in the Exodus. In which case, Joshua's 'renewal' of the Sinai Covenant in the shadow of these mountains was rather a successful offer of the Mosaic religion to these related tribes. When the confederation finally (10th c. BC) broke up into two kingdoms, Judah and Israel, these midland tribes regarded themselves as the True Israel, and made Shechem a rival capital to Jerusalem. The town only lost its importance fifty years later when King Omri moved the capital further west to Samaria (see p. 165).

The Assyrian invasion of the 8th c. BC created the hybrid race ever since known as the '**Samaritans**'. It was the Assyrian policy to control its dependencies by deporting whole populations. The foreigners who were deported into this area, intermarrying with the few local Israelites left here, accepted their religion. But this religion was highly suspect to their newly sensitive Jewish relatives returning from their exile, and mutual recriminations have left the two peoples at daggers drawn ever since. The Samaritans remained faithful to the five books of Moses (Pentateuch), but they rejected as scripture everything written later. Denied access to the Jerusalem Temple, they eventually in the 5th c. BC built their own on the natural high place of **Mount Gerizim,** and claimed (with some justification) that it fitted the specifications of the Pentateuch better than Jerusalem did. Over the years this mountain has acquired for them a more and more sacred character (to believe in Gerizim is one of their Ten Commandments) and has had associated with it all the stories they most treasure. It was here that Noah offered worship after the

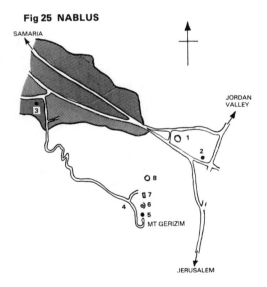

Fig 25 NABLUS

Flood, here that Abraham's sacrifice of Isaac took place, here that Melchizedek offered bread and wine, here that the Ark of the Covenant was deposited after the Exodus. It was even on this mountain that Adam and Eve first met each other. Yet the Samaritans remained so strongly attached to their faith that 10,000 of them died in the War against Rome.

Today's Samaritans remain a pitiable enough community. Numbering less than 400, even including the small colony near Tel Aviv, and forbidden to marry outside the clan, they suffer the inevitable genetic effects of intermarriage. Two thirds of the community are of priestly families, who are forbidden to earn a living by work. They occupy a small ghetto in upper Nablus (3), where they maintain a synagogue in which is displayed a fine manuscript of the Pentateuch which they like to think is the personal handiwork of Moses' great-grand-nephew (it dates from the 10th c. AD). They delight to receive Christian pilgrims, and their offerings. As their handbook puts it, 'They depend to some extent on the season of tourist by which they collect some gainings'. The biggest tourist attraction is the annual celebration of Passover on Mount Gerizim. For six weeks the community moves into houses near the summit, and at the full moon emerge to slaughter a lamb for each family in exact obedience to the 13th c. BC specifications of the book of Exodus.

The mountain top can be reached on foot, or more easily by car or coach (though some drivers express reluctance) on a hairpin road from the southwest of Nablus. The road reaches a plateau (4) which constitutes the Samaritan Easter holiday home, and boasts a synagogue in which their Pentateuch is exhibited when the community is on the mountain. The road rises a little further to the rock summit (5), from which a path leads to the ruins of a Byzantine church dedicated to Mary mother of Jesus (6), a mosque in honour of Abu Ghannam (7), and a view in the distance of a copse overlooking Nablus (8) where recent digs have revealed a Greek temple of the time of Hadrian (130 AD), probably on the foundations of the Samaritan Temple. The view all around is magnificent.

Over the past few years, Nablus has been the centre of strong Palestinian feeling against Israel's occupation of the West Bank, and these feelings can be vented against tourists. It would be as well to check with some authority about the current state of play before planning to go there.

Genesis 12[6–7]: Abram passed through the land of Canaan to the place at Shechem, to the oak of Moreh. At that time the Canaanites were in the land. Then the Lord appeared to Abram, and said, 'To your descendants I will give this land.' So he built there an altar to the Lord, who had appeared to him.

Genesis 48[21–22]: Israel [Jacob] said to Joseph, 'Behold, I am about to die, but God will be with you, and will bring you again to the land of your fathers. Moreover I have given to you rather than to your brothers one mountain slope' [one Shechem].

Joshua 24[1–26]: Joshua gathered all the tribes of Israel to Shechem ... and they presented themselves before God. And Joshua said to all the people, 'Thus says the Lord, the God of Israel, ... "I gave you a land on which you had not laboured, and cities which you had not built, and you dwelt therein; you eat the fruit of vineyards and oliveyards which you did not plant." Now therefore fear the Lord, and serve him in sincerity and faithfulness ... If you be unwilling to serve the Lord, choose this day whom you will serve ... As for me and my house, we will serve the Lord.'

Then the people answered, 'Far be it from us that we should forsake the Lord, to serve other gods; for it is the Lord our God who brought us and our fathers up from the land of Egypt ... Therefore we will serve the Lord, for he is our God.' ...

Then Joshua said to the people, 'You are witnesses against yourselves that you have chosen the Lord, to serve him.' And they said, 'We are witnesses.' ... So Joshua made a covenant with the people that day, and made statutes and ordinances for them at Shechem. And Joshua wrote these words in the book of the law of God; and he took a great stone, and set it up there under the oak in the sanctuary of the Lord.

2 Kings 17[23–41]: Israel was exiled from their own land to Assyria until this day. And the king of Assyria brought people from Babylon, Cuthah, Avva, Hamath and Sepharvaim, and placed them in the cities of Samaria instead of the people of Israel; and they took possession of Samaria, and dwelt in its cities ... They feared the Lord but also served their own gods, after the manner of the nations from among whom they had been carried away ... These nations feared the Lord, and also served their graven images; their children likewise, and children's children — as their fathers did, so they do to this day.

Luke 9[52–54]: Jesus sent messengers ahead of him, who went and entered a village of the Samaritans, to make ready for him; but the people would not receive him, because his face was set toward Jerusalem. And when his disciples James and John saw it, they said. 'Lord do you want us to bid fire come down from heaven and consume them?'

John 4[3–26]: Jesus left Judea and departed again to Galilee. He had to pass through Samaria. So he came to a city of Samaria, called Sychar, near the field that Jacob gave to his son Joseph. Jacob's well was there, and so Jesus, wearied as he was with his journey, sat down beside the well. It was about the sixth hour.

There came a woman of Samaria to draw water. Jesus said to her, 'Give me a drink.' ... The Samaritan woman said to him. 'How is it that you, a Jew, ask a drink from me, a woman of Samaria?' For Jews have no dealings with Samaritans. Jesus answered her, 'If you knew the gift of God, and who it is that is saying to you, "Give me a drink," you would have asked him, and he would have given you living water.' The woman said to him. 'Sir, you have nothing to draw with, and the well is deep; where do you get that living water? Are you greater than our father Jacob, who gave us the well, and drank from it himself, and his sons, and his cattle?' Jesus said to her, 'Every one who drinks of this water will thirst again, but whoever drinks of the water that I shall give him will never thirst; the water that I shall give him will become in him a spring of water welling up to eternal life.' The woman said to him, 'Sir, give me this water.... Our fathers worshipped on this mountain and you say that in Jerusalem is the place where men ought to worship.' Jesus said to her, 'Woman, believe me, the hour is coming, when neither on this mountain nor in Jerusalem will you worship the Father ... True worshippers will worship the Father in Spirit.' ... The woman said to him, 'I know the Messiah is coming ... he will show us all things.' Jesus said to her, 'I who speak to you am he.'

DH: Father, forgive us, for we so readily divide your one human family into neat groups with convenient labels, forgetting that you are the Father of us all. For ourselves and all your children, we confess the ills of our present world; for this land, where group is set against group, is only a parable of our whole world:

Catholics and Protestants are blind to the gifts you have given to each,
the North builds barriers of commerce to protect itself from the
poverty of the South,
black and white approach each other with suspicious fear,
and nation is set against nation.

Forgive us, Father;
we use religion as a weapon,
culture as a shield,
and make the rich variety of human experience a wall of division.
May we hear your Son, born and bred a Jew, speak to us again
as he praises the goodness of a Samaritan traveller,
receives a gift from a Samaritan woman by the well,
shows compassion to a Roman soldier,
and thus, in symbol, breaks down the false divisions of race, colour,
sex and nationality behind which we still hide.

In his name, we affirm:
we are members of one family,
all women are our sisters, and men our brothers,
we are parents to all children, children to all parents, kinsfolk to
every race;

and we will work, and pray, and serve until the unity which you created at the beginning, and promised for the end, is fulfilled in us.

NAIM   see p. 160

NAZARETH   30km. from Tiberias, 35km. from Haifa (fig. 26).

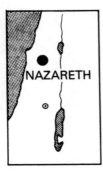

Nazareth lies in a lovely position, nestling as in a cocoon scooped out of the hillside. The sight of it as one approaches from the valley to the south, or better still at night time from the top of the hill to the north, is enchanting.

Closer contact tends to disappoint the visitor, especially after the neatness and walled compactness of Old Jerusalem. Noisy and dusty with traffic, it wears a shabby and neglected air, in spite of the ostentation of some of its religious monuments. Yet it remains precious to the Christian pilgrims as the town where Jesus grew up as a child and then spent thirty obscure years as a builder's apprentice. This is what was in the minds of the early Christians who established a presence here in the 3rd c. AD. This inspired the Franciscans who first came in 1260 within 40 years of Francis' death, and the recluse Charles de Foucauld who at the turn of this century came here to live the life of the Poor Man of Nazareth. He worked as a gardener for the Poor Clares before going to North Africa to devote his life to the Tuaregs, who killed him. The chapel where he used to pray is still used by the **Little Sisters of Jesus**, who continue to bear witness to his life of poverty, service and prayer. It is a good place in which to begin one's pilgrimage to Nazareth (1). The **Poor Clares** have recently moved to new and smaller quarters (up the lane opposite the Galilee Hotel), and keep some of Charles' poverty-stricken belongings to show visitors. Their simple and dignified chapel is well worth a visit (2).

The **Annunciation Basilica** with its gigantic dome dominates the small town (3) (closed 11.45 - 14.00, Sunday mornings, and after 18.00, 17.00 in winter. Toilets). Completed in 1969 at considerable expense, it replaces the simpler 200-year-old Franciscan church which collapsed in 1955. The work of reconstruction (see fig. 27) has allowed a thorough excavation of the site, and given visitors clearer access to the rock cave (a) which has been venerated since the 3rd c. AD as the dwelling place of Mary, mother of Jesus. Here the gospel of Luke envisages Mary as the person in whom Israel became what the prophets always hoped it would become.

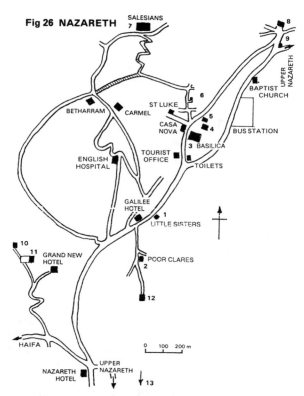

Fig 26 NAZARETH

The outline of the 5th c. Byzantine church built sideways on to the cave can be clearly seen (b), as well as the columns of the much larger 12th c. Crusader church which have now been incorporated into the new basilica's northern wall (c). The Crusader church stood for such a short while that six capitals, exquisitely carved in Normandy, were never installed. They are on display in the museum.

Stairs (d) lit by modern stained glass lead to the upper floor, which serves as the parish church for the local Latin Christians. Fellow Roman Catholics from many countries have striven to outdo each other in proclaiming the praises of Mary in its massive murals (continued in the groundfloor courtyard). The sanctuary is heavier still (150 square metres of mosaic) on the papacy. The fine prize-winning bronze doors at the entrances (e, e) are well worth inspecting. So is the freestanding baptistry outside the upper exit.

Adjoining the basilica is the Franciscan monastery of the **Terra Santa** (4), and at the far end of the square a church built on the reputed **House of Joseph** (5). The crypt leads to a cave which is said to have been his workshop.

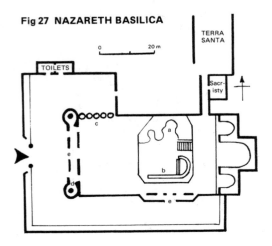

Fig 27 NAZARETH BASILICA

From the basilica, the road which continues uphill is Nazareth's **suk** or market. On a far smaller scale than Jerusalem's, it nonetheless offers the tourist similar fascinations, if at a slightly higher price. An archway on the right a little way up the suk leads into the small courtyard of the Greek Catholic church. To its left is the **Synagogue Church** (6), a simple Crusader vaulted building which a late tradition associated with the synagogue where Jesus proclaimed his determination to bring the Good News to the poor and set the downtrodden free. Ring the bell.

The suk ends as suddenly as it began, but it is worth continuing through an arcade up the twisting lane, and eventually up a series of steps, to the very top of the town, where the balcony of the **Salesian School** (7) offers a fine panorama of Nazareth and the Jezreel valley below, with Mount Carmel dipping into the sea on the west, and Mount Tabor rising in splendour on the east.

Depending on the amount of time available to visitors, Nazareth offers them these other places of interest:

The Greek Orthodox **Church of St Gabriel** lies at the north end of the town (8), near the well which once constituted Nazareth's water supply (9). The spring which supplies the well can be heard bubbling in the crypt of the church, a Byzantine foundation based on an apocryphal gospel of the 2nd c. AD which describes the angelic message to Mary as taking place while she was drawing water. The church has some fine ikons, and has recently been redecorated from ceiling to floor by the same artists who enlivened the Greek Catholic church in Jerusalem (p. 32). Closed 11.45 - 14.00.

At the other extremity of the town is the Convent of the **Annunciation Sisters** (10), whose exquisite new chapel has been embellished by the same artists. The domed chapel is clearly visible from the playground of the **Greek Catholic Seminary** (11), itself lying off a lane going steeply uphill from the Haifa road. The small community of nuns was recently settled here by the archbishop of Galilee primarily to revive the ancient tradition of ikon painting. Their liturgy, sung in Arabic morning and evening (17.30-18.30), is a joy to attend.

The church of **Mary's Dread** ('Spasm') (12) stands in a copse a little beyond the new convent of the Poor Clares. The church embroiders on the gospel story by imagining Jesus' mother's anguish as she sees his fellow countrymen threatening to throw him off the cliff. The unlikely **Mount of Precipitation** it has in view is the cliff below Nazareth, now a stone quarry (13).

The hill to the east is crowned by the new town of **Upper Nazareth** (Nazerat Illit). Nazareth was within Israel's boundaries even before 1967, and many of the Jewish immigrants of those days made their way here to establish a second Nazareth on the hills above the old one. It has brought a considerable amount of industry to the area, including textiles, chocolate and cars.

Zephaniah 3[14−17]: Shout, O Israel!
Rejoice and exult with all your heart,
O daughter of Jerusalem!...
The King of Israel, the Lord is in your midst [womb];
you shall fear evil no more ...
Do not fear, O Zion!...
The Lord, your God, is in your midst [womb],
a warrior who saves;
he will rejoice over you with gladness,
he will renew you with his love.

Luke 1[26−31]: The angel Gabriel was sent from God to a city of Galilee named Nazareth, to a virgin betrothed to a man whose name was Joseph, of the house of David; and the virgin's name was Mary. And he came to her and said, 'Hail [Rejoice], O favoured one, the Lord is with you ... Do not be afraid, Mary, for you have found favour with God. And behold, you will conceive in your womb and bear a son, and you shall call his name Jesus [the Lord saves].

Luke 2[39−40]: When they had performed everything according to the law of the Lord, they returned into Galilee, to their own city, Nazareth. And the child grew and became strong, filled with wisdom; and the favour of God was upon him.

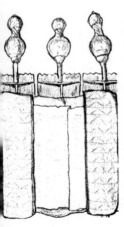

Luke 4[16−31]: Jesus came to Nazareth, where he had been brought up; and he went to the synagogue, as his custom was, on the sabbath day. And he stood up to read; and there was given to him the book of the prophet Isaiah. He opened the book and found the place where it was written,
The Spirit of the Lord is upon me,
because he has anointed me to preach good news to the poor.
He has sent me to proclaim release to the captive
and recovering of sight to the blind,
to set at liberty those who are oppressed,
to proclaim the acceptable year of the Lord.
And he closed the book, and gave it back to the attendant, and sat down; and the eyes of all in the synagogue were fixed on him. And he began to say to them, 'Today this scripture has been fulfilled in your hearing.' ... And they said, 'Is not this Joseph's son?' ... And he said, 'Truly, I say to you, no prophet is acceptable in his own country' ... When they heard this, all in the synagogue were filled with wrath. And they rose up and put him out of the

city, and led him to the brow of the hill on which their city was built, that they might throw him down headlong. But passing through the midst of them he went away. And he went down to Capernaum.

John 1[45–46]: Philip found Nathanael, and said to him, 'We have found him of whom Moses in the law and also the prophets wrote, Jesus of Nazareth, the son of Joseph.' Nathanael said to him, 'Can anything good come out of Nazareth?' Philip said to him, 'Come and see.'

Charles de Foucauld: What I dream of secretly is something very simple and very small, something like the very simple first communities of the early days of the Church ... A few souls gathered together to lead the life of Nazareth, to live by working like the Holy Family, to live by the values of Nazareth.

DH: It is the baby we remember; the baby who was just like any other baby and yet was God indeed.

It is the boy we remember; growing up like every other boy, knowing the joy and pain of growth and slowly learning more of himself and God.

It is the young man we remember; sometimes angry, sometimes uncertain; sometimes knowing, sometimes searching; but always holding the presence of God in his life and standing alongside ordinary people in love and compassion.

It is Jesus we remember; may the memory refresh us and bring us closer to you, O God, with thankful adoration and grateful praise.

BPB p. 96: Father, I thank you for what you have revealed of yourself
in Mary's virgin motherhood.
She was humble so you exalted her;
she was poor so you enriched her;
she was empty so you filled her;
she was your servant so you cared for her;
she had no future by reason of her virginity,
so you brought to birth in her
the world's future, Jesus Christ our Lord.

NCEC: Jesus, you lived as a boy in your home in Nazareth; bless our homes and protect our families.

Jesus, you lived under the authority of earthly parents; build bridges of tolerance and understanding between the generations in our homes and families.

Jesus, you lived in a carpenter's household; may we help each other to do our daily work honestly and wholeheartedly.

Jesus, you were content to be brought up quietly and without the limelight; make us ready to be unselfish and undemanding in our homes, so that our service to others may be service to you.

NEBO see p. 117

NEIN (NAIM)   18km. from Nazareth, or 6km. from Afula, just off the road to Mount Tabor.

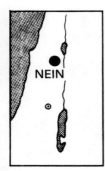

Most groups are content to photograph Nein from the distance at a convenient spot on the Afula road. Recently a tarmac road was laid in the hope of attracting Pope Paul VI there on his flying visit in 1964 (he didn't have the time), and it is now possible to drive right into the poor village.

All that is to be seen is a locked 18th c. church, which the people of the adjoining house will graciously open. It commemorates Luke's story of a raising from the dead, which was presumably not uninfluenced by the similar story told of Elisha at Shunem, which lies on the slopes of this same hill.

2 Kings 4[32–37]: When Elisha came into the house, he saw the child lying dead on his bed. So he went in and shut the door upon the two of them, and prayed to the Lord. Then he went up and lay upon the child ... and the child opened his eyes. Then he summoned Gehazi and said, 'Call this Shunammite.' So he called her. And when she came to him, he said, 'Take up your son.' She came and fell at his feet, bowing to the ground; then she took up her son and went out.

Luke 7[11–16]: Jesus went to a city called Nain, and his disciples and a great crowd went with him. As he drew near to the gate of the city, behold, a man who had died was being carried out, the only son of his mother, and she was a widow; and a large crowd from the city was with her. And when the Lord saw her, he had compassion on her and said to her, 'Do not weep.' And he came and touched the bier, and the bearers stood still. And he said, 'Young man, I say to you, arise.' And the dead man sat up, and began to speak. And he gave him to his mother. Fear seized them all; and they glorified God, saying, 'A great prophet has arisen among us!'

PETRA see p. 117

PRIMACY OF PETER Adjoining **Tabgha** (see p. 174 and 113), but access is only by another entrance 200m. further along the Capernaum road. Closed 11.45-14.00.

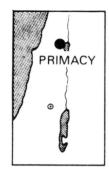

PRIMACY

This 1933 chapel, built of local black basalt, rests on the remains of a 4th c. church. It is perched on a rock jutting into the lake, and part of the rock forms the sanctuary. It has recently (1984) been refurbished, and a fine outdoor altar has been built to accommodate those who wish to hold a service here.

The gospels mention the way Jesus would control huge crowds by getting into a boat, presumably in a small harbour, and preaching to the people gathered on shore. This is one such harbour. The church

commemorates particularly the story in the appendix to John's gospel, where Peter is three times painfully reinstated after his three-fold betrayal of Jesus. Pope Paul VI, in his whirlwind visit in 1964, made a point of including this spot in his itinerary.

John 21[15-19]: Jesus said to Simon Peter, 'Simon, son of John, do you love me more than these?' He said to him, 'Yes, Lord; you know that I love you.' He said to him, 'Feed my lambs.' A second time he said to him, 'Simon, son of John, do you love me?' He said to him, 'Yes, Lord; you know that I love you.' He said to him, 'Tend my sheep.' He said to him the third time, 'Simon, son of John, do you love me?' Peter was grieved because he said to him the third time, 'Do you love me?' And he said to him, 'Lord, you know everything; you know that I love you.' Jesus said to him, 'Feed my sheep.' ... And after this he said to him, 'Follow me.'

DH: Build your Church, Lord Christ, on the rock of faith;
    a faith which stands firm in persecution,
    a faith which is constant in the search for truth,
    a faith which journeys on in pilgrimage,
    a faith which presents itself lovingly to the world,
    a faith which is strong to offer help to other seekers,

161

and open enough to receive their support,
a faith which rests not on our weakness, but on your strength.

QIRYAT YEARIM see p. 87

QUBEIBA see p. 119

QUMRAN 20km. south of Jericho, on the western bank of the Dead Sea. Closed 17.00 (16.00 on Fridays). Entrance fee (National Parks card). Restaurant, souvenirs & toilets.

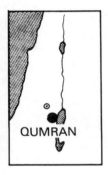

The present road to Qumran was not built till 1965. Until then the few who were interested in its story travelled across this desert precariously by jeep. Today the story is so well known that it attracts visitors by the coach load. In 1972 the road was extended south to Masada.

A stone thrown by a Bedouin boy to dislodge a goat that had strayed into a cave on this hillside brought to light a history hidden for 1,900 years. The stone hit an earthen jar. It contained a scroll, remarkably well preserved by the dry atmosphere, the work of a community which had once occupied the ruins of the plateau below. Expert opinion put the scroll at about New Testament times. Archaeologists were soon swarming over the hillside to inspect other caves, and the wily local Bedouins who had got there first were cutting up the priceless manuscripts and selling them by the square centimetre to the highest bidder. After a painstaking search of all the area it would seem that all the 'Dead Sea Scrolls' have now been recovered. They tell a remarkable tale.

About 150 BC a group of fifty rigorously orthodox Jews left Jerusalem to set up a commune in this desert. They were related to (if not identified with) the Essenes, whom the contemporary Jewish historian Josephus had described as so strict that they did not use the toilet on Saturdays. Disgusted (rather like the present Mea Shearim Jews, see p. 74) by the secularization of the priestly leaders of the time, they denounced them as having lost the faith, proclaimed themselves alone the True Israel — the 'Sons of Light' at permanent warfare with the 'Sons of Darkness' — and chose a spot with Exodus overtones to work for the coming of a new Kingdom of God. They lived a life of poverty, penance, and (apparently) celibacy, though their cemetery suggests that married people also belonged to the community. Under their guru, the 'Teacher of Righteousness', they saw themselves as the people of the 'New Testament', and awaited the coming of a priestly Messiah to prove them right. Their views were sectarian to the extreme, and it is quite possible that John the Baptist was once a member of the community, and was excommunicated for his universalist tendencies. In spite of this, there are occasional remarkable correspondences between their writings and those of the Christian 'New Testament'.

The community lived at Qumran for a hundred years, attracting more and more followers. The earthquake of 31 BC forced them to abandon the site for thirty years, but they eventually returned to repair and occupy it for another seventy years before the Roman army demolished it in the final mopping up operation of the Jewish War. Those who escaped fled down the coast to throw in their lot with the Zealots of Masada, and eventually to die with them. The ruined monastery was forgotten until 1947.

The buildings were used only as a community centre, where everyone met for work and worship. The living quarters were in tents and in the caves honeycombing the district. It was to these caves that they consigned their precious jars of documents (scripture texts, commentaries, psalms, rule books) when they were forced to flee. These are now preserved in the Israel Museum (see p. 63).

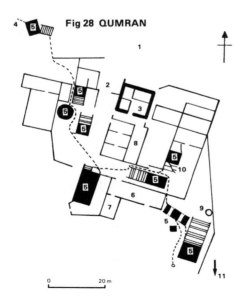

Fig 28 QUMRAN

From the carpark (fig. 28) (1) it is best to enter the area by the original main entrance (2) and climb its protecting tower (3). This provides a good overall view of the complex, and an understanding of how such a large community could exist in such a desert. Up on the hills they had built a dam to catch the occasional rainwater pouring down the wadi, and sent this by aqueduct (4) to a pool whose overflow fed the numerous stepped cisterns (5, 5, 5), some of which were for ritual purposes. The large community dining room (6) is clearly visible. In the adjoining scullery (7) enough piled bowls and plates were found to feed 700 people. Less discernible is the scriptorium (8) where there were found, fallen from the first floor, the writing table and inkwells used for the writing of the scrolls. The jars in which they had been stored were made in the community pottery, whose kilns are still visible (9). Close by is a cistern (10) whose steps still bear marks of the earthquake which made the community abandon the site, and of the rough and ready patching up done by those who returned. A little to the south of the ruins (11) it is possible to look across an eroded cleft to the closest of the caves (given the number '4'), a man-made dwelling where 40,000 fragments of documents were found. The original cave '1', and the thirty others used for accommodating the community, are in the cliffs to the northwest.

5km. further down the coast, at the freshwater springs of **Ein Fashkha,** excavations have revealed a small farm which grew food for the Qumran community on the hillside. This has now become a popular swimming resort and picnic area with all modern conveniences (entrance fee).

The waters of the Dead Sea are so dense with salts (calcium, magnesium, potassium and sodium) that they support no life, and the human body only sinks in minimally. Those who wish to test this personally (the Romans bound two of the Qumran non-swimmers and threw them in to do so) should be warned that the salts will hurt the eyes and smart on sores. Those who prefer to swim in fresh water will find delight (especially if they have just trudged round Qumran) in the pools into which the springs have been diverted just short of the Dead Sea.

DS Manual of Discipline 1[1–13]: Everyone who wishes to join the community must pledge himself to respect God and man; to live according to the communal rule; to seek God; to do what is good and upright in his sight, in accordance with what he has commanded through Moses and through his servants the prophets; to love all that he has chosen and hate all that he has rejected; to keep far from all evil and to cling to all good works; ... to bring into a bond of mutual love all who have declared their willingness to carry out the statutes of God; ... to love all the children of light ... and to hate all the children of darkness ...

All who declare their willingness to serve God's truth must bring all of their mind, all of their strength, and all of their wealth into the community of God, so that their minds may be purified, ... their strength controlled, ... and their wealth disposed in accordance with his just design.

DS Hymn of the Initiants: I shall hold it as one of the laws
engraven of old on the tablets
to offer God as my fruits
the praises of my tongue,
and to cull for him as my tithe
the skilled music of my lips.

DS Psalm 8[4—8]: I give thanks unto thee, O Lord,
for thou hast placed me where rills burst forth in dry land
where waters gush in thirsty soil,
where an oasis blooms in the desert;
like a fir or a pine or a cypress,
trees that never die,
that stand planted for thy glory alone ...
a tree whose stem is exposed to living waters,
which thrives beside a perpetual fount.

RACHEL'S TOMB   see p. 98

RAMAH   see p. 120

RAMAT EL KHALIL   see p. 128

SAFED   See p. 170

SAMARIA — SEBASTIYA

11km. northwest of Nablus, just off the Jenin road to the right. Entrance fee (National Parks card). Restaurant, souvenirs, antiquities, toilets. Closed 17.00.

The village clinging to the edge of this fine hill is still called Sebastiya, preserving the name Herod the Great gave to the city he built

165

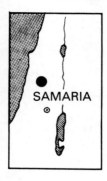

here in honour of the emperor Augustus (in Greek, Sebastos). It was an expansion, in typically expansive style, of a city with an already long history, having been chosen 850 years earlier by King Omri as the new capital of Israel. Shechem stood on the east side of Mount Ephraim; this stood on the west facing the Mediterranean coast, whose friendship he wanted to cultivate, and to whose Phoenician princess Jezebel he married off his son Ahab.

Omri gets only a few lines from the biblical author, whose yardstick was a purely religious one. In political terms he was so successful that for generations after, even when Israel was ruled by a new dynasty, Assyrian records refer to his kingdom as the 'House of Omri'. The prophets were less impressed by this political success: Elijah, Amos, Hosea and Isaiah all have harsh words for Samaria's decadent luxury and over-ecumenical religion. This was the town captured by the Assyrians and populated with the hybrid race known as the Samaritans (see p. 150). It began to lose its importance when Neapolis-Nablus was built.

The approach to Samaria is by the noble Roman west gate (fig. 29) (1) which gives on to a colonnaded street, once twelve metres wide and lined with shops (2). The spacious parking area was the Roman forum (3), and its sunken portion the town hall (4). Beyond the modern restaurant (5) a low wall (6) gives a view across the valley to the sports stadium (7), and an idea of the grand scale on which Herod and his successors built on this hill.

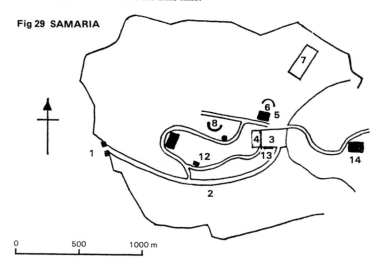

Fig 29 SAMARIA

0   500   1000 m

A path leads from the restaurant to a fine theatre cut into the hillside (8). The hill formed the acropolis, and a beautifully preserved round tower (4th c. BC) in its defensive wall can be seen on the ascent (9). The hill is crowned with the imposing temple which Herod dedicated to Augustus (10), its great flight of steps probably dating from later. The temple was built on top of the earlier royal palace (11), whose ruins yielded the ivory furniture inlays which probably gave their name to Ahab's House of Ivory. These are now displayed in the Jerusalem Rockefeller Museum (see p. 71).

On the descent there are the ruins of a church in memory of the death of John the Baptist (12). It was built by the Byzantines, who seem to have confused John's beheader, Herod Antipas, with Herod the Great, and who found Samaria in any case more accessible than Machaerus (see p. 117). The path leads back to the carpark, passing by a piece of wall (13) from the Israelite fortification of the town in the 9th c. BC. A second church of the Baptist, Crusader built and now a mosque, lies in the village (14).

*1 Kings 16*²³⁻²⁵: Omri began to reign over Israel, and reigned for twelve years ... He bought the hill of Samaria from Shemer for two talents of silver; and he fortified the hill, and called the name of the city which he built, Samaria, after the name of Shemer, the owner of the hill. Omri did what was evil in the sight of the Lord, and did more evil than all who were before him.

*1 Kings 22*³⁷⁻⁴⁰: King Ahab died, and was brought to Samaria; and they buried the king in Samaria ... The rest of the acts of Ahab, and all that he did, and the Ivory House which he built, and all the cities that he built, are they not written in the Book of the Chronicles of the Kings of Israel? So Ahab slept with his fathers.

*Amos 3*¹³⁻*6*⁶: 'Hear and testify against the house of Jacob,'
    says the Lord God, the God of hosts, ...
    'I will smite the winter house with the summer house;
    and the Houses of Ivory shall perish,
    and the great houses shall come to an end ...
    Hear this word, you cows of Bashan,
    who are in the mountains of Samaria,
    who oppress the poor, who crush the needy,
    who say to their husbands,
    "Bring, that we may drink!"
    The Lord God has sworn by his holiness
    that, behold, the days are coming upon you,
    when they shall take you away with hooks ...
    Woe to those who lie upon beds of ivory,
    and stretch themselves upon couches, ...
    who sing idle songs to the sound of the harp, ...

who drink wine in bowls,
and anoint themselves with the finest oils,
but are not grieved over the ruin of Joseph!
Therefore they shall now be the first
of those to go into exile.'

SAMARITANS see p. 150

SEA OF GALILEE 31km. east of Nazareth.

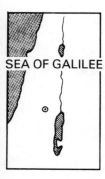

SEA OF GALILEE

Most of the gospel stories about Jesus have the Sea of Galilee as thei
background. Its popularity with pilgrims is therefore not surprising
especially since in its most charming aspects it has changed far les:
than most other sites since New Testament times. Peter and Andrew
knew it well, being citizens of Capernaum, which Jesus more or les:
made the centre of his Galilean ministry. Matthew also worked there
'at the receipt of custom'. John, James and Philip came from nearby
Bethsaida, though its site is unknown, as also is the Gadarene cliff or
the eastern shore.

The Sea has been variously known through history as the **Sea o**
Tiberias (after its most important town), **Kinnereth** (after its harp-
like shape), and **Gennesareth** (after the region). It is about 21km
north to south (as long as Lake Windermere therefore) and 12km
across at its widest point. Its position in the wind-tunnel formed by
the hills makes it very susceptible to storms. It sinks to 48m. at its
deepest point, and has been famous throughout history for its fish.
Pilgrims today are offered 'St Peter's fish', rather bony but with a
delicate taste, and with a coin-like shape on its tongue — possibly the
origin of the humorous story in Matthew 17$^{24-27}$.

The Sea lies 200m. below sea level, and is best first viewed from a
panoramic lay-by on the right coming from Nazareth, just above the
sea-level sign before entering the town of Tiberias. On the skyline to
the west are the distinctive **Horns of Hattin** (a small hillock just off
the road with a projection at each end) where the Crusaders were
finally defeated by Saladin in 1187. To the north (on a clear day) one
can see the snowclad slopes of **Mount Hermon** and the hills of
Lebanon. To the east are the Golan Heights which mark the boun-
dary with Syria. To the south the Jordan valley, where Israel borders
with Jordan.

The prosperous and expanding town of **Tiberias** lies below, first
built in Jesus' own lifetime by Herod Antipas in honour of the

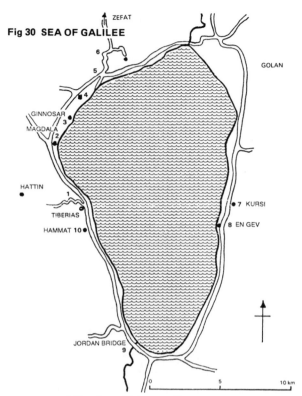

Fig 30 SEA OF GALILEE

Roman emperor Tiberius. Being a Roman rather than a Jewish town, it does not figure in Jesus' ministry in the gospel story. Its Jewish fame came later, when it became the home of the refugee rabbis from Jerusalem in 70 AD, and eventually the birthplace of the Talmud, the Jewish commentary on Scripture. The famous rabbis Akiba (2nd c.) and Maimonides (12th c.) are buried here. The fortifications still visible date from Turkish times. Boat excursions to Capernaum and En Gev may be booked from here.

Along the lake shore going clockwise from Tiberias (fig. 30):
1. Several excellent 'beaches' (entrance fee), ideal for swimming, sunbathing and walking on the water (on skis).
2. The remains of **Magdala** (from which the famous Magdalene took her name) now largely under water, the lake having risen several metres since New Testament times. Just north, the YMCA have a fine lakeside chapel, Peniel.

169

3. The guesthouse (Nof) of the **kibbutz Ginnosar**, an ideal place to have a meal (it would be best to book), to swim in the lake, and to learn something of the history of the collective settlements known as the kibbutzim. Founded in 1934, it now supports 600 people on its thriving fishing industry, and farms bananas, avocados, grapefruit and cereals in the surrounding fields. Fine cafeteria and shops. They cash travellers' cheques at the desk.

4. The heavily fortified pumping station which pushes a billion kgs. of water daily up to the Nazareth hills, thence to be piped throughout the country. The water channel alongside the road siphons off the minerals harmful to irrigation.

5. The turn right for **Tabgha** and **Capernaum** (see pp. 174 and 112).

6. Here the road rises into the hills of Upper Galilee. Shortly on the right is the entrance to the **Mount of Beatitudes** (see p. 144), and a little further on to the right the lane leading to the ruins of **Korazin** (Chorozain) — not as visually interesting as those of Capernaum (National Parks card). 16km. further north is **Safed** or **Zefat**, prominent 850m. up on the hillside like a 'town that cannot be hid' (Matthew 5[14]) — though obviously any hill town could merit such a general observation. It has no biblical connexions, but the town is well worth a visit for its Crusader remains and its beautiful 16th c. synagogues. It is a favourite resort of artists, and commands magnificent views of the lake and of the Mediterranean coast.

7. Round to the east side of the lake, under the imposing Golan Heights, a new road leads to the newly excavated and quite delightful remains of the 4th c. Byzantine 'Church of the Gadarenes' at **Kursi** (National Parks card).

8. The road continues along the lakeside to the small and vulnerable kibbutz of **En Gev**. It is much frequented by tourists since it is on the steamer itinerary, and boasts a fine restaurant. Swimming and boating.

9. To the south, where the Jordan issues, lies the **Jordan Bridge** (Gesher Yarden), where new facilities are now provided for pilgrims who wish to renew their baptismal vows (or just simply to paddle) in the gentle Jordan waters now that the traditional site near Jericho has become a forbidden military zone. Refreshments and toilets.

10. Returning north, the hot springs of Tiberias (140°F, 60°C), amidst which the famous 2nd c. rabbi Meir, 'Revealer and Wonderworker', has his shrine. The neighbouring Synagogue has a fine 4th c. mosaic floor.

Mark 1[16−18]: Passing along by the Sea of Galilee, Jesus saw Simon and Andrew the brother of Simon casting a net in the Sea; for they were fishermen. And Jesus said to them, 'Follow me and I will make you become fishers of men.' And immediately they left their nets and followed him.

Mark 2[13]: Jesus went out again beside the Sea; and all the crowd gathered about him, and he taught them.

Mark 3[7]: Jesus withdrew with his disciples to the Sea, and a great multitude from Galilee followed.

Mark 4[1]: Again Jesus began to teach beside the Sea. And a very large crowd gathered about him, so that he got into a boat and sat in it on the Sea; and the whole crowd was beside the Sea on the land.

Mark 4[35−41]: When evening had come, Jesus said to them, 'Let us go across to the other side.' After leaving the crowd, they took him with them in the boat, just as he was. And other boats were with him. And a great storm of wind arose, and the waves beat into the boat, so that the boat was already filling. But he was in the stern, asleep on the cushion; and they woke him and said to him, 'Teacher, do you not care if we perish?' And he awoke and rebuked the wind, and said to the Sea, 'Peace! Be still!' And the wind ceased, and there was a great calm. He said to them, 'Why are you afraid? Have you no faith?' And they were filled with awe, and said to one another, 'Who then is this, that even wind and sea obey him?'

Mark 6[47−51]: When evening came, the boat was out on the Sea, and Jesus was alone on the land. And he saw that they were making headway painfully, for the wind was against them. And about the fourth watch of the night he came to them, walking on the Sea. He meant to pass by them, but when they saw him walking on the Sea they thought it was a ghost, and cried out; for they all saw him and were terrified. But immediately he spoke to them and said, 'Take heart, it is I; have no fear.' And he got into the boat with them and the wind ceased. And they were utterly astounded.

The excerpts quoted above illustrate how frequently the Sea of Galilee provides the background to Jesus' ministry. Almost every page of the first six chapters of Mark (and the parallels in Matthew and Luke) refer to the lakeside. See also:

Mark 1^{21-22}	Teaching in the synagogue
Mark $1^{23}-2^{12}$	Cures of demoniacs, lepers and paralytics
Mark 2^{13-17}	Call of Levi (Matthew?)
Mark 3^{7-12}	The crowds
Mark 4^{1-34}	Parables on the lakeside
Mark 5^{1-20}	Gadarene swine
Mark 5^{25-34}	The sick woman
Mark 5^{35-43}	Jairus' daughter
Mark 6^{30-44}	Loaves and fishes
Mark 6^{53-56}	Cures
Matthew 5—7	Sermon on the Mount
Matthew 17^{24-27}	The Temple tax
John 6	Preaching in the synagogue
John 21	The risen Christ

SEDOM   see p. 116

SHECHEM   see p. 149

SHEPHERDS' FIELD   see p. 100

SHILOH   35km. north of Jerusalem, off the Nablus road.

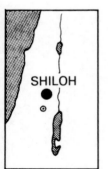

SHILOH

Shortly after the signpost for Sinjil (named after the Crusader Raymund de St Gilles), a right hand turn leads to the village of Turmus Aiya. A few km. beyond, a field and a low mound are all that is left of Shiloh, Israel's one time religious centre, where Moses' Ark of the Covenant provided a rallying point for the tribes over the two hundred years following the Exodus in the 13th c. BC. There is little for the non-expert to see.

1 Samuel 1—4: There was a certain man ... whose name was Elkanah ... who used to go up year by year from his city to worship and to sacrifice to the Lord of hosts at Shiloh ... His wife Hannah conceived and bore a son, and she called his name Samuel, for she said, 'I have asked him of the Lord.' ... She prayed and said,
  'My heart exults in the Lord,
  my strength is exalted in the Lord ...
  because I rejoice in thy salvation ...
  The Lord makes poor and makes rich;

he brings low, he also exalts.
He raises up the poor from the dust;
he lifts the needy from the ash heap ...'
The boy ministered to the Lord, in the presence of Eli the priest ... He continued to grow both in stature and in favour with the Lord and with men ... The Lord was with him and let none of his words fall to the ground. And all Israel from Dan to Beersheba knew that Samuel was established as a prophet of the Lord. And the Lord appeared again at Shiloh, for the Lord revealed himself to Samuel at Shiloh by the word of the Lord. And the word of Samuel came to all Israel.

Now Israel went out to battle against the Philistines ... The people sent to Shiloh, and brought from there the ark of the covenant to the Lord of hosts, who is enthroned on the cherubim ... The Philistines fought, and Israel was defeated, and they fled, every man to his home; and there was a very great slaughter, for there fell of Israel 30,000 foot soldiers. And the ark of God was captured ...

A man from Benjamin ran from the battle line, and came to Shiloh the same day, with his clothes rent and with earth upon his head. When he arrived, Eli was sitting upon his seat by the road watching, for his heart trembled for the ark of God ... When he mentioned the ark of God, Eli fell over backward from his seat by the side of the gate; and his neck was broken and he died, for he was an old man, and heavy ... His daughter-in-law named her child Ichabod, saying, 'The glory has departed from Israel.'

SOLOMON'S POOLS 4km. south of Bethlehem on the Hebron road. The car park lies off the road left. From there one must walk a few hundred metres to the pools. Entrance is free.

These three vast water reservoirs, partly cut out of the solid rock in an area rich with springs, were probably installed in New Testament times by Pilate. Jerusalem continued to depend on this water supply until very recent times. Traces of the Roman aqueduct leading from this high ground down to Jerusalem are still visible along the road to Bethlehem, outside the Jaffa Gate, and in the courtyard of the American Colony Hotel in Jerusalem. Further aqueducts feed the pools from the hills to the south. The fortress guarding the reservoirs dates from Turkish times.

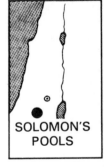

SOLOMON'S
POOLS

A tradition has associated the pools with King Solomon. The tradition is mistaken, but a reading of the Song of Solomon could enliven a picnic on this beautiful shady spot.

Song of Solomon 4[12-16]: A garden locked is my sister, my bride,
a garden locked, a fountain sealed.
Your shoots are an orchard of pomegranates

173

with all choicest fruits, henna with nard,
nard and saffron, calamus and cinnamon,
with all trees of frankincense,
myrrh and aloes, with all chief spices —
a garden fountain, a well of living water,
and flowing streams from Lebanon.

Awake, O north wind,
and come, O south wind!
Blow upon my garden,
let its fragrance be wafted abroad.
Let my beloved come to his garden,
and eat its choicest fruits.

TABGHA   14km. north of Tiberias, at the right hand turn for Capernaum (see p. 113). Toilets, drinks, and a very full collection of postcards and slides. Closed 17.00.

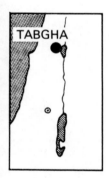

Tabgha is a corruption of the name **Heptapegon** which means Seven Springs. The whole area still gives evidence of how well watered it has always been.

The gospels locate the story of the feeding of the thousands on the east side of the lake, but because that was difficult of access, pilgrims from the earliest times have commemorated the story here on the west side. The remains of the 4th c. mosaics have recently (1984) been brilliantly incorporated into a fine reconstruction of the Byzantine basilica, and the flora and fauna of the Palestine of the time are again on resplendent display. The famous 'loaves and fishes' mosaic is in the sanctuary, eloquently summing up this church's theme, where all creatures are being fed by the hand of God. The church of **Peter's Primacy** is adjoining. (see p. 161)

Psalm 34: Taste and see that the Lord is good.

I will bless the Lord at all times,
his praise always on my lips;
in the Lord my soul shall make its boast.
The humble shall hear and be glad.

Taste and see that the Lord is good.

John 6[1-14]: After this Jesus went to the other side of the Sea of Galilee, which is the Sea of Tiberias. And a multitude followed him, because they saw the signs which he did on those who were diseased. Jesus went up on the mountain, and there sat down with his disciples. Now the Passover, the feast of the Jews, was at hand. Lifting up his eyes, then, and seeing that a multi-

tude was coming to him, Jesus said to Philip, 'How are we to buy bread, so that these people may eat?' This he said to test him, for he himself knew what he would do. Philip answered him. 'Two hundred days' wages would not buy enough bread for each of them to get a little.' One of his disciples, Andrew, Simon Peter's brother, said to him, 'There is a lad here who has five barley loaves and two fish; but what are they among so many?' Jesus said, 'Make the people sit down.' Now there was much grass in the place; so the men sat down, in number about five thousand. Jesus then took the loaves, and when he had given thanks, he distributed them to those who were seated; so also the fish, as much as they wanted. And when they had eaten their fill, he told his disciples, 'Gather up the fragments left over, that nothing may be lost.' So they gathered them up and filled twelve baskets with fragments from the five barley loaves, left by those who had eaten. When the people saw the sign which he had done, they said, 'This is indeed the prophet who is to come into the world!'

BPB p. 94: Father, you have given us Jesus Christ
   who is the true bread from heaven.
  He is the manna of the new covenant
   which came down from heaven
    and gives life to the world.
  Jesus said,
   'I am the bread of life;
   he who comes to me will not hunger,
    and he who believes in me will never thirst.'
  Father, deepen my faith in Christ
   so he may fill me with eternal life
    and raise me up on the last day.
  Feed me with Christ's own body and blood,
   for unless I eat his flesh and drink his blood
    I will not have life in me ...
  Father, let me live by Christ your Son
   as he lives by you;
  and then the Spirit of holiness
   by whom you raised Jesus from the dead

will dwell in me as in his temple;
and he will raise me from the dead at judgment day.
Father, I thank you for inviting me to eat at your table,
so enabling me to taste for myself
that the Lord is very sweet.

TABOR   see p. 146

TANTUR   see p. 98

TIBERIAS   see p. 168

UMMAYAD PALACE   see p. 133

YAFO   see p. 131

ZEFAT   see p. 170

RESOURCE MATERIAL FOR WORSHIP

The liturgical material which follows has been taken from four sources: the Roman Catholic *Missal* (RC); the Church of England *Alternative Services Book* (CE); the *Order of Worship for the Lord's Supper* of the United Reformed Church (URC); and Huub Oosterhuis' *Ten Table Prayers* (HO). No complete text of any one service is offered. Instead, enough material is provided for Christians of any tradition to use as they see fit in their own customary pattern of Communion, Eucharist, Mass or Lord's Supper.

1. **Introduction**

    a. (RC)   The grace and peace of God our Father
                  and the Lord Jesus Christ be with you.
                  And also with you.

    b. (URC) This is the day which the Lord has made;
                  Let us rejoice and be glad in it.
                  It is good to give thanks to the Lord;
                  For his love endures for ever.

2. **Opening Prayers** (URC)

    Almighty God,
    to whom all hearts are open,
    all desires known,
    and from whom no secrets are hidden:
    cleanse the thoughts of our hearts
    by the inspiration of your Holy Spirit,
    that we may perfectly love you,
    and worthily magnify your holy Name;
    through Christ our Lord. **Amen.**

    Almighty God, infinite and eternal
    in wisdom, power and love: we
    praise you for all that you are,
    and for all that you do for the
    world. You have shown us your
    truth and your love in our Saviour

Jesus Christ. Help us by your
Spirit to worship you in spirit
and in truth; through Jesus Christ
our Lord.   **Amen.**

3. **Prayers of Penitence**

a. (RC)   You were sent to heal the contrite: Lord, have mercy.
Lord, have mercy.
You came to call sinners: Christ, have mercy.
Christ, have mercy.
You plead for us at the right hand of the Father: Lord, have mercy.
Lord, have mercy.
May almighty God have mercy on us,
forgive us our sins,
and bring us to everlasting life.
Amen.

b. (CE)   **Almighty God, our heavenly Father,**
we have sinned against you and against our fellow men,
in thought and word and deed,
through negligence, through weakness,
through our own deliberate fault.
We are truly sorry,
and repent of all our sins.

For the sake of your Son Jesus Christ, who died for us,
forgive us all that is past;
and grant that we may serve you in newness of life
to the glory of your name.   Amen.

c. (URC)   **Lord God most merciful,**
we confess that we have sinned,
through our own fault,
and in common with others,
in thought, word and deed,
and through what we have left undone.

We ask to be forgiven.

By the power of your Spirit
turn us from evil to good,
help us to forgive others,
and keep us in your ways

of righteousness and love;
through Jesus Christ our Lord.   Amen.

4. Assurance of Pardon

a. (URC) God so loved the world that he
gave his only Son, that whoever
believes in him should not perish
but have eternal life.

To all who repent and believe, we
declare, in the name of the Father,
the Son and the Holy Spirit: God
grants you the forgiveness of
your sins.

b. (CE)   Almighty God,
who forgives all who truly repent,
have mercy upon *you*,
pardon and deliver *you* from all *your* sins,
confirm and strengthen *you* in all goodness,
and keep *you* in life eternal;
through Jesus Christ our Lord.   **Amen.**

5. Gloria in Excelsis

Glory to God in the highest,
and peace to his people on earth.

Lord God, heavenly King,
almighty God and Father,
we worship you, we give you thanks,
we praise you for your glory.

Lord Jesus Christ, only Son of the Father,
Lord God, Lamb of God,
you take away the sin of the world:
have mercy on us;
you are seated at the right hand of the Father:
receive our prayer.

For you alone are the Holy One,
you alone are the Lord,

**you alone are the Most High,
Jesus Christ, with the Holy Spirit,
in the glory of God the Father.   Amen.**

6. Scripture Readings

7. The Creed

I believe in God the Father Almighty,
Creator of heaven and earth;
and in Jesus Christ his only Son our Lord,
who was conceived by the Holy Ghost,
born of the Virgin Mary;
suffered under Pontius Pilate,
was crucified, dead, and buried;
he descended into hell;
the third day he rose again from the dead;
he ascended into heaven,
sitteth at the right hand of God the Father Almighty;
from thence he shall come to judge the living and the dead.
I believe in the Holy Ghost;
the holy Catholic Church;
the communion of saints;
the forgiveness of sins;
the resurrection of the body,
and life everlasting.   **Amen.**

8. **Intercessions** (URC)

Almighty God, whose Spirit helps
us in our weakness and guides us
in our prayers; we pray for the
Church and for the world in the
name of Jesus Christ.

Renew the faith and life of the
Church; strengthen its witness; and
make it one in Christ. Grant that
we and all who confess that he is
Lord may be faithful in service and
filled with his spirit, and that
the world may be turned to him.

Guide the nations in the ways of
justice, liberty and peace; and help
them to seek the unity and welfare
of mankind. Give
to all in authority wisdom to know
and strength to do what is right.

Grant that men and women in their
various callings may have grace to
do their work well; and may the
resources of the earth be wisely
used, truth honoured and preserved,
and the quality of our life enriched.

Comfort those in sorrow; heal the
sick in body or in mind; and
deliver the oppressed. Give us
active sympathy for all who suffer;
and help us so to bear the burdens
of others that we may fulfil the
law of Christ.

Keep us and the members of our
families united in loyalty and in
love, and always in your care; and
may our friends and neighbours,
and all for whom we pray, receive
the help they need, and live in
peace.

We remember those who have died

Eternal God, accept our thanks and
praise for all who have served you
faithfully here on earth, and
especially for those dear to our
own hearts ... May we and all your
people, past, present and to come,
share the life and joy of your
kingdom; through Jesus Christ our
Lord. **Amen.**

Other suitable intercessory prayers may be found on pages 39, 96, 114, 121,
148, 161.

9. Gracious Words and Invitation (URC)

> Come to me, all who labour and are
> heavy-laden, and I will give you
> rest.
>
> I am the bread of life; he who
> comes to me shall not hunger, and
> he who believes in me shall never
> thirst.
>
> Him who comes to me I will not
> cast out.

10. Narrative of the Institution (URC)

> I received from the Lord what I
> also delivered to you, that the
> Lord Jesus on the night when he
> was betrayed took bread, and when
> he had given thanks, he broke it,
> and said, 'This is my body which
> is for you. Do this in
> remembrance of me.' In the same
> way also the cup, after supper,
> saying, 'This cup is the new
> covenant in my blood. Do this,
> as often as you drink it, in
> remembrance of me.' For as often
> as you eat this bread and drink
> the cup, you proclaim the Lord's
> death until he comes.   (*1 Corinthians 11*$^{23-26}$)

11. Eucharistic Prayer

a. (RC)   The Lord be with you.
          And also with you.
          Lift up your hearts.
          We lift them up to the Lord.
          Let us give thanks to the Lord our God.
          It is right to give him thanks and praise.

> Father, it is our duty and our salvation,
> always and everywhere

to give you thanks
through your beloved Son, Jesus Christ.
He is the Word through whom you made the universe,
the Saviour you sent to redeem us.
By the power of the Holy Spirit
he took flesh and was born of the Virgin Mary.
For our sake he opened his arms on the cross;
he put an end to death
and revealed the resurrection.
In this he fulfilled your will
and won for you a holy people.
And so, we join the angels and saints
in proclaiming your glory:
Holy, holy, holy, Lord, God of power and might,
heaven and earth are full of your glory.
 Hosanna in the highest.
Blessed is he who comes in the name of the Lord.
 Hosanna in the highest.

Father, you are holy indeed,
and all creation rightly gives you praise.
All life, all holiness comes from you
through your Son, Jesus Christ our Lord,
by the working of the Holy Spirit.
From age to age you gather a people to yourself,
so that from east to west
a perfect offering may be made
to the glory of your name.
And so, Father, we bring you these gifts.
We ask you to make them holy by the power of your Spirit,
that they may become the body and blood
of your Son, our Lord Jesus Christ,
by whose command we celebrate this eucharist.
On the night he was betrayed,
he took bread and gave you thanks and praise.
He broke the bread, gave it to his disciples, and said:
Take this, all of you, and eat it:
this is my body which will be given up for you.

When supper was ended, he took the cup.
Again he gave you thanks and praise,
gave the cup to his disciples, and said:
Take this, all of you, and drink from it:

this is the cup of my blood,
the blood of the new and everlasting covenant.
It will be shed for you and for all men
so that sins may be forgiven.
Do this in memory of me.

Let us proclaim the mystery of faith:

1 **Christ has died,**
   Christ is risen,
   Christ will come again.

2 **Dying you restored our death,**
   rising you restored our life.
   Lord Jesus, come in glory.

3 **When we eat this bread and drink this cup,**
   we proclaim your death, Lord Jesus,
   until you come in glory.

4 **Lord, by your cross and resurrection**
   you have set us free.
   You are the Saviour of the world.

Father, calling to mind the death your Son endured for our
   salvation,
his glorious resurrection and ascension into heaven,
and ready to greet him when he comes again,
we offer you in thanksgiving this holy and living sacrifice.
Look with favour on your Church's offering,
and see the Victim whose death has reconciled us to yourself.
Grant that we, who are nourished by his body and blood,
may be filled with his Holy Spirit,
and become one body, one spirit in Christ.
May he make us an everlasting gift to you
and enable us to share in the inheritance of your saints,
with Mary, the virgin Mother of God;
with the apostles, the martyrs,
(Saint N. — *the patron saint or saint of the day*) and all your saints,
on whose constant intercession we rely for help.

Lord, may this sacrifice,
which has made our peace with you,
advance the peace and salvation of all the world.
Strengthen in faith and love your pilgrim Church on earth;

your servant, Pope N., our bishop N.,
and all the bishops,
with the clergy and the entire people your Son has gained for you.
Father, hear the prayers of the family you have gathered here
before you.
In mercy and love unite all your children
wherever they may be.
Welcome into your kingdom our departed brothers and sisters,
and all who have left this world in your friendship.
We hope to enjoy for ever the vision of your glory,
through Christ our Lord, from whom all good things come.
Through him,
with him,
in him,
in the unity of the Holy Spirit,
all glory and honour is yours,
almighty Father,
for ever and ever.
Amen.

b. (CE) The Lord be with you *or* The Lord is here.
And also with you.   His Spirit is with us.

Lift up your hearts.
We lift them to the Lord.

Let us give thanks to the Lord our God.
It is right to give him thanks and praise.

It is indeed right,
it is our duty and our joy,
at all times and in all places
to give you thanks and praise,
holy Father, heavenly King,
almighty and eternal God,
through Jesus Christ your only Son our Lord.

For he is your living Word;
through him you have created all things from the beginning,
and formed us in your own image.

Through him you have freed us from the slavery of sin,
giving him to be born as man and to die upon the cross;
you raised him from the dead
and exalted him to your right hand on high.

185

Through him you have sent upon us
your holy and life-giving Spirit,
and made us a people for your own possession.

Therefore with angels and archangels,
and with all the company of heaven,
we proclaim your great and glorious name,
for ever praising you and saying:

Holy, holy, holy Lord,
God of power and might,
heaven and earth are full of your glory.
Hosanna in the highest.
Blessed is he who comes in the name of the Lord.
Hosanna in the highest.

Accept our praises, heavenly Father,
through your Son our Saviour Jesus Christ;
and as we follow his example and obey his command,
grant that by the power of your Holy Spirit
these gifts of bread and wine
may be to us his body and his blood;

Who in the same night that he was betrayed,
took bread and gave you thanks;
he broke it and gave it to his disciples, saying,
Take, eat; this is my body which is given for you;
do this in remembrance of me.
In the same way, after supper
he took the cup and gave you thanks;
he gave it to them, saying,
Drink this, all of you;
this is my blood of the new covenant,
which is shed for you and for many for the forgiveness of sins.
Do this, as often as you drink it,
in remembrance of me.

Christ has died:
Christ is risen:
Christ will come again.

Therefore, heavenly Father,
we remember his offering of himself
made once for all upon the cross,
and proclaim his mighty resurrection and glorious ascension.
As we look for his coming in glory,

we celebrate with this bread and this cup
his one perfect sacrifice.

Accept through him, our great high priest,
this our sacrifice of thanks and praise;
and as we eat and drink these holy gifts
in the presence of your divine majesty,
renew us by your Spirit,
inspire us with your love,
and unite us in the body of your Son,
Jesus Christ our Lord.

Through him, and with him, and in him,
by the power of the Holy Spirit,
with all who stand before you in earth and heaven,
we worship you, Father almighty,
in songs of everlasting praise:

**Blessing and honour and glory and power
be yours for ever and ever. Amen.**

c. (URC) Lift up your hearts.
We lift them to the Lord.
Let us give thanks to the Lord our God.
It is right to give him thanks and praise.
With joy we give you thanks and
praise, Almighty God, Source of
all life and love, that we live
in your world, that you are always
creating and sustaining it by your
power, and that you have so made
us that we can know and love you,
trust and serve you. We give you
thanks that you loved the world so
much that you gave your only Son,
so that everyone who has faith in
him may not die but have eternal
life.

We thank you that Jesus was born
among us; that he lived our common
life on earth; that he suffered
and died for us; that he rose again;
and that he is always present
through the Holy Spirit.

187

We thank you that we can live in
the faith that your kingdom will
come, and that in life, in death
and beyond death you are with us.

Therefore with all the company of
heaven, and with all your people
of all places and times, we proclaim
your greatness and sing your praise.

Holy, holy, holy Lord
God of power and might,
Heaven and earth are full of your glory.
Hosanna in the highest.

Blessed is he
who comes in the
name of the Lord.
Hosanna in the highest.

Holy Lord God,
by what we do here
in remembrance of Christ
we celebrate
    his perfect sacrifice on the Cross
    and his glorious resurrection and ascension;
we declare
    that he is Lord of all;
and we prepare for
    his coming in his kingdom.

We pray that
through your Holy Spirit
this bread may be for us
    the body of Christ
and this wine
    the blood of Christ.

Accept our sacrifice of praise;
and as we eat and drink
at his command
unite us to Christ
as one body in him,
and give us strength
to serve you in the world.

And to you,
one holy and eternal God,
Father, Son and Holy Spirit,
we give praise and glory,
now and for ever. **Amen.**

d. (HO)   The Lord be with you.
        The Lord will preserve you.
        Lift up your hearts.
        Our hearts are with the Lord.
        Let us thank the Lord our God.
        He is worthy of our gratitude.

We thank you
for you are a God of people,
for we may call you our God and our Father,
for you hold our future in your hands,
for this world touches your heart.

You called us and broke through our deafness,
you appeared in our darkness,
you opened our eyes with your light,
you ordered everything for the best for us
and brought us to life.

Blessed are you, the source of all that exists.
We thirst for you,
because you have made us thirsty.
Our hearts are restless
until we are secure in you,
with Jesus Christ our Lord.

With all who have gone before us in faith,
We praise your name, O Lord our God.
You are our hope
and we thank you, full of joy,
adoring you with the words:

Holy, holy, holy,
Lord of all powers.
Heaven and earth
are full of your glory.
Come and deliver us,
Lord most high.
Blessed is he who comes
in the name of the Lord.

189

**Come and deliver us,
Lord most high.**

We thank you
for the sake of your beloved Son,
whom you called and sent
to serve us and to give us light,
to bring your kingdom
to the poor,
to bring redemption
to all captive people,
and to be forever
and for all mankind
the likeness and the form
of your constant love and goodness.

We thank you
for this unforgettable man
who has fulfilled everything
that is human —
our life and death.
We thank you
because he gave himself,
heart and soul, to this world.

For, on the night that he was delivered up,
he took bread into his hands
and raising his eyes to you,
God, his almighty Father,
he gave thanks
and broke the bread
and gave it to his friends
with the words:
Take and eat,
this is my body for you.
Do this in memory of me.

He also took the cup
and, giving thanks to you, said:
This cup is the new covenant in my blood
shed for you and for all mankind
so that sins may be forgiven.
Every time you drink this cup,
you will do it in memory of me.

So whenever we eat of this bread
and drink from this cup
we proclaim the death of the Lord
until he comes.

Therefore, Lord our God,
we present this sign of our faith
and therefore we call to mind
the suffering and death of your Son,
his resurrection from the dead,
his entry into your glory,
recalling that he
who is exalted at your right hand
will intercede for us
and that he will come
to do justice to the living and the dead
on the day that you have appointed.

Send us your Spirit
who is life, justice and light.
O God,
you want the well-being of all men,
not their unhappiness
and not death.
Take all violence away from us.
Curb the passion
that makes us seek each others' lives.
Give us peace on earth
by the power of Jesus Christ,
your Son here among us.
We ask and implore you
to grant us this.

Then your name will be made holy,
through him and with him and in him,
everywhere on earth and here and now,
and forever and ever.
Amen.

12. Communion

We break this bread
to share in the body of Christ.
**Though we are many, we are one body,
because we all share in one bread.**

Lamb of God, you take away the sins of the world: have mercy on us.

Lamb of God, you take away the sins of the world: have mercy on us.

Lamb of God, you take away the sins of the world: grant us peace.

Jesus, Lamb of God: have mercy on us.
Jesus, bearer of our sins: have mercy on us.
Jesus, redeemer of the world: give us your peace.

Draw near with faith. Receive the body of our
Lord Jesus Christ which he gave for you, and his
blood which he shed for you.

Eat and drink in remembrance that he died for
you, and feed on him in your hearts by faith with
thanksgiving.

13. Concluding Prayers

a. (URC) Most gracious God,
we praise you
for what you have given
and for what you have promised us here.

You have made us one
with all your people
in heaven and on earth.
You have fed us
with the bread of life,
and renewed us for your service.

Now we give ourselves to you;
and we ask
that our daily living
may be part of the life of your kingdom,

and that our love
may be your love reaching out into the life of the world;
through Jesus Christ our Lord. **Amen.**

b. (CE)   Father of all, we give you thanks and praise, that when we were still far off you met us in your Son and brought us home. Dying and living, he declared your love, gave us grace, and opened the gate of glory. May we who share Christ's body live his risen life; we who drink his cup bring life to others; we whom the Spirit lights give light to the world. Keep us firm in the hope you have set before us, so we and all your children shall be free, and the whole earth live to praise your name; through Christ our Lord. **Amen.**

c. (CE)   Almighty God,
we thank you for feeding us
with the body and blood of your Son
   Jesus Christ.
Through him we offer you our souls and bodies
to be a living sacrifice.
Send us out
in the power of your Spirit
to live and work
to your praise and glory. **Amen.**

14. Blessing

a. (CE)   The peace of God, which passes all understanding, keep your hearts and minds in the knowledge and love of God, and of his Son Jesus Christ our Lord; and the blessing of God almighty, the Father, the Son, and the Holy Spirit, be among you, and remain with you always. **Amen.**

Go in peace to love and serve the Lord.
In the name of Christ. Amen.

or Go in the peace of Christ.
Thanks be to God.

b. (URC) Go in peace to serve the Lord;
and the blessing of God Almighty,
the Father, the Son and the Holy
Spirit, be with you always. **Amen.**

193

c. (RC)   The Lord be with you.
And also with you.

May almighty God bless you,
the Father, and the Son, and the Holy Spirit.
Amen.

Go, in the peace of Christ.
or The Mass is ended, go in peace.
or Go in peace to love and serve the Lord.
Thanks be to God.

A WAY OF THE CROSS (fig. 31)

The tradition of following Jesus on his journey to the cross is a very old one. The route now followed by pilgrims, and indeed the marking of it by fourteen 'Stations', is more recent, dating only from the 13th c. Still, that is long enough to encourage pilgrims to join hands with the millions of Christians of all races and denominations who have come here over the years to meditate on the Passion of Christ.

Many Protestants will be unfamiliar with this devotion. Coming to it with fresh minds, they may hopefully find fresh significance in this ancient practice. If they have reservations about the five stations (3, 4, 6, 7, 9) not based on biblical evidence, this need not deter them from drawing inspiration from a pattern of prayer which Christians of other traditions have long found helpful.

The traditional route passes through lanes which are noisy and at times thick with visitors intent on shopping, sightseeing and refreshment. This ought not to

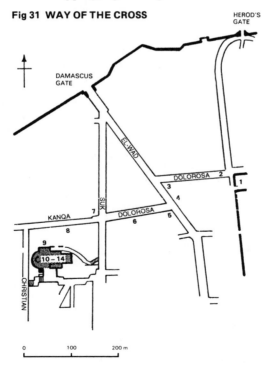

Fig 31 WAY OF THE CROSS

make pilgrims resentful. Jesus' own way of the cross passed through a similar scene, and people were no doubt offering to sell him postcards too. God can be found in the midst of this hubbub, not only in the cloisters.

An official Way of the Cross is conducted every Friday at 15.00. Groups who wish to do their own thing may find the following texts and prayers useful. Suggestions have been added for those who feel the occasion calls for song. The selection of hymns below offers further possibilities.

1. JESUS IS CONDEMNED TO DEATH

A new assembly point for large groups has recently been set up just inside St Stephen's Gate. But the first station has traditionally been kept in the playground of the al-Omariya school in the Via Dolorosa. Entrance is up a ramp parallel with the road, open outside school hours. Together with the Sion convent opposite, this once formed part of the Antonia fortress, the Roman garrison guarding the Temple. If Pilate held court there, this is where Jesus was tried, scourged and condemned.

We adore thee, O Christ, and we praise thee.
Because by thy holy cross thou hast redeemed the world.

Mark 15[1-15]: As soon as it was morning the chief priests, with the elders and the scribes, and the whole council held a consultation; and they bound Jesus and led him away and delivered him to Pilate. And Pilate asked him, 'Are you the King of the Jews?' And he answered him, 'You have said so.' ...

Now at the feast he used to release for them one prisoner for whom they asked. And among the rebels in prison, who had committed murder in the insurrection, there was a man called Barabbas. And the crowd came up and began to ask Pilate to do as he was wont to do for them. And he answered them, 'Do you want me to release for you the King of the Jews?' ... But the chief priests stirred up the crowd to have him release for them Barabbas instead. And Pilate again said to them, 'Then what shall I do with the man whom you call the King of the Jews?' And they cried out again, 'Crucify him.' And Pilate said to them, 'Why, what evil has he done?' But they shouted out all the more, 'Crucify him.' So Pilate, wishing to satisfy the crowd, released for them Barabbas; and having scourged Jesus, he delivered him to be crucified.

Spirit of the living God, fall afresh on me.
Spirit of the living God, fall afresh on me.
Break me, melt me, mould me, fill me.
Spirit of the living God, fall afresh on me.

2. JESUS RECEIVES HIS CROSS

This Station is usually celebrated on the roadway outside the Sion convent, under the famous Ecce Homo arch. Small groups could ask permission to enter the convent (closed 12.30 - 14.00 and Sundays) where the prayers can more aptly be said on the magnificent Roman pavement which could well be the 'Lithostrotos' mentioned in John's Passion.

We adore thee, O Christ, and we praise thee.
Because by thy holy cross thou hast redeemed the world.

John 19[13-17]: Pilate brought Jesus out and sat [him] down on the judgment seat at a place called The Pavement [Lithostrotos] and in Hebrew, Gabbatha. Now it was the day of Preparation of the Passover; it was about the sixth hour. He said to the Jews, 'Behold your King!' They cried out, 'Away with him, away with him, crucify him!' Pilate said to them, 'Shall I crucify your King?' The chief priests answered. 'We have no king but Caesar.' Then he handed him over to them to be crucified. So they took Jesus, and he went out, bearing his own cross, to the place called the place of a skull, which is called in Hebrew Golgotha.

Let all that is within me cry holy.
Let all that is within me cry holy.
Holy, holy, holy is the Lamb that was slain.

3. JESUS FALLS FOR THE FIRST TIME

The road goes downhill to a T junction. Turn left. Immediately on the left is a small chapel attached to the Polish hospice marked with a III. The roadway outside has recently incorporated some of the underlying paving stones which go back to New Testament times. Elsewhere they remain a few metres down.

We adore thee, O Christ, and we praise thee.
Because by thy holy cross thou hast redeemed the world.

Isaiah 53[4-7]: Surely he has borne our griefs
            and carried our sorrows;
            yet we esteemed him stricken,
            smitten by God, and afflicted.
            But he was wounded for our transgressions,
            he was bruised for our iniquities;
            upon him was the chastisement that made us whole,
            and with his stripes we are healed.
            All we like sheep have gone astray;
            we have turned every one to his own way;
            and the Lord has laid on him
            the iniquity of us all.
            He was oppressed, and he was afflicted,
            yet he opened not his mouth;
            like a lamb that is led to the slaughter,
            and like a sheep that before its shearers is dumb,
            so he opened not his mouth.

John 1[29]: John saw Jesus coming towards him, and said, 'Behold the Lamb of God, who takes away the sin of the world!'

Let all that is within me cry worthy.
Let all that is within me cry worthy.
Worthy, worthy, worthy is the Lamb that was slain.

4. JESUS MEETS HIS MOTHER

A little further along this same road is a chapel on the left marked IV. Just before it through a courtyard is the parish church of the Catholic Armenians. It is possible to ask permission to go down from the right aisle of the church into the crypt, where the Byzantines beautifully captured the heart of this Station with a mosaic of a pair of women's sandals turning in the roadway to meet Jesus.

We adore thee, O Christ, and we praise thee.
Because by thy holy cross thou hast redeemed the world.

Luke 2[48–49]: Jesus' mother said to him, 'Son, why have you treated us so? Behold, your father and I have been looking for you anxiously.' And he said to them, 'How is it that you sought me? Did you not know that I must be about my Father's business?'

Luke 2[34–35]: Simeon said to Mary,
      'Behold, this child is set for the fall
      and rising of many in Israel,
      and for a sign that is spoken against;
      and a sword will pierce through your own soul also.'

John 19[26–27]: When Jesus saw his mother, and the disciple whom he loved standing near, he said to his mother, 'Woman, behold, your son!' Then he said to the disciple. 'Behold, your mother!' And from that hour the disciple took her to his own home.

Someone's crying, Lord, kum ba yah!
Someone's crying, Lord, kum ba yah!
Someone's crying, Lord, kum ba yah!
O Lord, kum ba yah!

5. SIMON OF CYRENE HELPS JESUS CARRY HIS CROSS

A short way along the same road, the Via Dolorosa turns right uphill. On the corner a chapel bears the mark V. One has to imagine Simon 'coming in from the country' along the road from Damascus Gate we have just walked.

We adore thee, O Christ, and we praise thee.
Because by thy holy cross thou hast redeemed the world.

Mark 15[21]: The soldiers compelled a passer-by, Simon of Cyrene, who was coming in from the country, the father of Alexander and Rufus, to carry his cross.

Mark 8³⁴: Jesus called to him the multitude with his disciples, and said to them, 'If any man would come after me, let him deny himself and take up his cross and follow me.'

2 Timothy 2³: Share in suffering as a good soldier of Christ Jesus.

When I needed a neighbour, were you there, were you there?
When I needed a neighbour, were you there?
And the creed and the colour and the name won't matter,
Were you there?

6. VERONICA WIPES THE FACE OF JESUS

Half way up this stepped street, on the left, the Little Sisters of Charles de Foucauld have turned a Crusader vaulted room into a simple and prayerful chapel. Their work among the poor puts into concrete terms the legend that a woman offered to wipe Jesus' face with her headcloth, which was then left permanently imprinted with the *verum ikon* (or true image) of his face.

We adore thee, O Christ, and we praise thee.
Because by thy holy cross thou hast redeemed the world.

Isaiah 53²⁻³: He grew up before the Lord like a young plant,
and like a root out of dry ground;
he had no form or comeliness that we should look at him,
and no beauty that we should desire him.
He was despised and rejected by men;
a man of sorrows, and acquainted with grief;
and as one from whom men hide their faces
he was despised, and we esteemed him not.

John 1¹⁰⁻¹²: He was in the world,
and the world was made through him,
yet the world knew him not.
He came to his own home,
and his own people received him not.
But to all who received him,
who believed in his name,
he gave them power to become children of God.

Matthew 25⁴⁰: The King will answer those at his right hand, 'Truly, I say to you, as you did it to one of the least of these my brethren, you did it to me.'

When I needed a healer, were you there, were you there?
When I needed a healer, were you there?
And the creed and the colour and the name won't matter.
Were you there?

7. JESUS FALLS THE SECOND TIME

The top of this street meets the north-south thoroughfare of Old Jerusalem which is the Suk or market. Dead opposite, by a pillar which was part of the colonnade lining the street, the Station is marked with VII.

We adore thee, O Christ, and we praise thee.
Because by thy holy cross thou hast redeemed the world.

Psalm 38[6–22]: I am utterly bowed down and prostrate;
       all the day I go about mourning.
       For my loins are filled with burning,
       and there is no soundness in my flesh.
       I am utterly spent and crushed;
       I groan because of the tumult of my heart ...
       Do not forsake me, O Lord!
       O my God, be not far from me!
       Make haste to help me,
       O Lord, my salvation!

Hebrews 2[17–18]: He had to be made like his brethren in every respect, so that he might become a merciful and faithful high priest in the service of God, to make expiation for the sins of the people. For because he himself has suffered and been tempted, he is able to help those who are tempted.

Let all that is within me cry blessed.
Let all that is within me cry blessed.
Blessed, blessed, blessed is the Lamb that was slain.

8. JESUS SPEAKS TO THE WOMEN OF JERUSALEM

Just to the left of the pillar, the east-west road continues uphill (El Kanqa Street). A short way up on the left, opposite the shops, a small cross set into the wall with the words IC XC NIKA (Jesus Christ Wins) marks the 8th Station.

We adore thee, O Christ and we praise thee.
Because by thy holy cross thou hast redeemed the world.

Luke 23[27–31]: There followed Jesus a great multitude of the people, and of women who bewailed and lamented him. But Jesus turning to them said, 'Daughters of Jerusalem, do not weep for me, but weep for yourselves and your children. For behold, the days are coming when they will say, "Blessed are the barren, and the wombs that never bore, and the breasts that never gave suck!" Then they will begin to say to the mountains, "Fall on us"; and to the hills, "Cover us". For if they do this when the wood is green, what will happen when it is dry?'

Matthew 7[21]: Jesus said, 'Not every one who says to me, "Lord, Lord," shall enter the kingdom of heaven, but he who does the will of my Father who is in heaven.'

Someone's lonely, Lord, kum ba yah!
Someone's lonely, Lord, kum ba yah!
Someone's lonely, Lord, kum ba yah!
O Lord, kum ba yah!

9. JESUS FALLS THE THIRD TIME

We are now close to the end of our journey at Holy Sepulchre church, but because the church is now smaller than it once was, we have to retrace our steps down to the Suk. The right turn takes us through part of the market, which will probably be crowded. The first fork right, about a hundred metres along, is a stone stairway. Go up this and follow the winding alley to the end, where a pillar at the door marks the 9th Station. The Ethiopian monks and nuns who live beyond will happily allow the group into their courtyard, which forms the roof of St Helena's chapel in Holy Sepulchre church.

We adore thee, O Christ, and we praise thee.
Because by thy holy cross thou hast redeemed the world.

Psalm 37[23–24]: The steps of a man are from the Lord,
and he establishes him in whose way he delights;
though he fall he shall not be cast headlong,
for the Lord is the stay of his hand.

Hebrews 4[15–16]: We have not a high priest who is unable to sympathize with our weaknesses, but one who in every respect has been tempted as we are, yet without sin. Let us then with confidence draw near to the throne of grace, that we may receive mercy and find grace to help in time of need.

Let all that is within me cry Jesus.
Let all that is within me cry Jesus.
Jesus, Jesus, Jesus is the Lamb that was slain.

10. JESUS IS STRIPPED OF HIS GARMENTS

The monks may here allow you to enter the Holy Sepulchre church through their property. If not, the complicated route again needs a retracing of steps. Return along the alley and down the steps into the Suk. Turn right and take the next entrance to the right. This does a double bend before leading through a stone doorway into Holy Sepulchre Square. The rest of the Stations can be observed in this square if the church is too crowded to allow the group convenient access. Otherwise the 10th Station is kept inside the main door, at the foot of the steps which lead up on the right to Calvary.

We adore thee, O Christ, and we praise thee.
Because by thy holy cross thou hast redeemed the world.

John 19[23–24]: When the soldiers had crucified Jesus they took his garments and made four parts, one for each soldier; also his tunic. But the tunic was without seam, woven from top to bottom; so they said to one another, 'Let us not tear it, but cast lots for it to see whose it shall be.'

Psalm 22[16–18]: Yea, dogs are round about me;
a company of evildoers encircle me;
they have pierced my hands and feet —
I can count all my bones —
they stare and gloat over me;
they divide my garments among them.
and for my raiment they cast lots.

I was cold, I was naked, were you there, were you there?
I was cold, I was naked, were you there?
And the creed and the colour and the name won't matter,
were you there?

11. JESUS IS NAILED TO THE CROSS

The stone steps to the right lead up to the hill of Calvary, whose sides have been cut straight, and the top flattened and paved, to allow pilgrims easier access. Upstairs, the right hand chapel is served by the Latins. A mural depicts the nailing.

We adore thee, O Christ, and we praise thee.
Because by thy holy cross thou hast redeemed the world.

Luke 23[33–43]: When they came to the place which is called The Skull, there they crucified Jesus, and the criminals, one on the right and one on the left. And Jesus said, 'Father, forgive them, for they know not what they do.' And they cast lots to divide his garments ... There was also an inscription over him, 'This is the King of the Jews'.

One of the criminals who were hanged railed at him, saying 'Are you not the Christ? Save yourself and us!' But the other rebuked him, saying, 'Do you not fear God, since you are under the same sentence of condemnation? And we indeed justly; for we are receiving the due reward for our deeds; but this man has done nothing wrong.' And he said, 'Jesus, remember me when you come into your kingdom.' And he said to him, 'Truly, I say to you, today you will be with me in Paradise.'

Were you there when they crucified my Lord?
Were you there when they crucified my Lord?
O, sometimes it causes me to tremble, tremble, tremble;
Were you there when they crucified my Lord?

12. JESUS DIES ON THE CROSS

The Greek Orthodox chapel to the left displays a large crucifix over the altar. Underneath pilgrims may stoop one at a time to put their hand through a hole in the paving and touch the rock in which the cross is thought to have been set.

We adore thee, O Christ, and we praise thee.
Because by thy holy cross thou hast redeemed the world.

John 19[28-37]: After this Jesus, knowing that all was now finished, said (to fulfil the scripture), 'I thirst.' A bowl full of vinegar stood there; so they put a sponge full of vinegar on hyssop and held it to his mouth. When Jesus had received the vinegar, he said, 'It is finished'; and he bowed his head and gave up his Spirit ...
The soldiers came and broke the legs of the first, and of the other who had been crucified with him; but when they came to Jesus and saw that he was already dead, they did not break his legs. But one of the soldiers pierced his side with a spear, and at once there came out blood and water ... These things took place that the scripture might be fulfilled, 'Not a bone of him shall be broken', and 'They shall look on him whom they have pierced.'

Were you there when they nailed him to the tree?
Were you there when they nailed him to the tree?
O, sometimes it causes me to tremble, tremble, tremble;
Were you there when they nailed him to the tree?

13. JESUS IS TAKEN DOWN FROM THE CROSS

Back to ground level again, at the foot of the Calvary steps, a piece of marble has been set into the floor, and decorated with hanging lamps. Here Greeks and Armenians commemorate the anointing of Jesus' body before burial.

We adore thee, O Christ, and we praise thee.
Because by thy holy cross thou hast redeemed the world.

John 19[38-40]: After this Joseph of Arimathea ... asked Pilate that he might take away the body of Jesus, and Pilate gave him leave. So he came and took away the body. Nicodemus also ... came bringing a mixture of myrrh and aloes about a hundred pounds' weight. They took the body of Jesus, and bound it in linen cloths with the spices, as is the burial custom of the Jews.

Psalm 22[14-15]: I am poured out like water,
and all my bones are out of joint;
my heart is like wax,
it is melted within my breast;
my strength is dried up like potsherd,
and my tongue cleaves to my jaws;
thou dost lay me in the dust of death.

Spirit of the living God, fall afresh on me;
Spirit of the living God, fall afresh on me;
Break me, melt me, mould me, fill me.
Spirit of the living God, fall afresh on me.

14. JESUS IS LAID IN THE SEPULCHRE

The traditional tomb of Jesus is in the centre of the church, isolated from the rock face which once lay beyond. It is enclosed in a little house, and only half a dozen or so pilgrims can enter it at a time, since it has no exit other than the entrance. A simple stone slab marks the empty tomb.

We adore thee, O Christ, and we praise thee.
Because by thy holy cross thou hast redeemed the world.

Mark 15[46–47]: Joseph of Arimathea bought a linen shroud, and taking him down, wrapped him in the linen shroud, and laid him in a tomb which had been hewn out of the rock; and he rolled a stone against the door of the tomb. Mary Magdalene and Mary the mother of Joses saw where he was laid.

Romans 6[3–11]: Do you not know that all of us who have been baptized into Christ Jesus were baptized into his death? We were buried therefore with him by baptism into death, so that as Christ was raised from the dead by the glory of the Father, we too might walk in newness of life ... So you must consider yourselves dead to sin and alive to God in Christ Jesus.

Someone's buried, Lord, kum ba yah!
Someone's buried, Lord, kum ba yah!
Someone's buried, Lord, kum ba yah!
O Lord, kum ba yah!

15. The Stations of the Cross, in keeping with the theology of the age in which the devotion grew up, end with the burial of Jesus. A more recent theology prefers (like the church of the Holy Sepulchre itself) not to dissociate Jesus' death and resurrection: the one must throw light on the other.

 The altar of St Mary Magdalene, close by on the right, commemorates the revelation of the risen Christ to one of his first disciples in the garden in which the tomb was then set. The closing prayers might well be said there, or alternatively downstairs in the Armenian crypt where St Helena is said to have found the discarded cross.

John 20[1–18]: On the first day of the week Mary Magdalene came to the tomb early, while it was still dark, and saw that the stone had been taken away from the tomb ... And she saw two angels in white, sitting where the body of Jesus had lain, one at the head and one at the feet. They said to her, 'Woman, why are you weeping?' She said to them, 'Because they have taken away my Lord, and I do not know where they have laid him.' Saying this, she turned round and saw Jesus standing, but she did not know that it was Jesus. Jesus said to her, 'Woman, why are you weeping? Whom do you seek?' Supposing him to be the gardener, she said to him, 'Sir, if you have carried him away, tell me where you have laid him, and I will take him away.' Jesus said to her, 'Mary.' She turned and said to him in Hebrew, 'Rabboni!' (which means Teacher). Jesus said to her, 'Do not hold me, for I have not yet ascended to the Father; but go to my brethren and say to them, I am ascending to my Father and your Father, to my God and your God.' Mary Magdalene went and said to the disciples, 'I have seen the Lord.'

Christ has died, Christ is risen, Christ will come again.

He is Lord, he is Lord,
he is risen from the dead and he is Lord.
Every knee shall bow, every tongue confess
that Jesus Christ is Lord.

A SELECTION OF HYMNS
(in alphabetical order)

1   *All glory, laud and honour,*
to thee, Redeemer King,
to whom the lips of children
made sweet hosannas ring.

Thou art the King of Israel,
thou David's royal Son,
who in the Lord's name comest,
the King and blessed one.

The company of angels
are praising thee on high,
and mortal men and all things
created make reply.

To thee before thy passion
they sang their hymns of praise;
to thee now high exalted
our melody we raise.

Thou didst accept their praises,
accept the prayers we bring,
who in all good delightest,
thou good and gracious King.
St Theodulph of Orleans, tr. J. M. Neale

2   All people that on earth do dwell,
sing to the Lord with cheerful voice;
him serve with fear, his praise forth tell,
come ye before him and rejoice.

The Lord, ye know, is God indeed,
without our aid he did us make;

we are his folk, he doth us feed
and for his sheep he doth us take.

O enter then his gates with praise,
approach with joy his courts unto;
praise, laud and bless his name always,
for it is seemly so to do.

To Father, Son and Holy Ghost,
the God whom heaven and earth adore,
from men and from the angel-host
be praise and glory evermore.

William Kethe, Day's Psalter

3   Amazing grace! How sweet the sound
that saved a wretch like me.
I once was lost but now I'm found
was blind, but now I see.

'Twas grace that taught my heart to fear,
and grace my fears relieved.
How precious did that grace appear
the hour I first believed.

Through many dangers, toils and snares
I have already come.
'Tis grace hath brought me safe thus far,
and grace will lead me home.

The Lord has promised good to me;
his word my hope secures.
He will my shield and portion be
as long as life endures.

John Newton

4   Angels we have heard on high
sweetly singing o'er our plains,
and the mountains in reply
echo still their joyous strains.
Gloria in excelsis Deo.

Shepherds, why this jubilee?
Why your rapturous strain prolong?
Say, what may your tidings be,
which inspire your heavenly song?

Come to Bethlehem and see
him whose birth the angels sing:
come adore on bended knee
the infant Christ, the new-born King.

James Chadwick

5   At the name of Jesus
every knee shall bow,
every tongue confess him
King of glory now.
'Tis the Father's pleasure
we should call him Lord,
who from the beginning
was the mighty Word.

Humbled for a season,
to receive a name
from the lips of sinners
unto whom he came,
faithfully he bore it
spotless to the last,
brought it back victorious,
when from death he passed.

Name him, brothers, name him
with love strong as death,
but with awe and wonder,
and with bated breath;
he is God the Saviour,
he is Christ the Lord,
ever to be worshipped,
trusted and adored.

Brothers, this Lord Jesus
shall return again,
with his Father's glory,

with his angel train;
for all wreaths of empire
meet upon his brow,
and our hearts confess him
King of glory now.

Caroline Maria Noel

6

Be still and know that I am God. (3 times)
I am the Lord that healeth thee. (3 times)
In thee O Lord I put my trust. (3 times)

Anon

7

Blessed assurance — Jesus is mine!
O what a foretaste of glory divine!
Heir of salvation, purchase of God;
born of his Spirit, washed in his blood.
This is my story, this is my song,
praising my Saviour all the day long.
(Repeat)

Perfect submission, perfect delight,
vision of rapture burst on my sight;
angels descending bring from above
echoes of mercy, whispers of love.

Perfect submission, all is at rest,
I in my Saviour am happy and blest;
watching and waiting, looking above,
filled with his goodness, lost in his love.

Fanny J. Crosby

8

Break thou the Bread of Life,
dear Lord, to me,
as thou didst break the bread
beside the sea;
beyond the sacred page
I seek thee, Lord,
my spirit longs for thee,
thou living Word.

Thou art the Bread of Life,
O Lord, to me,
thy holy Word the truth
that saveth me;
give me to eat and live
with thee above,
teach me to love thy truth,
for thou art love.

O send thy Spirit, Lord,
now unto me,
that he may touch my eyes
and make me see;
show me the truth concealed
within thy Word,
and in thy Book revealed,
I see thee, Lord.

Mary A. Lathbury

9 *By the rivers of Babylon,*
there we sat down;
there we wept
when we remembered Zion.

When the wicked
carried us away to captivity
they required of us a song;
now how shall we sing the Lord's song
in a strange land?

Let the words of our mouth
and the meditation of our heart
be acceptable in thy sight
here tonight.

10 Christ has died (alleluia),
Christ is risen (alleluia),
Christ will come again (alleluia).

11   Colours of day dawn into the mind,
the sun has come up, the night is behind.
Go down in the city, into the street,
and let's give the message to the people we meet.

So light up the fire and let the flame burn,
open the door, let Jesus return.
Take seeds of his Spirit, let the fruit grow,
tell the people of Jesus, let his love show.

Go through the park, on into the town;
the sun still shines on, it never goes down.
The light of the world is risen again;
the people of darkness are needing our friend.

Open your eyes, look into the sky,
the darkness has come, the sun came to die.
The evening draws on, the sun disappears,
but Jesus is living, and his Spirit is near.

Sue McClellan, John Pac and Keith Ryecroft

12   Crown him with many crowns,
The Lamb upon his throne:
hark how the heavenly anthem drowns
all music but its own.
Awake, my soul, and sing
of him who died for thee,
And hail him as thy matchless King
through all eternity.

Crown him the Lord of life,
who triumphed o'er the grave,
and rose victorious in the strife
for those he came to save.
His glories now we sing
who died and rose on high,
who died eternal life to bring,
and lives that death may die.

Crown him the Lord of love;
behold his hands and side,
those wounds yet visible above,

in beauty glorified.
All hail, Redeemer, hail!
for thou hast died for me:
thy praise shall never, never fail
throughout eternity.
Matthew Bridges and Godfrey Thring

13   *Day by day in the market place*
I play my flute all day.
I have piped to them all,
but nobody dances.
Day by day in the market place
I play my flute all day,
and whoever you be,
won't you dance with me?

At Cana, when my mother pleaded
that they were short of wine,
I gave them all the wine they needed;
their happiness was mine.

Once, when I found poor Peter quaking,
I let him walk the sea.
I filled their fishing nets to breaking
that day in Galilee.

While all the world despised the sinner
I showed him hope again,
and gave the honours at that dinner
to Mary Magdalene.

Lazarus from the tomb advancing
once more drew life's sweet breath.
You too will leave the churchyard dancing,
for I have conquered death.
Aimé Duval

14   Dear Lord and Father of mankind,
forgive our foolish ways!
Reclothe us in our rightful mind,

in purer lives thy service find,
in deeper reverence praise.

In simple trust like theirs who heard
beside the Syrian sea,
the gracious calling of the Lord,
let us, like them, without a word,
rise up and follow thee.

O Sabbath rest by Galilee!
O calm of hills above,
where Jesus knelt to share with thee
the silence of eternity,
interpreted by love!

Drop thy still dews of quietness,
till all our strivings cease;
take from our souls the strain and stress,
and let our ordered lives confess
the beauty of thy peace.
John Greenleaf Whittier

15 Give me joy in my heart, keep me praising,
give me joy in my heart I pray.
Give me joy in my heart keep me praising.
Keep me praising till the end of day.

Sing hosanna! Sing hosanna!
Sing hosanna to the King of Kings!
Sing hosanna! Sing hosanna!
Sing hosanna to the King!

Give me peace in my heart, keep me resting,
give me peace in my heart I pray.
Give me peace in my heart, keep me resting.
Keep me resting till the end of day.

Give me love in my heart, keep me serving,
give me love in my heart, I pray.
Give me love in my heart, keep me serving,
keep me serving till the end of day.
Traditional

16   Glory to God, glory to God,
glory to the Father.
Glory to God, glory to God,
glory to the Father.
To him be glory for ever.
To him be glory for ever.
Alleluia, amen.
Alleluia, amen,
alleluia, amen,
alleluia, amen.

Glory to God, glory to God,
Son of the Father.

Glory to God, glory to God,
glory to the Spirit.

Peruvian

17   God is love,
and he who abides in love
abides in God, and God in him.

18   God's Spirit is in my heart.
He has called me and set me apart.
This is what I have to do,
what I have to do.

*He's sent me to give the Good News to the poor,
tell prisoners that they are prisoners no more,
tell blind people that they can see,
and set the downtrodden free,
and go tell ev'ryone
the news that the Kingdom of God has come,
and go tell ev'ryone
the news that God's Kingdom has come.*

Just as the Father sent me,
so I'm sending you out to be
my witnesses throughout the world,
the whole of the world.

By dying I'm going away,
but I'll be with you every day
as the Spirit of love in your heart,
the love in your heart.

Hubert Richards

19 Go, the Mass is ended,
children of the Lord.
Take his Word to others
as you've heard it spoken to you.
Go, the Mass is ended,
go and tell the world
the Lord is good, the Lord is kind,
and he loves ev'ryone.

Go, the Mass is ended,
take his love to all.
Gladden all who meet you,
fill their hearts with hope and courage.
Go, the Mass is ended,
fill the world with love,
and give to all what you've received
— the peace and joy of Christ.

Go, the Mass is ended,
strengthened in the Lord,
lighten ev'ry burden,
spread the joy of Christ around you.
Go, the Mass is ended,
take his peace to all.
This day is yours to change the world
— to make God known and loved.

Sister Marie Lydia Pereira

20 Gracious Spirit, Holy Ghost,
taught by thee, we covet most,
of Thy gifts at Pentecost,
holy, heavenly love.

Love is kind, and suffers long,
love is meek, and thinks no wrong,

215

love than death itself more strong;
therefore give us love.

Prophecy will fade away,
melting in the light of day;
love will ever with us stay;
therefore give us love.

Faith will vanish into sight;
hope be emptied in delight;
love in heaven will shine more bright;
therefore give us love.

Faith and hope and love we see,
joining hand in hand, agree;
but the greatest of the three,
and the best, is love.

Christopher Wordsworth

21   Guide me, O thou great Redeemer,
pilgrim through this barren land;
I am weak, but thou are mighty,
hold me with thy powerful hand;
Bread of heaven,
feed me till I want no more.

Open now the crystal fountain
whence the healing stream doth flow;
let the fire and cloudy pillar
lead me all my journey through;
strong Deliverer,
be thou still my strength and shield.

When I tread the verge of Jordan,
bid my anxious fears subside;
Death of death, and hell's Destruction,
land me safe on Canaan's side;
Songs of praises
I will ever give to thee.

William Williams; tr. Peter Williams and others

22 He is Lord, he is Lord,
he is risen from the dead and he is Lord.
Every knee shall bow, every tongue confess
that Jesus Christ is Lord.

Traditional

23 He's got the whole world in his hands,
He's got the whole world in his hands,
He's got the whole wide world in his hands,
He's got the whole world in his hands.

He's got you and me, brother, in his hands.

He's got you and me, sister, in his hands.

He's got the little bitty baby in his hands.

Traditional

24 Holy God, we praise thy name;
Lord of all, we bow before thee!
All on earth thy sceptre own,
all in heaven above adore thee.
Infinite thy vast domain,
everlasting is thy reign.

Hark! the loud celestial hymn,
angel choirs above are raising;
Cherubim and Seraphim,
in unceasing chorus praising,
fill the heavens with sweet accord,
holy, holy, holy Lord,

Holy Father, holy Son,
Holy Spirit, three we name thee.
While in essence only one.
Undivided God we claim thee;
and adoring bend the knee,
while we own the mystery.

C. A. Walworth

25   Holy, holy, holy, holy,
holy, holy, holy Lord
   God almighty.
And we lift our hearts before you
   as a token of our love.
Holy, holy, holy, holy.

Gracious Father, gracious Father,
we are glad to be your children,
   gracious Father.
And we lift our heads before you
   as a token of our love,
gracious Father, gracious Father.

Risen Jesus, risen Jesus,
we are glad that you've redeemed us,
   risen Jesus.
And we lift our hands before you
   as a token of our love,
risen Jesus, risen Jesus.

Holy Spirit, holy Spirit,
come and fill our hearts anew,
   O holy Spirit.
And we lift our voice before you
   as a token of our love,
holy Spirit, holy Spirit.
Jimmy Owens

26   Holy, holy, holy!
   Lord God almighty!
Early in the morning
   our song shall rise to thee;
holy, holy, holy!
   Merciful and mighty!
God in three persons,
   blessed Trinity!

Holy, holy, holy!
   All the saints adore thee,
casting down their golden crowns
   around the glassy sea;

Cherubim and Seraphim
    falling down before thee,
which wert, and art,
    and evermore shalt be.

Holy, holy, holy!
    Though the darkness hide thee,
though the eye of sinful man
    thy glory may not see,
only thou art holy,
    there is none beside thee,
perfect in power,
    in love, and purity.

Holy, holy, holy!
    Lord God almighty!
All thy works shall praise thy name,
    in earth, in sky, and sea;
holy, holy, holy!
    Merciful and mighty!
God in three persons,
    blessed Trinity!

Reginald Heber

27   *I am the resurrection and the life;*
        He who believes in me will never die.

I have come to bring the truth;
I have come to bring you life;
if you believe, then you shall live.

In my word all men will come to know,
it is love which makes the spirit grow;
if you believe, then you shall live.

Keep in mind the things that I have said;
remember me in the breaking of the bread;
if you believe, then you shall live.

As my Father created with his breath,
so I too will call you from your death;
if you believe, then you shall live.

Ray Repp and others

28　　I danced in the morning
when the world was begun,
and I danced in the moon
and the stars and the sun,
and I came down from heaven
and I danced on the earth,
at Bethlehem
I had my birth.

Dance, then, wherever you may be,
I am the Lord of the Dance, said he.
And I'll lead you all
　　wherever you may be,
and I'll lead you all
　　in the dance, said he.

I danced for the scribe
and the pharisee,
but they would not dance
and they wouldn't follow me.
I danced for the fishermen,
for James and John;
they came with me
and the dance went on.

I danced on the Sabbath
and I cured the lame.
The holy people
they said it was a shame.
They whipped and they stripped
and they hung me on high,
and they left me there
on the cross to die.

I danced on a Friday
when the sky turned black.
It's hard to dance
with the devil on your back.
They buried my body
and they thought I'd gone
but I am the dance
and I still go on.

They cut me down
and I leapt up high.
I am the life
that'll never, never die.
I'll live in you
if you'll live in me;
I am the Lord
of the Dance, said he.

Sydney Carter

29   In Christ there is no East or West,
in him no South or North,
but one great fellowship of love
throughout the whole wide earth.

In him shall true hearts everywhere
their high communion find,
his service is the golden cord
close-binding all mankind.

Join hands, then, brothers of the faith,
whate'er your race may be!
Who serves my Father as a son
is surely kin to me.

In Christ now meet both East and West,
in him meet South and North,
all Christly souls are one in him,
throughout the whole wide earth.

John Oxenham

30   Jerusalem, Jerusalem,
Lift up your voice and sing;
Hosanna, in the highest,
Hosanna to your king!

31   Jesus Christ is risen today,
alleluia!
Our triumphant holy day,
alleluia!

Who did once, upon the cross,
  alleluia!
Suffer to redeem our loss,
  alleluia!

Hymns of praise then let us sing,
  alleluia!
Unto Christ, our heavenly king,
  alleluia!
Who endured the cross and grave,
  alleluia!
Sinners to redeem and save,
  alleluia!

But the pains that he endured,
  alleluia!
Our salvation have procured;
  alleluia!
Now above the sky he's king,
  alleluia!
Where the angels ever sing,
  alleluia!
  Lyra Davidica (1708) and the Supplement (1816).
  Based partly on 'Surrexit Christus hodie' (14th c.)

32   Jesus is Lord. (4 times)
Alleluia. (4 times)

And I love him ...

Christ is risen ...

Send your Spirit ...

Alleluia, alleluia,
alleluia, alleluia,
alleluia, alleluia,
alleluia, alleluia.

33   Jesus, stand among us
in thy risen power;

let this time of worship
be a hallowed hour.

Breathe the Holy Spirit
into every heart;
bid the fears and sorrows
from each soul depart.

Thus with quickened footsteps
we'll pursue our way,
watching for the dawning
of eternal day.

William Pennefather

34 Keep in mind that Jesus Christ has died for us
and is risen from the dead.
He is our saving Lord,
he is joy for all ages.

Lucien Deiss

35 Kum ba yah, my Lord, kum ba yah!
kum ba yah, my Lord, kum ba yah!
Kum ba yah, my Lord, kum ba yah!
O Lord, kum ba yah!

Someone's crying, Lord ...

Singing ...

Praying ...

Hungry ...

Suffering ...

Lonely ...

Spiritual

36 *Laudato sii, O mi Signore* (4 times)

Praise to you in all your creatures,
brother sun and sister moon;

223

in the stars and in the wind,
air and fire and flowing water.

For our sister, mother earth,
she who feeds us and sustains us;
for her fruits, her grass, her flowers,
for the mountains and the oceans.

Praise for those who spread forgiveness,
those who share your peace with others,
bearing trials and sickness bravely!
Even sister death won't harm them.

For our life is but a song,
and the reason for our singing
is to praise you for the music;
join the dance of your creation.

Praise to you, Father most holy,
praise and thanks to you, Lord Jesus,
praise to you, most holy Spirit,
life and joy of all creation!

Damian Lundy

37   Lead, kindly light
            amid th'encircling gloom,
        lead thou me on;
        the night is dark
            and I am far from home,
        lead thou me on.
        Keep thou my feet;
            I do not ask to see
        the distant scene;
            one step enough for me.

        I was not ever thus,
            nor prayed that thou
        shouldst lead me on;
        I loved to choose
            and see my path; but now
        lead thou me on.

I loved the garish day,
  and, spite of fears,
pride ruled my will;
  remember not past years.

So long thy power
  hath blest me, sure it still
will lead me on
o'er moor and fen,
  o'er crag and torrent, till
the night is gone;
and with the morn
  those angel faces smile
which I have loved
  long since, and lost awhile.
          John Henry Newman

38 Let all mortal flesh keep silence
and with fear and trembling stand,
ponder nothing earthly-minded:
for with blessing in his hand,
Christ our God on earth descendeth,
our full homage to demand.

King of kings, yet born of Mary,
as of old on earth he stood,
Lord of lords, in human vesture,
in the Body and the Blood.
He will give to all the faithful
his own self for heavenly food.

Rank on rank the host of heaven
spreads its vanguard on the way,
as the Light of Light descendeth
from the realms of endless day,
that the powers of hell may vanish
as the darkness clears away.

At his feet the six-winged Seraph;
Cherubim with sleepless eye,
veil their faces to the Presence,
as with ceaseless voice they cry,
Alleluia, alleluia,
alleluia, Lord most high.
      Liturgy of St James, tr. G. Moultrie

39   Let all that is within me cry holy.
Let all that is within me cry holy.
Holy, holy, holy is the Lamb that was slain.

Let all that is within me cry mighty ...

Worthy ...

Blessed ...

Jesus ...

Risen ...

Traditional

40   Let all the world in every corner sing,
"My God and King!"
The heavens are not too high,
his praise may thither fly:
the earth is not too low,
his praises there may grow.
Let all the world in every corner sing,
"My God and King!"

Let all the world in every corner sing,
"My God and King!"
The Church with psalms must shout,
no door can keep them out:
but, above all, the heart
must bear the longest part.
Let all the world in every corner sing,
"My God and King!"

George Herbert

41   Let us break bread together on our knees.
Let us break bread together on our knees.
When I fall on my knees
with my face to the rising sun,
O Lord, have mercy on me.

Let us drink wine together ...

Let us praise God together ...

Traditional

42   Living, he loved me: dying, he saved me;
buried, he carried my sins far away;
rising, he justified freely for ever;
one day he's coming — Oh, glorious day!

Traditional

43   Lord Jesus Christ,
you have come to us,
born as one of us,
   Mary's Son.
Led out to die on Calvary,
risen from death to set us free,
living Lord Jesus, help us see
   you are Lord.

Lord Jesus Christ,
I would come to you,
live my life for you,
   Son of God.
All your commands I know are true,
your many gifts will make me new,
into my life your power breaks through,
   living Lord.

Patrick Appleford

44   Low in the grave he lay,
Jesus, my Saviour;
waiting the coming day,
Jesus, my Lord.

Up from the grave he arose,
with a mighty triumph o'er his foes:
he arose a victor from the dark domain,

227

and he lives for ever with his saints to reign:
he arose! he arose! Hallelujah! Christ arose!

Vainly they watch his bed,
Jesus, my Saviour;
vainly they seal the dead,
Jesus, my Lord.

Death cannot keep his prey,
Jesus, my Saviour;
he tore the bars away,
Jesus, my Lord.

Robert Lowry

45   Make me a channel of your peace.
Where there is hatred,
  let me bring your love.
Where there is injury,
  your pardon, Lord.
And where there's doubt,
  true faith in you.

Make me a channel of your peace.
Where there's despair in life,
  let me bring hope.
Where there is darkness
  only light,
and where there's sadness
  ever joy.

Oh, Master,
  grant that I may never seek
so much to be consoled
  as to console,
to be understood as to understand,
to be loved, as to love,
  with all my soul.

Make me a channel of your peace.
It is in pardoning
  that we are pardoned,
in giving to all men

that we receive,
and in dying that we're
    born to eternal life.
        Sebastian Temple

46   May the peace of Christ
    be with you today,
may the peace of Christ
    be with you today,
may the love of Christ,
the joy of Christ,
may the peace of Christ be yours.
        Kevin Mayhew

47   Mine eyes have seen the glory
    of the coming of the Lord.
He is trampling out the vintage
where the grapes of wrath are stored.
He has loosed the fateful lightning
    of his terrible swift sword.
His truth is marching on.

Glory, glory halleluja! (3 times)
His truth is marching on.

He has sounded forth the trumpet
    that shall never sound retreat.
He is sifting out the hearts of men
    before his judgment seat.
O, be swift my soul to answer him,
    be jubilant my feet!
Our God is marching on.

In the beauty of the lilies
    Christ was born across the sea
with a glory in his bosom
    that transfigures you and me.
As he died to make men holy,
    let us die to make men free,
whilst God is marching on.
        Julia Ward Howe

48   My song is love unknown,
my Saviour's love to me;
love to the loveless shown,
that they might lovely be.
O who am I,
that for my sake
my Lord should take
frail flesh, and die?

They rise and needs will have
my dear Lord made away;
a murderer they save,
the Prince of life they slay;
yet cheerful he
to suffering goes,
that he his foes
from thence might free.

In life, no house, no home
my Lord on earth might have
in death, no friendly tomb,
but what a stranger gave.
What may I say?
Heaven was his home;
but mine the tomb
wherein he lay.

Here might I stay and sing,
no story so divine;
never was love, dear King!
Never was grief like thine.
This is my Friend,
in whose sweet praise
I all my days
could gladly spend.

Samuel Crossman

49   Nearer, my God, to thee,
nearer to thee!
E'en though it be a cross
that raiseth me;

still all my song shall be,
  'Nearer, my God, to thee,
    nearer to thee!'

Though, like the wanderer,
  the sun gone down,
darkness comes over me,
  my rest a stone;
yet in my dreams I'd be
nearer, my God, to thee,
    nearer to thee.

There let my way appear
  steps unto heaven,
all that thou sendest me
  in mercy given;
angels to beckon me
nearer, my God, to thee,
    nearer to thee.

Then, with my waking thoughts
  bright with thy praise,
out of my stony griefs
  Bethel I'll raise;
so by my woes to be
nearer, my God, to thee,
    nearer to thee.

Genesis 28[11–19]
Sarah F. Adams

50   Now the green blade riseth
  from the buried grain,
wheat that in the dark earth
  many days has lain;
love lives again,
  that with the dead has been:
love is come again
  like wheat that springeth green.

In the grave they laid him,
  Love whom men had slain,
thinking that never

he would wake again,
laid in the earth
like grain that sleeps unseen:
love is come again
like wheat that springeth green.

Forth he came at Easter,
like the risen grain,
he that for three days
in the grave had lain,
quick from the dead
my risen Lord is seen:
love is come again
like wheat that springeth green.

When our hearts are wintry,
grieving or in pain,
thy touch can call us
back to life again,
fields of our heart
that dead and bare have been:
love is come again
like wheat that springeth green.

J. M. C. Crum

51   O come, all ye faithful,
joyful and triumphant,
O come ye, O come ye to Bethlehem;
come and behold him,
born the king of angels:

O come, let us adore him,
O come, let us adore him,
O come, let us adore him,
Christ the Lord.

True God of true God,
Light of Light eternal,
lo! He abhors not the Virgin's womb,
Son of the Father,
begotten, not created:

Sing, choirs of angels,
sing in exultation,
sing all ye citizens of heaven above,
Glory to God
in the highest:

Yea, Lord, we greet thee,
born this happy morning;
Jesus, to thee be glory given,
Word of the Father,
now in flesh appearing:

18th c., tr. Frederick Oakeley

52 O for a thousand tongues, to sing
my dear Redeemer's praise,
the glories of my God and King,
the triumphs of his grace!

Jesus! the name that charms our fears,
that bids our sorrows cease;
'tis music in the sinner's ears,
'tis life, and health, and peace.

See all your sins on Jesus laid;
the Lamb of God was slain,
his soul was once an offering made
for every soul of man.

My gracious Master and my God,
assist me to proclaim,
to spread through all the earth abroad
the honours of thy name.

Charles Wesley

53 O little town of Bethlehem,
how still we see thee lie!
Above thy deep and dreamless sleep
the silent stars go by.
Yet, in thy dark streets shineth
the everlasting light;

the hopes and fears of all the years
are met in thee tonight.

O morning stars, together
proclaim the holy birth,
and praises sing to God the King,
and peace to men on earth;
for Christ is born of Mary;
and, gathered all above,
while mortals sleep, the angels keep
their watch of wondering love.

How silently, how silently,
the wondrous gift is given!
So God imparts to human hearts
the blessings of his heaven.
No ear may hear his coming;
but in this world of sin,
where meek souls will receive him, still
the dear Christ enters in.

Philip Brooks

54　O Lord, my God,
　　when I in awesome wonder,
consider all the worlds
　　thy hand has made,
I see the stars,
　　I hear the rolling thunder,
thy pow'r throughout
　　the universe displayed.

Then sings my soul,
　　my Saviour God to thee:
How great thou art,
　　how great thou art.

And when I think
　　that God, his Son not sparing,
sent him to die,
　　I scarce can take it in,
that on the cross,

my burden gladly bearing,
he bled and died
   to take away my sin.

When Christ shall come
   with shout of acclamation
and take me home,
   what joy shall fill my heart;
when I shall bow
   in humble adoration,
and there proclaim;
   my God, how great thou art.
                              Anon

55   Once in royal David's city
          stood a lowly cattle shed,
          where a Mother laid her baby
          in a manger for his bed:
          Mary was that Mother mild,
          Jesus Christ her little child.

          He came down to earth from heaven
          who is God and Lord of all,
          and his shelter was a stable
          and his cradle was a stall;
          with the poor and mean, and lowly,
          lived on earth our Saviour holy.

          Not in that poor lowly stable,
          with the oxen standing by,
          we shall see him; but in heaven,
          set at God's right hand on high;
          when like stars his children crowned
          all in white shall wait around.
                    Cecil Francis Alexander

56   *Our God reigns, our God reigns,*
          our God reigns, our God reigns!

          How lovely on the mountains are the feet of him
          who brings good news, good news,

announcing peace, proclaiming news of happiness:
Our God reigns, our God reigns.

The watchmen raise their voices in a shout of joy
as they see the Lord,
they see the Lord returning to Jerusalem:
Our God reigns, our God reigns.

Break forth with joy, waste places of Jerusalem:
the Lord has brought us peace;
his saving power the ends of all the earth shall see:
Our God reigns, our God reigns.

Isaiah 52[7–10]

57 O worship the Lord in the beauty of holiness,
bow down before him, his glory proclaim;
with gold of obedience, and incense of lowliness,
kneel and adore him, the Lord is his name.

Low at his feet lay thy burden of carefulness,
high on his heart he will bear it for thee,
comfort thy sorrow and answer thy prayerfulness,
guiding thy steps as may best for thee be.

Fear not to enter his courts in the slenderness
Of the poor wealth thou would'st reckon as thine;
truth in its beauty, and love in its tenderness,
these are the offerings to lay on his shrine.

These, though we bring them in trembling and
    fearfulness,
he will accept for the name that is dear;
mornings of joy give for evenings of tearfulness,
trust for our trembling, and hope for our fear.

John Samuel Bewley Monsell

58 Peace is flowing like a river,
flowing out through you and me,
spreading out into the desert,
setting all the captives free.

Love is flowing like a river ...

Joy is flowing like a river ...

Hope is flowing like a river ...

Anon

59   Praise him, praise him,
praise him in the morning,
praise him in the noontime.
Praise him, praise him,
praise him when the sun goes down.

Love him, love him.

Trust him, trust him.

Serve him, serve him.

Jesus, Jesus.

Anon

60   Praise, my soul, the King of heaven;
to his feet thy tribute bring.
Ransomed, healed, restored, forgiven,
who like thee, his praise should sing?
Praise him! Praise him!
Praise him! Praise him!
Praise the everlasting King.

Praise him for his grace and favour
to our fathers in distress;
praise him, still the same for ever,
slow to chide and swift to bless.
Praise him! Praise him!
Praise him! Praise him!
Glorious in his faithfulness.

Father-like, he tends and spares us;
well our feeble frame he knows;
in his hands, he gently bears us,

237

rescues us from all our foes.
Praise him! Praise him!
Praise him! Praise him!
Widely as his mercy flows.

Angels, help us to adore him;
Ye behold him face to face;
sun and moon, bow down before him,
dwellers all in time and space.
Praise him! Praise him!
Praise him! Praise him!
Praise with us the God of grace.

Henry Francis Lyte

61   Praise to the Holiest in the height,
and in the depth be praise;
in all his words most wonderful,
most sure in all his ways!

O loving wisdom of our God!
When all was sin and shame,
a second Adam to the fight
and to the rescue came.

O wisest love! that flesh and blood,
which did in Adam fail,
should strive afresh against the foe,
should strive and should prevail.

O generous love! that he who smote
in man for man the foe,
the double agony in man
for man should undergo.

Praise to the Holiest in the height,
and in the depth be praise:
in all his words most wonderful,
most sure in all his ways!

John Henry Newman

62   Rejoice in the Lord always,
and again I say rejoice.

Rejoice in the Lord always,
and again I say rejoice.
Rejoice, rejoice,
and again I say rejoice.
Rejoice, rejoice,
and again I say rejoice.
Philippians 4[4]

63   Seek ye first the kingdom of God
and his righteousness,
and all these things shall be added unto you.
Allelu, Alleluia.
Alleluia. (4 times)

Ask and it shall be given unto you,
seek and ye shall find.
Knock and the door will be opened unto you.
Allelu, alleluia.

Therefore consider the lilies of the field;
they neither toil nor spin.
Yet even Solomon was not arrayed like them.
Allelu, alleluia.
Matthew 6—7

64   Shalom my friends, shalom my friends,
shalom, shalom.
May God be with you, may God be with you,
shalom, shalom.
Traditional

65   Silent night, holy night,
all is calm, all is bright,
round yon virgin mother and child;
holy infant so tender and mild:
sleep in heavenly peace,
sleep in heavenly peace.

Silent night, holy night.
Shepherds quake at the sight,

glories stream from heaven afar,
heavenly hosts sing alleluia:
Christ, the Saviour is born,
Christ the Saviour is born.

Silent night, holy night.
Son of God, love's pure light
radiant beams from thy holy face,
with the dawn of redeeming grace:
Jesus, Lord, at thy birth,
Jesus, Lord, at thy birth.

Joseph Mohr, tr. J. Young

66   Spirit of the living God,
  fall afresh on me.
Spirit of the living God,
  fall afresh on me.
Break me, melt me,
  mould me, fill me.
Spirit of the living God,
  fall afresh on me.

Michael Iverson

67   *Take our bread, we ask you,*
take our hearts, we love you,
take our lives, oh Father,
we are yours, we are yours.

Yours as we stand
  at the table you set,
yours as we eat the bread
  our hearts can't forget.
We are the signs
  of your life with us yet;
we are yours, we are yours.

Your holy people
  stand washed in your blood,
Spirit filled, yet hungry,
  we await your food.

Poor though we are,
  we have brought ourselves to you:
we are yours, we are yours.
              Joseph Wise

68   Tell out, my soul, the greatness of the Lord!
Unnumbered blessings, give my spirit voice;
tender to me the promise of his word;
in God my Saviour shall my heart rejoice.

Tell out, my soul, the greatness of his name!
Make known his might, the deeds his arm
    has done;
his mercy sure, from age to age the same;
his holy name — the Lord, the Mighty One.

Tell out, my soul, the greatness of his might!
Powers and dominions lay their glory by.
Proud hearts and stubborn wills are put to flight,
the hungry fed, the humble lifted high.

Tell out, my soul, the glories of his word!
Firm in his promise, and his mercy sure.
Tell out, my soul, the greatness of the Lord
to children's children and for evermore!
          Based on the Magnificat
            T. Dudley-Smith

69   The Lord's my shepherd, I'll not want,
he makes me down to lie
in pastures green. He leadeth me
the quiet waters by.

My soul he doth restore again,
and me to walk doth make
within the paths of righteousness,
e'en for his own name's sake.

Yea, though I walk in death's dark vale,
yet will I fear none ill.
For thou art with me, and thy rod
and staff me comfort still.

My table thou hast furnishéd
in presence of my foes,
my head thou dost with oil anoint,
and my cup overflows.

Goodness and mercy all my life
shall surely follow me.
And in God's house for evermore
my dwelling place shall be.

Paraphrased from Ps. 23
in the "Scottish Psalter" 1650

70   Thine be the glory, risen, conquering Son,
endless is the victory thou o'er death hast won;
angels in bright raiment rolled the stone away,
kept the folded grave-clothes, where
    thy body lay.

Thine be the glory, risen, conquering Son,
endless is the victory thou o'er death hast won.

Lo! Jesus meets us, risen from the tomb;
lovingly he greets us, scatters fear and gloom;
let the Church with gladness hymns of
    triumph sing,
for the Lord now liveth; death hast lost its sting.

E. L. Budry
tr. R. B. Hoyle

71   This is the day (this is the day)
that the Lord has made (that the Lord has made).
Let us rejoice (let us rejoice)
and be glad in it (and be glad in it).
This is the day that the Lord has made.
Let us rejoice and be glad in it.
This is the day (this is the day)
that the Lord has made.

This is the day that he rose again ...

This is the day that the Spirit came ...

Anon

72   This joyful Eastertide,
away with sin and sorrow,
my love, the Crucified,
hath sprung to life this morrow:

Had Christ, that once was slain,
ne'er burst his three-day prison,
our faith has been in vain:
but now hath Christ arisen.

My flesh in hope shall rest,
and for a season slumber:
till trump from east to west
shall wake the dead in number:

Death's flood hath lost his chill,
since Jesus crossed the river:
lover of souls, from ill
my passing soul deliver:
                    George Ratclife Woodward

73   Thou wilt keep him in perfect peace (3 times)
whose mind is stayed on thee.

Marvel not, I say unto you (3 times)
you must be born again.

Though your sins as scarlet be (3 times)
they shall be white as snow.

If the Son shall set you free (3 times)
you shall be free indeed.
                    Anon

74   To God be the glory! Great things he hath done!
So loved he the world that he gave us his Son,
who yielded his life an atonement for sin,
and opened the life-gate that all may go in.

Praise the Lord! praise the Lord!
Let the earth hear his voice!
Praise the Lord! praise the Lord!
Let the people rejoice!
O come to the Father through Jesus the Son;
And give him the glory — great things he hath done!

O perfect redemption, the purchase of blood!
To every believer the promise of God;
the vilest offender who truly believes,
that moment from Jesus a pardon receives.

Great things he has taught us, great things he hath done,
and great our rejoicing through Jesus the Son:
but purer and higher and greater will be
our wonder, our transport, when Jesus we see!

Fanny J. Crosby

75   We are gathering together unto him,
we are gathering together unto him.
Unto him shall the gathering of the people be.
We are gathering together unto him.

We are offering together unto him.

We are singing together unto him.

We are praying together unto him.

Anon

76   Were you there when they crucified my Lord?
Were you there when they crucified my Lord?
O, sometimes it causes me to tremble, tremble, tremble!
Were you there when they crucified my Lord?

Were you there when they nailed him to the tree?

Were you there when they pierced him in the side?

Were you there when they laid him in the tomb?

Were you there when God raised him from the dead?

Spiritual

77 When I needed a neighbour, were you there, were you there?
When I needed a neighbour, were you there?
And the creed and the colour and the name won't matter,
    were you there?

I was hungry and thirsty, were you there, were you there?

I was cold, I was naked, were you there, were you there?

When I needed a shelter, were you there, were you there?

When I needed a healer, were you there, were you there?

Wherever you travel, I'll be there, I'll be there,
wherever you travel, I'll be there.
And the creed and the colour and the name won't matter,
    I'll be there.

Sydney Carter

78 When I survey the wondrous cross
on which the Prince of glory died,
my richest gain I count but loss,
and pour contempt on all my pride.

See from his head, his hands, his feet,
sorrow and love flow mingled down:
did e'er such love and sorrow meet,
or thorns compose so rich a crown?

Were the whole realm of nature mine,
that were an offering far too small;
love so amazing, so divine,
demands my soul, my life, my all!

Isaac Watts

Do not seek for the City of God on earth, for it is not built of wood or stone; but seek it in the soul of man who is at peace with himself.

Philo (1st c. AD)

A HOLY LAND TIMETABLE

DATE	EVENTS	PLACES LISTED IN THIS BOOK
Old Stone Age: 200,000 BC		Mt. Carmel Man
Middle Stone Age: 10,000 BC		Jericho
New Stone Age: 6000 BC	First buildings	Jericho tower Megiddo Bet Shean Banyas
Chalcolithic Age: 4000 BC		En Gedi temple
Early Bronze Age: 3000 BC	Egyptian domination	Megiddo Hazor
Middle Bronze Age: 2000 BC	Canaanites Hyksos Israelite tribes emigrate to Egypt	Megiddo altar
Late Bronze Age: 1500 BC	Hyksos driven out of Egypt Thutmosis III takes Megiddo Egyptian domination Israelite exodus from Egypt	Shechem walls and temple Megiddo walls Hazor
Judges: 1200 BC	Israelite occupation of Land Philistine domination	Gibeon tunnel Shiloh
Kings: 1000 BC	Saul against Philistines David conquers Philistines Solomon's Empire Temple Schism of North and South Assyrian domination Israel exiled	 Jerusalem: Solomon's Quarry Hazor Banyas-Dan shrine Samaria palace Megiddo tunnel Jerusalem: Hezekiah's tunnel

		Babylonian domination Judah exiled Samaritans	
Persians:	550 BC	Return of Jewish exiles Rebuilding of temple	
Greeks:	300 BC	Alexander the Great Maccabee rebellion Hasmonean dynasty	Samaria tower Jerusalem: Kidron tombs Qumran
Romans:	60 BC	Pompey Herod the Great	 Jerusalem: Antonia Citadel Temple Bethesda pools Family tomb Herodium Masada Jericho palace Hebron Caesarea theatre and aqueduct Mamre Bet Shean theatre Samaria
	6 BC	Jesus of Nazareth Roman procurators Jewish War	Banyas—Caesarea Philippi Solomon's Pools Zealots at Masada
	70 AD	Destruction of Jerusalem Bar Kokhba Hadrian's Aelia Capitolina Jewish Galilee settlements	 Jerusalem: Ecce Homo Tombs of Kings Samaria forum and theatre Capernaum synagogue Corozain Tiberias Bet Shearim
Byzantines:	300 AD	Constantine	Bethlehem Nativity church Jerusalem: Holy Sepulchre Eleona Ascension Armenian Mosaic St Stephen

		Justinian	Kursi
			Mar Saba
			Jerusalem: Bethesda
			Tomb of Virgin
			Bethlehem
		Christian pilgrimages	Capernaum House of Peter
			Tabgha
			Nazareth Byzantine church
			Samaria church of John
			Bet Shean monastery
			Masada monastery
			Bet Alfa
		Persian invasion	
Arabs:	600 AD	Omayyad Dynasty	Jerusalem: Dome of the Rock
			El Aksa
		Turkish invasion	Omayyad palace
Crusaders:	1100 AD	Crusaders	Jerusalem: Holy Sepulchre
			St Anne
			St James
			Cenacle
			Ascension
			Citadel
			Monastery of Cross
			Samaria: Church of John
			Bethany
			Hebron
			Belvoir
			Caesarea
			En Karem
			Acre fortification
			Mt Tabor
			Abu Ghosh
			Emmaus
			Nazareth church
		Crusaders defeated	Horns of Hattin
		End of Christian rule	
Mamelukes:	1250 AD		Acre
			Jerusalem: palaces
			synagogues
Turks:	1500 AD	Suleiman the Magnificent	Jerusalem: old city walls
			Safed synagogues

249

			Tiberias walls
			Acre: khans
			    walls
			    mosque

		First Jewish immigrants	Jerusalem: Mea Shearim
			    Dormition
			    St George
			Bethphage chapel

British Mandate:	1920 AD	Jewish immigration	Tel Aviv founded
			Jerusalem: Gethsemane
			    Dominus Flevit
			    Rockefeller
			Mt Tabor church
			Mt of Beatitudes church
			Shepherds Field

		Arab resistance: War	

Israel:	1948 AD	State of Israel	Bahai shrine
			Bethany church
			Jerusalem: Hebrew university
			    Israel museum
			    Knesset
			    Kennedy
			      memorial
			    Yad Vashem
			    Hadassah
			    Model of
			      Jerusalem
			Nazareth basilica

	1967 AD	Six Day War	
	1973 AD	Yom Kippur War	
	1980 AD	Jerusalem capital of Israel	

INDEX OF BIBLE TEXTS

INDEX OF PLACES

PILGRIMAGE

'Where are you going?'
  'From nowhere to somewhere.'
'How long will it take you?'
  'From now until then.'
'What will you find there?'
  'The past as a present.'
'How will you use it?'
  'I know not. Amen.'

'What are you packing?'
  'A suitcase of sleeping.'
'Why is it heavy?'
  'It bulges with night.'
'In what is its value?'
  'Goods one can trade with.'
'How will you bargain?'
  'I know not. Amen.'

'Who will go with you?'
  'A child and an old man.'
'How will they travel?'
  'On the backs of the dead.'
'What will they live on?'
  'Bread, wine and blessings.'
'Will they survive then?'
  'I trust so. Amen.'

'What will the land be?'
  'Sand, thorns and granite.'
'Why do you want it?'
  'As the garden I need.'
'How will you shape it?'
  'With songs keen as sickles.'
'When will it flower?'
  'From now until then.'
Nadine Brummer, 1982